The Modern Grievance Procedure in the United States

Recent Titles from Quorum Books

The Modern Grievance Procedure in the United States

David Lewin
and
Richard B. Peterson

Quorum Books

New York • Westport, Connecticut • London

Library of Congress Cataloging-in-Publication Data

Lewin, David.
  The modern grievance procedure in the United States / David Lewin
and Richard B. Peterson.
    p. cm.
  Bibliography: p.
  Includes index.
  ISBN 0-89930-149-5 (lib. bdg. : alk. paper)
  1. Grievance procedures—United States. I. Peterson, Richard B.
II. Title.
HF5549.5.G7L49 1988
331.88'96—dc19   87-32612

British Library Cataloguing in Publication Data is available.

Library of Congress Catalog Card Number: 87-32612
ISBN: 0-89930-149-5

First published in 1988 by Quorum Books

Greenwood Press, Inc.
88 Post Road West, Westport, Connecticut 06881

Printed in the United States of America

The paper used in this book complies with the
Permanent Paper Standard issued by the National
Information Standards Organization (Z39.48-1984).

10 9 8 7 6 5 4 3 2 1

Contents

Figures and Tables

Preface

This study has been a long time in the making. We first conceived the idea of undertaking a field study of grievance procedures in the United States in 1979, subsequently received funding for the research from the National Science Foundation (NSF), and began the research in 1981. Data collection proceeded over the next three years, which was far longer than initially envisioned.

Toward the end of this period, we encountered a most unusual opportunity to extend the study of grievance procedure effectiveness to include the post-grievance settlement behavior of employees and supervisors/managers in four large organizations. We seized that opportunity, but the additional data collection and analysis requirements meant that we could not begin to write up the study until mid-1986. This volume represents the culmination of our efforts, and we now better understand why so few industrial relations scholars who preceded us have attempted large-scale, multistage field studies of any topic, let alone grievance procedures.

Despite this, we believe that the data assembled for this study, which cover the 1980-1983 period, are the most comprehensive and richest ever obtained about the grievance procedure. The data base includes 77 employer organizations distributed among steel manufacturing, retail department stores, nonprofit hospitals, and local public schools; several hundred management and union officials who responded to lengthy questionnaires about grievance handling; 36 management and union officials in the aforementioned four industries and sectors who willingly sat for personal interviews and supplied us with valuable qualitative data about the grievance process; and detailed grievance and personnel file information for almost 3,000 grievants and non-grievants as well as their respective supervisors/managers.

All of these data have been incorporated into this study, which fundamentally seeks to identify the determinants and measures of grievance procedure effectiveness and the consequences of grievance procedure usage at the individual level. While the study, like others, has its conceptual and empirical limitations, we have attempted to advance our knowledge of grievance procedures dynamics and outcomes and, in the process, to demonstrate that it is indeed possible to conduct behaviorally oriented research into modern industrial relations. Ultimately, of course, the success of our efforts will be judged by readers of this volume—which, in our view, is as it should be.

1
Introduction

This is a study of the modern grievance procedure in the United States that focuses on four industries and sectors, namely, steel manufacturing, retail trade, nonprofit hospitals, and local public schools. Steel and public education are highly unionized, while retail trade and hospitals are moderately unionized. In all four cases, however, grievance procedures are spelled out in written collective bargaining agreements, and it is the grievance filing, processing, settlement, and post-settlement behavior of the parties to these procedures that serve as the focus of this study.*

Industrial relations research flourished during the 1940s and 1950s, stagnated during the 1960s (though more so in the United States than abroad), and resurged during the 1970s and especially the 1980s. But despite the recent resurgence of industrial relations research, few contemporary studies of grievance procedures exist. Those that have emerged, such as by Peach and Livernash (1974), Goldberg (1982), Katz, Kochan, and Gobeille (1983), Norsworthy and Zabala (1985), Knight (1986), and Ichniowski (1986), are confined to small samples of respondents, a few plants, or a single firm, industry, or subunit of government and, therefore, do not permit broader generalizations to be drawn. Some more comprehensive studies of grievance procedures have been conducted outside the United States, such as those by Thomson and Murray (1976) and Hyman (1972). But for the United States, the works of

*This study was supported by a grant from the National Science Foundation (Grant #SES-80-23041). The views expressed here are solely those of the authors and should not be attributed to the Foundation.

Slichter, Healy, and Livernash (1960) and Kuhn (1961) remain the best known and most substantial, yet the data on which those studies are based are three decades or more old. Hence, the primary objective of this study is to present and analyze new data about grievance procedures in several settings and thereby help to inform both academics and practitioners about the dynamics and consequences of this process.

GRIEVANCE DEFINITIONS AND CONSIDERATIONS

What is a grievance? In its broadest conception, a grievance is any employee complaint about the employment relationship. Some labor agreements describe a grievance in this fashion. More commonly, however, a grievance is defined as a dispute that "relates in some manner to the proper interpretation or application of the collective bargaining agreement" (Rand, 1980, p. 50). Such a definition narrows the occurrence of grievances to unionized settings and to written contract language that expressly deals with grievances—although some labor agreements do not contain grievance procedures and grievancelike dispute resolution procedures are present in some nonunion settings.[1]

One pragmatic advantage of narrowing grievances to alleged violations of labor agreements is that both union and management officials are freed from handling a potentially large volume of employee complaints, including those that are not well articulated. A possible disadvantage of a narrow definition of grievances is that certain important employee complaints may go unheeded and may, in turn, contribute to low product quality, high turnover, absenteeism and strikes, and internal union turmoil. In any case, we use the term "grievance" to refer to any alleged violation of the labor agreement between the parties where the grievance takes a written form and where it pertains to written contract language. The term "grievance procedure," which is more fully defined in Chapter 2, refers to the system established by the parties for the processing and settlement of grievances. This system is shaped by certain environmental forces, union and management organizational characteristics and policies, employee characteristics and attitudes, and the nature and structure of the bargaining relationship between the parties.

Our interest in studying grievance procedures in unionized settings is motivated by several considerations. First, the literature on the grievance procedure is inadequate. Industrial relations textbooks, for example, rarely provide in-depth treatment of this subject, and the few that do typically devote most of their attention to arbitration.[2] While arbitration is unquestionably an important step in the grievance process and while provisions for its use are widespread in labor agreements, the reality is that most grievances are settled short of arbitration. Hence, an overly strong textbook emphasis on grievance arbitration detracts from both the study and appreciation of much of the dynamics of grievance processing.

Second, and related, the industrial relations literature provides much more substantial treatments of collective bargaining than of contract administration. Perhaps this is because the bargaining process is more amenable to conceptualization and measurement than the contract administration process, or because the bargaining process is more readily linked to organizational outcomes than the contract administration process. In any event, the irony of this disparate literature treatment is that union and management officials devote far more time to contract administration, which is an ongoing process, than to collective bargaining, which is a periodic process in the U.S. system of industrial relations. And, in the unionized setting, it is the grievance procedure that lies at the heart of the contract administration process.

Third, and from a research perspective, the grievance procedure literature is largely a qualitative literature. Despite the contributions that this literature has made to our knowledge of the grievance process, and recognizing that quantification can also be carried to excess, it is nevertheless true that the recent resurgence of research on certain industrial relations topics—for example, strikes, bargaining theory, contract arbitration, and union political activity—has featured substantial and widespread use of quantitative methods of analysis.[3] If the grievance procedure is to compete favorably with other industrial relations topics for the attention of researchers, it must be shown that the procedure is more amenable to quantiative examination than is reflected in the prevailing literature. We intend to provide such quantitative analysis in this study.

Fourth, and from an applied or practitioner's perspective, judgments about the relative effectiveness of grievance handling and settlement must be made in order to formulate and redesign employee relations policies and practices. Unfortunately, the literature on the grievance procedure is not helpful in this respect because virtually no attention has been given to the conceptualization and measurement of grievance procedure effectiveness.[4] Yet recent research on the strategic choice of industrial relations and human resource policy and practice suggests that the grievance procedure can be approached from an "effectiveness" perspective.[5] By assessing the effectiveness of grievance procedures in four settings and over several years, this study will provide some evidence that should be useful to practitioners in making strategic choices about grievance procedure policy and practice.

THE IMPORTANCE OF GRIEVANCE ACTIVITY

What is important about the grievance procedure and grievance activity is unionized settings? An answer to this question depends in part on whose perspective is taken, namely, that of employees, union officials, management, or the public.

For employees, the grievance procedure is a mechanism that presumably legitimizes the filing of complaints about the employment relationship. The grievance mechanism exists, it is expected to be used, provisions for filing and responding to grievances are set out, and settlement procedures are explicit. Also provided is representation for an employee whose grievance proceeds through higher levels of the grievance procedure.

Typically after the first step of the procedure, a shop steward, grievance committeeman, union grievance committee or all of these representatives take over the processing of grievances; the individual employee does not constantly have to be on the firing line representing himself directly to management. Before this, however, an individual employee-complainant can decide if his grievance has been satisfactorily dealt with in formal and informal discussions with his immediate supervisor. Whether or not it is explictly set out in contract language, such oral discussion is the actual first step of virtually all grievance procedures. The individual employee thus has the option of accepting a settlement of his grievance at this oral step or pursuing it further in writing.

These characteristics of the grievance procedure indicate that the procedure's main benefit to employees is serving as a due process mechanism for treating complaints about the employment relationship. For an individual employee, this potential benefit must be weighed against the potential cost of grievance filing, where the cost can take the form of managerial retribution, formally or otherwise, against grievance filers.

From union officials' perspective, provisions for grievance processing constitute a bargaining achievement and underscore the importance of these officials' role as representatives of the membership. Actual grievance processing by union officials may provide them with benefits in the form of power, expertise, and recognition by union members, management officials, or both, of such power and expertise. Conversely, union members may judge their grievances to have been ineffectively handled by their representatives, management may reach a similar conclusion about union officials, and some union officials may judge other union officials to be ineffective grievance handlers. Clearly, for union officials the grievance procedure and grievance activity offer certain opportunities but also certain threats to the viability of their leadership.

For management, the grievance procedure offers several potential benefits. First, and unlike labor-management relations in other developed countries, the workplace conflicts represented by grievances filed rarely are accompanied by strikes or work slowdowns in the United States. Indeed, in most situations the production of goods or services continues while grievances are being resolved. Second, the grievance procedure provides information to management that can be used for decision making. The information may pertain to a particular condition of employment, such as work scheduling; to an interpersonal matter involving supervisory relations; or to an item that may subsequently become a matter for collective bargaining, such as subcontracting. In all of these examples, the fact that grievances are formally filed, eventually resolved, and generate written records permits this aspect of labor-management relations to be treated as part of an organization's management information system.

Third, the involvement of union officials in grievance handling—for example, determining whether grievances have merit, representing employees in grievance proceedings, and dealing with employees who lose their grievance claims—represents a (partial) substitution of these officials' time for the time that management would otherwise spend on grievance processing and resolution. Though it is rarely accounted for in any formal way, even a modest opportunity cost valuation of management's time suggests that management can benefit from the "managerial" role that union officials play with respect to the grievance process.

The costs of grievance filing and processing to management include, of course, the time and financial resources that management expends on this activity. Such costs may be enlarged when management is faced with union officials who promote grievance filing for political purposes or who are determined to achieve through the grievance process what could not be achieved through collective bargaining. Also a potential cost to management is the reversal of managerial actions through arbitrators' decisions. Still a further potential cost in this regard, one rarely discussed in the literature and even more rarely studied, is the demoralization of supervisors and middle-level managers whose decisions are reversed by higher-level management or through arbitration. Such demoralization may translate into lower supervisory performance, inhibit supervisors' future decision-making effectiveness, and even reduce supervisors' organizational mobility and job tenure.

From a public or societal perspective, the grievance procedure (and contract administration more broadly) has been described as an important component of "industrial justice," one that provides a Constitution-like form of checks and balances on employer decisions (Slichter, 1947). Indeed, the presence of grievance procedures in unionized settings may help to explain why radical unions, if not radical politics, have played so limited a role in the United States. But even if political democracy in the workplace is enhanced by grievance procedures, others argue that certain economic benefits accrue to society from the presence and use of grievance procedures.

The most forceful advocates of this view are Freeman and Medoff (1984), who describe the grievance procedure as a "voice" mechanism and analogize it to the voice exercised by consumers who complain to a company about the price, quality, or other attributes of its products. Such complaints are said to improve product quality and company operations, thereby benefiting consumers as a whole.[6] Similarly, employee voice exercised through the grievance procedure is said to reduce employee turnover, increase employee job tenure, enhance the training and skill of employees, and improve productivity—all with consequent benefits to society. Unfortunately, Freeman and Medoff provide little direct evidence on the use and consequences of grievance procedures at the individual enterprise, plant, or employee levels.

A different view of grievance procedures is proffered by Katz, Kochan, and Weber (1985). They contend that a "displacement effect" is at work in grievance processing, where displacement refers to the paid employee hours required to process a grievance that otherwise could have been devoted directly to productive activity. From this conception of grievance processing can be derived the hypothesis that grievance filing rates will be negatively related to firm or organizational subunit performance. Katz, Kochan, and Weber provide evidence that confirms this hypothesis, but that evidence is confined to a (nonrandom) sample of 25 plants of a large automobile manufacturing firm. Despite this limited evidential base, the displacement effect approach to the grievance process leads to fundamentally different conclusions about the outcomes or consequences of grievance processing from those derived from the voice approach to the grievance process.

In sum, grievance procedures offer an array of potential benefits but also potential costs to employees, union officials, managers, and the public as a whole. Some of these benefits and costs have been discussed in the literature, but few in-depth, recent, quantitative assessments of them are extant. Thus, at present, it is hardly possible to answer the question, "How effective are unionized grievance procedures in the United States?" This is one of the two central questions that will be addressed in this study.

A second question about grievance procedures is "What are the consequences of using the procedure?" Because grievance procedures are intended to resolve workplace conflict while both production and the employment relationship continue in place, these procedures may be thought to be "impact neutral" as between grievance filers and nonfilers. However, the aforementioned exit-voice model implies that grievance filers will benefit from use of the grievance procedure because they are bringing useful productivity-enhancing information to management. In contrast, organization punishment-industrial discipline models (Scott, 1965; O'Reilly and Weitz, 1980; Arvey and Jones, 1985) strongly suggest that grievance filers (that is, organizational "dissidents") will be sanctioned or subject to retribution for bringing conflict to the surface. Heretofore, no research on unionized grievance procedures has examined the post-grievance settlement behaviors of the parties so that we simply do not know which of these different perspectives on the consequences of grievance procedure usage has empirical validity. Hence, this issue and the second question noted above will also be addressed in this study.

EXTENT OF GRIEVANCE ACTIVITY

How many grievances are filed under a collective bargaining agreement in a given year? Does the volume of grievances vary over time, with the business cycle, by union and management organizational changes, or with the occurrence of bargaining itself? Answers to these questions are extremely hard to come by, for there is no comprehensive data base from which answers can be derived. Further and for the following reasons, it is unlikely that such a data base, especially a recurring data base, can be established.

A basic limitation in this regard is that, as noted earlier, the first step of most grievance procedures involves oral discussion and does not provide for written documentation. The grievant and the immediate supervisor are asked or required to discuss the grievance and to attempt to resolve it without resort to more formal proceedings. Only if a grievance cannot be resolved at this step will a grievance be reduced to writing. Hence the problem of unobserved or omitted variables is a substantial one in this regard, and, in addition, those grievances that are reduced to writing may present an upwardly biased picture of unresolved workplace conflict.

Not only are the volume of grievances and the determinants of grievance resolution largely unknown to researchers, they are often unknown to an enterprise's management. Consider that grievances are initiated and most are settled at the local workplace level, not at a centralized corporate or other macro-organization level. Supervisors who deal with workplace grievances typically do not have to report such grievances to higher levels unless the grievances go unresolved. In fact, certain unresolved grievances will be reported to higher organizational levels only if grievants decide to put their cases in writing and pursue them to higher steps of the grievance procedure. Thus, an enterprise's employee relations staff and its middle and senior management will, at best, only be informed about a subset—probably a very small subset—of all employee grievances in the organization.

One way of estimating the total annual volume of grievance activity in unionized settings is to use published data on arbitration cases. These are furnished annually by the U.S. Federal Mediation and Conciliation Service (FMCS) and the American Arbitration Association (AAA) for the number of cases filed (or panels requested) and arbitration awards rendered; the data are shown in Tables 1.1 and 1.2.

In 1986 the FMCS received about 31,500 panel requests, and the number of such requests averaged about 24,000 annually over the 1971-1986 period. The number of arbitration awards made under FMCS auspices totaled about 4,400 in 1985 (the last year for which data are available) and averaged about 5,600 annually over the 1977-1985 period. The AAA reports approximately 18,000 arbitration cases filed and approximately 2,600 arbitration awards rendered in 1986. The average annual volume of cases filed and awards rendered under AAA auspices over the 1971-1986 period were 14,400 and 5,200, respectively.

How many grievance cases might arise annually in unionized settings, based on the FMCS and AAA data? Let us assume that (1) FMCS and AAA grievance arbitration cases are independent of each other, (2) no nonunion grievance cases are contained in the FMCS and AAA data, (3) unionized grievance procedures contain four written steps, with arbitration being the fourth step, (4) panel requests and grievance cases constitute one-quarter of all cases that reach the third step of grievance procedures, (5) one-third of all second-step grievances are carried to the third step of grievance procedures, and (6) one-half of all first-step grievances are taken to the second step of grievance procedures. By this reckoning and beginning with a combined FMCS-AAA total of grievance panels requested and grievance cases filed (about 50,000), some 1,200,000 written grievance cases would have occurred in the United States in 1986.

Following the dominant view expressed in the grievance literature, namely, that most grievances are never put into writing, suppose that six grievances are resolved at the oral discussion stage for each grievance that is put in writing. On this basis, about 7,200,000 grievances would have occurred in unionized workplaces in 1986. If the ratio of oral to written grievances is 9/1, as is suggested by some students of this subject (Kuhn, 1961), then the volume of grievances occurring in 1986 would have approached 11,000,000. And this does not include grievances that employees failed to bring to the attention of supervisors, even in an informal way. Lest this last calculation be regarded as wildly off the mark, consider that 11,000,000 grievances translates into roughly one grievance annually for every two unionized workers in the U.S. economy. Further, 1,200,000 written grievances translates into approximately one grievance annually for every 20 unionized workers in the economy.

None of this, of course, establishes the precise number or perhaps even a close approximation of the volume of grievance activity in unionized settings that occurs at any point in time. Rather, the discussion under-

Table 1.1
Panel Requests and Grievance Arbitration Awards
Filed with the U.S. Federal Mediation
and Conciliation Service, 1971-1986

Year	Number of Panel Requests[1]	Number of Arbitration Awards[2]
1971	12,327	NA[3]
1972	13,005	NA
1973	13,626	NA
1974	15,445	NA
1975	18,619	NA
1976	20,732	NA
1977	23,474	4,574
1978	25,639	5,529
1979	27,189	5,655
1980	29,906	7,539
1981	30,050	6,967
1982	30,734	7,120
1983	30,706	6,096
1984	30,159	5,834
1985	31,222	4,406
1986	31,515	NA

[1]Includes interest arbitration panel requests which are less than one percent of total annual requests.
[2]Does not include awards unidentified by the FMCS due to inadequate reporting by arbitrators.
[3]Not Available.

Source: FMCS Annual Reports and communication to the authors, February 16, 1987

Table 1.2
Cases Filed with and Grievance Awards
Rendered by the American Arbitration
Association, 1971-1986

Year	Cases Filed	Awards Rendered
1971	6,658	3,837
1972	7,657	3,854
1973	8,569	4,239
1974	10,261	5,213
1975	13,251	6,784
1976	14,333	7,127
1977	14,661	7,195
1978	16,437	7,713
1979	16,669	7,525
1980	17,062	7,382
1981	17,664	7,256
1982	17,038	3,917
1983	17,511	6,956
1984	17,211	6,434
1985	17,527	6,119
1986	17,872	2,592

Source: Director of Case Administration, American Arbitration
          Association, February 1987.

scores that the extent of workplace conflict cannot readily be judged from data that pertain only to the last stage of formal conflict resolution procedures (that is, arbitration). Yet, unfortunately, these are the only systematic data in existence about grievance activity in the United States. While we are not conducting an economy-wide study, the data obtained in this research from employers and unions in four sectors of the economy are intended to provide better information on the volume of grievance activity and grievance resolution in unionized settings.

THE EVOLUTION OF GRIEVANCE PROCEDURES

The grievance procedure in the United States has undergone considerable changes. For example, prior to World War II, it was common practice to use mediation rather than arbitration where the parties were unable to resolve a grievance that arose during the life of the labor agreement (Fleming, 1965; Prasow and Peters, 1983). In fact, some of the early labor arbitrators initially served as grievance mediators.

During World War II, the War Labor Board was created to establish machinery that would minimize the effects of strikes and other forms of workplace conflict on industrial production. Since most strikes were technically illegal during that time, it became necessary to develop mechanisms to address employee grievances that arose while labor agreements were in force; what emerged was grievance arbitration. If labor and management could not resolve their differences, then members of the War Labor Board would render decisions on the issues in dispute. Initially the process worked well because the parties accepted the underlying national interest that gave rise to it, even though no legal requirement existed to compel participation in arbitration proceedings.

This continued to be the case until the early 1950s (Prasow and Peters, 1983). Thereafter, the parties began to reject arbitrators' decisions. In other instances, one or the other of the parties to the labor agreement was unwilling to enter into arbitration even if contract language called for such a proceeding. Consequently, labor and management began to negotiate more directly over conflict resolution processes. Multistep grievance procedures became increasingly common and arbitration commonly became the last step of the grievance process. Unionists favored arbitration because it provided a vehicle for resolving workplace disputes without the need to conduct strikes against employers. Management, though reluctant to permit a third party to render a final and binding decision about a workplace dispute, sought and achieved no-strike provisions in labor agreements in return for multistep grievance procedures that included arbitration as the final step.

As to public policy governing labor-management relations, prior to 1947 Congress refrained from requiring federal enforcement of collective bargaining agreements. This changed, however, with the passage in 1947 of the Labor-Management Relations (Taft-Hartley) Act. Section 301 of the act permitted cases to be brought before U.S. district courts where violations of labor agreements were alleged to have occurred. The decisions of the U.S. Supreme Court in the Lincoln Mills (1957) and Steelworkers Trilogy (1960) cases provided the legal foundation for enforcement of labor arbitration awards and, indeed, of labor contracts as a whole (Prasow and Peters, 1983). Moreover, the Supreme Court took the position that arbitration was preferable to the courts in resolving workplace disputes that arose during the life of labor agreements.

An exception to this general position concerns cases involving allegations of race or sex discrimination. Here, the Supreme Court ruled in the *Gardner v. Denver* (1973) case that arbitration was not necessarily the final route of grievance resolution. In such cases and where employees lose their appeals in arbitration, the employees are not precluded from turning to the courts for the adjudication of their grievances. Some analysts predicted that the *Gardner-Denver* decision would spell the demise of grievance arbitration, but this judgment proved to be inaccurate. In fact, discrimination cases came to be heard by arbitrators who developed expertise in employment discrimination law.

As the unionized grievance procedure evolved during the third quarter of the twentieth century, complaints proliferated about delays in grievance processing. The gap between initial grievance filing and the rendering of an arbitration award was alleged to have increased substantially, exceeding a full year in some cases. To counter the contention that "justice delayed was justice denied" under the grievance procedure, labor and management began in the 1970s to experiment with expedited arbitration procedures for certain types of workplace disputes (Zalusky, 1976). A detailed review of these procedures will be provided in Chapter 2. Despite their emergence and growth, however, expedited grievance procedures have not been systematically examined for their consequences or in relation to more conventional grievance procedures. Because expedited grievance procedures are widely used in one and sporadically used in another of the sectors included in this study, we will examine the effectiveness of these procedures and compare them to the effectiveness of nonexpedited, or conventional, grievance procedures.

An even more recent development is the reemergence of grievance mediation as a method of resolving grievances short of arbitration (Gregory and Rooney, 1980; Goldberg and Brett, 1983). At first glance, grievance mediation appears to reduce the costs and shorten the time involved in grievance processing relative to more conventional procedures. Such mediation may also be superior to arbitration where there has been a breakdown in the grievance system, such as in the coal mining industry (Brett, Goldberg, and Ury, 1980). However, and as with expedited arbitration, systematic analysis of the costs and benefits of grievance mediation compared to other grievance resolution procedures is lacking. More will be said about this matter in the detailed review of the grievance literature presented in Chapter 2.

In sum, substantial changes in grievance procedures have occurred over the last several decades. Chief among these, perhaps, is that the grievance procedure has become largely an adjudicative process whereas it was once largely a problem-solving process. In recent years, moreover, an emphasis on problem solving has reemerged as labor and management have experimented with expedited grievance procedures and grievance mediation. Whatever its particular form, however, an analytical model of the grievance procedure is required if progress is to be made in the empirical study of this conflict resolution mechanism. This is the subject of the next section.

GRIEVANCE PROCEDURE DYNAMICS AND MODELING

Most of the literature on the grievance process is atheoretical, so that Thomson's 1974 observation still holds: "So far no theory of the grievance process has evolved." Only a few studies (Peach and Livernash, 1974; Thomson and Murray, 1976) have offered conceptual models of the grievance procedure, and even fewer have generated testable hypotheses by which to study grievance procedures. We intend to remedy both these weaknesses.

Figure 1.1 presents a partial model of the grievance procedure that incorporates concepts drawn from other grievance models as well as from the collective bargaining literature (see Lewin, Feuille, Kochan, and Delaney, 1988). The model shows that grievance activity is influenced by (1) environmental forces, including economic, political, legal, and techological forces; (2) characteristics of the union and management organizations, including centralization, internal conflict, the nature of supervision, and the ratio of union stewards to members; (3) union and management grievance policies, including the formality of and consistency with which management policies are applied and union policies with respect to filing certain types of grievances and challenging a certain proportion of grievance rulings; (4) characteristics of the labor-management relationship, including the degree of trust or hostility between the parties and the extent to which the parties engage in problem-solving behavior; and (5) characteristics of the employer's work force (and the union's membership), including size, occupational composition, age, sex, race, education, and work experience. These variables are expected to determine the structure of the grievance process, the scope of grievance issues, the volume and types of grievances filed, and the extent to which grievances are taken to higher steps

Figure 1.1
A Partial Model of the Grievance Procedure

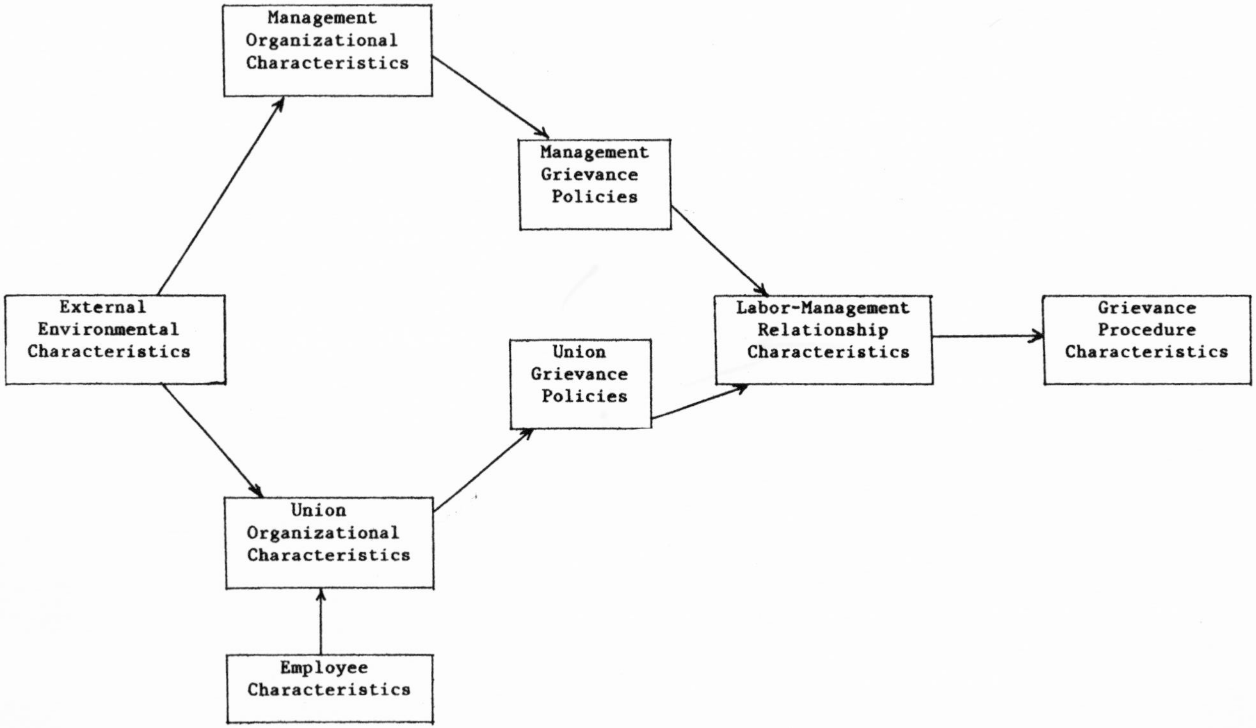

of the grievance procedure. In this model, the grievance procedure is a dependent variable, and its structure, functions, and utilization are determined by key environmental, organizational, and individual variables.

Alternatively, and as with the collective bargaining process, the grievance procedure may be modeled as an independent variable that influences certain labor relations outcomes, notably the resolution of grievances. From this perspective, the characteristics of the grievance procedure are expected to affect the level and speed of grievance settlement and the substance of grievance decisions, including the frequency with which management's or the union's position is upheld, the reinstatement of workers to their jobs, and the awarding of back pay and benefits.

Of course, grievance outcomes will be influenced not only by the characteristics of the grievance procedure, but by the independent variables—environmental, organizational, and individual—that also shape the grievance procedure itself. In other words, some of these variables will influence grievance resolution directly while other variables will have indirect effects that are transmitted through the grievance process. Consequently, the grievance procedure is most suitably modeled not as a dependent or an independent variable but, instead, as an intervening variable, the characteristics of which are shaped by environmental, organizational, and individual variables and that, in turn, influences grievance resolution. This model reflects a systems view of the grievance procedure in which certain inputs (for example, organizational characteristics) are transformed into certain outputs (for example, grievance resolution). Figure 1.2 depicts this systems model of the grievance procedure.

Also shown in Figure 1.2 is a post-grievance resolution variable. This refers to the behavior manifested by the parties to grievances after grievances have been resolved. For example, turnover among grievance filers may be higher than among nonfilers in the immediate post-grievance settlement period. Or promotion rates among grievance filers may be lower than among nonfilers in the period following grievance settlement. Similarly, supervisors who are direct parties to grievances filed may have higher turnover rates and lower promotion rates in the post-grievance settlement period than supervisors who are not directly involved in grievance activity. The received grievance literature is silent on these matters, but both organizational behavior and management science research suggest that a complete systems model of the grievance process should include a post-grievance settlement variable (Nadler and Tushman, 1979).

GRIEVANCE PROCEDURE EFFECTIVENESS

How effective are grievance procedures and how can grievance procedure effectiveness be operationalized and measured? While these mat-

Figure 1.2
A Systems Model of the Grievance Procedure

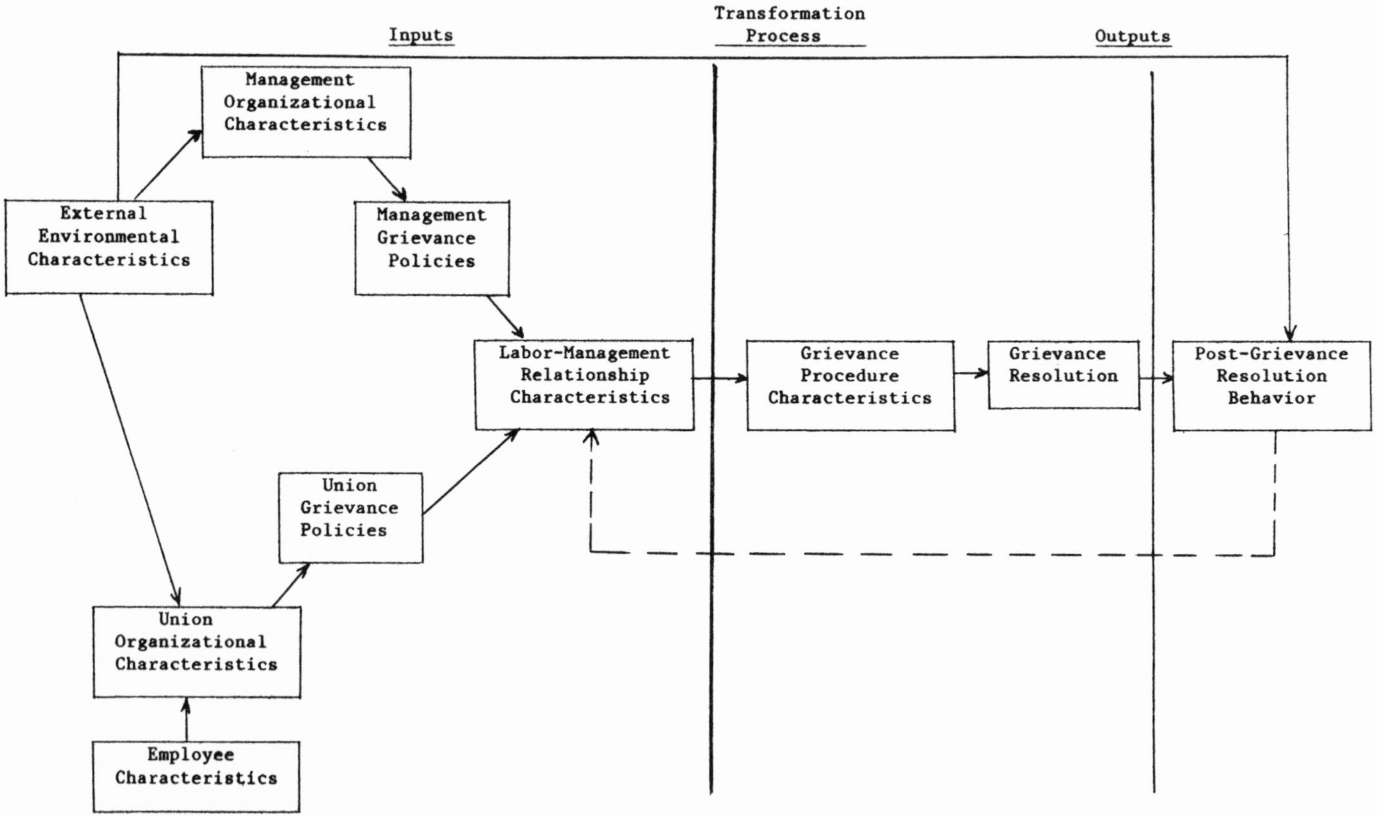

Inputs | Transformation Process | Outputs

- External Environmental Characteristics
- Management Organizational Characteristics
- Management Grievance Policies
- Union Grievance Policies
- Union Organizational Characteristics
- Employee Characteristics
- Labor-Management Relationship Characteristics
- Grievance Procedure Characteristics
- Grievance Resolution
- Post-Grievance Resolution Behavior

ters will be more fully taken up in Chapter 3, a few observations about grievance procedure effectiveness will be made here. First, no single measure of grievance procedure effectiveness has been agreed to by researchers, although the grievance filing rate is the most commonly used measure. Second, effectiveness may be judged by behavioral data, such as the grievance rate or the arbitration rate, and by attitudinal data, such as the parties' perceived equity of grievance settlement. Third, effectiveness is an "interim" concept in that it is used to measure a process, not the outcomes of a process. Unlike the concept of efficiency, which is used to measure directly the outcomes of certain economic processes, measures of grievance procedure effectiveness must be constructed.

In this study we will use several measures of grievance procedure effectiveness, including the grievance rate, the level of settlement, the speed of settlement, the arbitration rate, the percentage of grievances settled in favor of one or the other party, and the parties' perceived equity of grievance settlement. Some of these are behavioral measures and others are attitudinal measures, but apparently they have never been used in combination to measure grievance procedure effectivenss. This study of grievance procedure effectiveness will be guided by the systems model of the grievance procedure shown in Figure 1.2.

POST-GRIEVANCE SETTLEMENT BEHAVIOR

What are the consequences of grievance procedure usage and settlement and how can these be operationalized and measured? While these matters will also be more fully taken up in Chapter 3, a few relevant points should be noted here. First and as with grievance procedure effectiveness, no single indicator or measure of post-grievance settlement is likely to be adequate; certainly none has even been provided by previous researchers. Second, post-grievance settlement consequences are probably best judged by behavioral data, such as turnover rates, promotion rates, or performance measures. Note, however, that for many jobs and employees, including those included in this study, performance measures take the form of supervisory ratings, which themselves are largely attitudinal or perceptual in nature. Hence, it may not be possible to assess post-grievance settlement consequences strictly by behavioral data or measures. Third, some post-grievance settlement consequences, such as voluntary and involuntary turnover, result in termination of the employment relationship, while other consequences, such as lowered promotion rates or performance ratings for grievance filers, do not (necessarily) do so. Therefore, in a longitudinal analysis of post-grievance settlement consequences only certain behaviors can be sequentially or repeatedly studied and measured.

In this study, we will use several measures of post-grievance settlement consequences, including voluntary and involuntary turnover rates, work attendance rates, promotion rates, and performance ratings. The research approach will be to examine these measures over time for samples of grievance filers and nonfilers, and to compare these measures both prior to and following the filing and settlement of grievances. Advantage will also be taken of a unique opportunity to examine the post-grievance settlement behavior of supervisors and managers against whom grievances were and were not filed during the period under study. This portion of the research will also be guided by the systems model of the grievance procedure shown in Figure 1.2.

SUMMARY AND REMAINING CHAPTERS

In this opening chapter, we addressed (1) the definition of grievances and the rationale for studying unionized grievance procedures, (2) the importance of grievance activity, (3) the extent of grievance activity, (4) the evolution of grievance procedures, and (5) the concept of grievance procedure effectiveness. The remainder of the book is organized as follows.

Chapter 2 provides a detailed review and an assessment of the grievance procedure literature, especially that portion of the literature that has emerged since 1960. Chapter 3 sets forth the research design for the study, including the specification of hypotheses, operationalization of variables, identification of research sites and sources, sample selection, data collection methods, and methods of data analysis. Chapters 4 and 5 report the empirical analysis and findings about grievance procedure effectiveness in steel manufacturing, retail department stores, nonprofit hospitals, and local public schools. Survey data obtained for the study are emphasized in Chapter 4, while both survey and interview data are incorporated into Chapter 5. The post-grievance settlement behavior of the parties to grievance activity in four organizations is examined in Chapter 6. The final chapter summarizes the major findings and conclusions of the study, derives implications for theory building and further research into the grievance procedure, and offers recommendations to practitioners for improving the functioning and effectiveness of grievance procedures.

NOTES

1. Grievance procedures are pervasive in industrial union contracts where employees work for a single employer, but are generally not present in craft union contracts where employees move from employer to employer on a job shop basis, such as in the construction industry. For evidence that a majority of large U.S. companies maintain grievancelike appeal and complaint systems for

nonunion employees, see Berenbeim (1980). For evidence of the uses and behavioral consequences of nonunion grievance procedures, see Lewin (1986, 1987a).

2. See, for example, Sloane and Witney (1985) and Davey, Bognanno, and Estenson (1982).

3. See, for example, Kaufman (1982), Svejnar (1980), Bloom (1981), and Masters (1985).

4. However, see Anderson (1979), Briggs (1982), and Knight (1986).

5. See Kochan, McKersie, and Cappelli (1984) and Lewin (1987b).

6. The consumer analogy and the conceptual basis of Freeman and Medoff's work may be found in Hirschman (1970).

2

The Grievance Procedure in Practice and Research: Review and Assessment

What is meant by the term "grievance procedure"? Chamberlain (1965) offers the following definition:

The grievance procedure is thus a many splendored thing. It is in part the judicial process of applying the terms of the agreement to particular situations, as it is most frequently pictured. It is also the mechanism through which the first-line representatives of union and management engage in a continuing contest over the exercise of authority in the shop—a contest which may be relatively quiescent, at the one extreme, or almost brutal, at the other, but which is always present in some degree. The grievance process is also a device which strategic groups within the union can use to engage in fractional bargaining on their own behalf, sometimes challenging the authority of the union in the doing but more often able to clothe their purpose in "grievances" which have at least the air of legitimacy about them. And finally, the grievance process, in the hands of sophisticated practitioners, can be made an instrument for more effective administration within the shop. (p. 247)

Put more succinctly, "the essence of the grievance procedure is to provide a means by which an employee, without jeopardizing his job, can express a complaint about his work or working conditions and obtain a fair hearing through progressively higher levels of management" (Steiber, 1968).

In this chapter we will review the grievance procedure literature and focus on definitional components of the procedure. We begin by exam-

We express our appreciation to Tom Pearce and Karen Evans for research assistance provided to the authors in the preparation of this chapter. Pearce is now on the faculty of Oklahoma State University, and Evans is at the University of Massachusetts at Amherst.

ining the mechanics and functioning of grievance procedures in union-ized settings. Next some of the strengths and weaknesses of the griev-ance procedure are discussed. In this regard it may be asked whether the grievance procedure is truly a "many splendored thing" or merely a thorn in the sides of both management and union. Then we examine expedited arbitration and grievance mediation, two relatively new tech-niques apparently gaining in popularity as methods of workplace conflict resolution. Next we identify the key studies of grievance procedures and the key variables contained in these studies. In the final section of the chapter, we provide an overall assessment of the grievance procedure literature.

THE GRIEVANCE PROCEDURE IN
THE UNIONIZED SETTING

As a prelude to discussing the mechanics and functions of the griev-ance procedure, it is important to recognize the significant roles that attitudes, beliefs, and perceptions play in all grievance procedures. As Veglahn (1977) notes, "The mechanics of the process are far less impor-tant than the participant's attitude toward the procedure" (p. 150). Thomson and Murray (1976), who offer a generalized framework for the analysis of grievance procedures, also emphasize the importance of the attitudes and perceptions of the parties. Their summary is worth quoting at length:

1. All industrial situations contain conditions and events which can be potentially dissatisfying to employees (latent issues). A grievance begins with some sort of "triggering event" which transforms a latent issue into a conscious one.

2. This event creates a "cognitive" or psychological reaction in the mind of the employee affected.

3. Assuming one decides to act on the feelings of dissatisfacton, several choices are possible. One may seek out fellow employees to see if they have the same sense of grievance (potential allies). If they do, a process of building a sense of group cohesion around the grievance may begin. The other typical action is to confront someone who is seen as being able to correct the grievance.

4. Once the grievance is made manifest the parties involved usually engage in mutual probing to establish how strongly the other feels about the issue, what the other "really" wants and intends to do about it, etc. This position clari-fication stage may be as perfunctory as a single question or it may involve lengthy meetings or "behind the scenes" investigation.

5. Once a management representative has received a grievance and obtained some clarification of the grievant's position on the matter he is the one who must now make several decisions. He can choose to ignore the matter; try to handle it himself; consult with colleagues; ask for a superior's advice; or turn the matter over to a superior for a decision.

6. Once a first decision on the grievance is reached and communicated a "reaction phase" begins. Assuming the decision is unsatisfactory, the grievant can choose to live with the dissatisfying situation, to seek out allies or agents for support, or to pursue the matter further on his own.

7. The person on the management side who receives the grievant's reaction to the initial management response must go through the same cognitive process.

8. The final outcome may involve a compromise, "total victory" for one side or the other, or a solution in which both parties are better off than previously. The outcome also contains an aftermath: it will affect the attitudes of each side about the overall continuing relationship between them. The whole issue then rejoins the latent pool from which it originally arose. (pp. 19-20)

ELEMENTS OF THE GRIEVANCE PROCEDURE

The actual machinery used to process grievances in unionized settings has often been discussed in the literature. For example, Slichter, Healy, and Livernash (1960) observe that:

In a broad sense the formal grievance procedures found in various labor agreements are very similar. Since they are appeal procedures, there are always several steps involved. Usually there are two lower steps and one or two higher steps followed by arbitration. . . . Grievances involving established policy and precedent are expected to be settled at lower steps. . . . The higher steps are usually required for grievances calling for a new policy or precedent and also for a few grievances too "hot" for lower-step settlement. (p. 722)

Slichter, Healy, and Livernash also note, however, that there are distinctive characteristics of individual labor agreements and wide variation in details among them. Further, the grievance procedures outlined in most labor contracts are really more complicated than a casual reading might suggest because the written procedure only hints at the involved and intricate practice. Nevertheless, one generally finds that grievance procedures vary according to degree of formality, character of representation, regulation of grievance activity, and other special grievance activities.

Degree of Formality

Degree of formality is the extent to which the procedure includes such factors as specifications for written grievances, time limits for responses at each step, and the designation of grievance handling representatives at each step of the procedure. According to Veglahn (1977), the greater the number of steps in the grievance process the more formal is the process. The trend in recent years apparently has been toward more formal grievance procedures. One reason for this is that the existence of a more formalized procedure seems to encourage employee use of the procedure. Another reason is that the writing up of a grievance at the first step and the requirement of a written answer at that step encourages the clarification of the issue, the dropping of complaints with inadequate substance, and more thorough investigation before a written answer is given (Slichter, Healy, and Livernash, 1960).

Character of Representation

The character of union and management representation in grievance procedures varies widely. For example, structural differences among union organizations lead to differences in representation. Some unions leave representation in grievance disputes up to the local officials while others bring in a national or international representative in the later stages of grievance processing. Some enterprises emphasize the role of supervisors and lower-level managers in grievance processing, while other enterprises emphasize the role of middle and senior management. Degree of formality of the grievance procedure also affects grievance representation. Some contracts specify precisely who will be represented by both sides at each step of the process, while other contracts are more general in this regard.

Regulation of Grievance Activity

Grievance procedures also tend to vary in terms of the regulation of grievance handling. Most contracts require the employer to compensate union representatives for work-time lost while processing grievances, and some contracts even provide that the employer will pay for full-time union representatives in the plant. Usually upper limits are placed on how much time a union representative can spend on grievance handling and on leaving the job without supervisory permission.

Handling "Special" Grievances

Another factor that brings about variation in unionized grievance procedures is the manner in which the parties handle "special" grievances (Slichter, Healy, and Livernash, 1960). A common practice is to expedite discharge, suspension, and layoff cases either by filing such grievances at the third step or advancing such grievances rapidly to that step. However, the practice may not necessarily be spelled out in the contract.

Some disagreement exists in the literature about the number of steps that should be included in a grievance procedure. Thomson and Murray (1976) advise:

The lowest feasible number of steps within a plant is probably three: supervisor, departmental or other middle management, and senior management. The decision reached is almost entirely a function of the size of plant and the number of levels of management and not, in this instance, of the level of conflict. Essentially, wherever there is a significant level of effective authority, there should be a step. However, too many steps within the internal plant procedure could lead to delay and repetition and encourage by-passing. In general the guiding rule should probably be: if in doubt, choose fewer rather than more steps and add to them later if necessary. (p. 140)

Slichter, Healy, and Livernash (1960) report that:

there are two-step, three-step, four-step, five-step and six-step procedures. It does not follow that large companies always have complex appeal procedures while small companies have simple procedures. For example, one very large company has a two-step procedure plus arbitration, and many small companies match each level of supervision with a separate grievance step. (p. 722)

Thus, there is no consensus about the proper or optimal number of steps to be included in a unionized grievance procedure. Note, further, that no research has been done to determine whether the number of steps in unionized grievance procedures is larger or smaller, on average, than those in nonunion grievance procedures, though it is likely that there is more variation in this regard in nonunion than in unionized settings.

FUNCTIONS OF THE UNIONIZED GRIEVANCE PROCEDURE

The unionized grievance procedure has several functions. One function is to insure that there is *compliance* with the collective bargaining agreement. In the case of the early craft unions, the business agent or working delegate visited the worksite to check working conditions and see that both employees and employers abided by the contract. Following the unionization of industrial workers in the 1930s, the shop steward came to serve the role of a contract "policeman," but often without the powers to compel the employer to conform to the agreement. Typically, management felt obligated only to hear complaints and to dispose of them only in terms of management's conception of its own rights (Kuhn, 1961).

Following Kuhn (1961), the second function of the grievance process is *adjudicative* in nature. This function emerged out of the War Labor Board experience and the early post–world War II period when binding arbitration of unresolved grievances emerged. The adjudicative role was strengthened by key Supreme Court decisions in the late 1950s and early 1960s (for example, the Steelworkers Trilogy cases) that gave legal sanctions to arbitrators' awards. No longer were industrial relations officers regarded as "judges." A neutral third party would serve as the judge in a grievance case if the parties were unable to resolve their differences at earlier steps of the grievance procedure.

The third function of the grievance process is the *administrative* function. In this regard, both management and union representatives serve as expert problem solvers and members of administrative bodies (such as grievance committees and tripartite arbitration boards) established under the collective bargaining agreement. Their decisions in grievance cases help to establish precedents and administer the work-related aspects of the enterprise.

The fourth function of the grievance process, one often neglected by researchers, is a *political* function in which pressure is brought to bear on management to gain particular concessions for one or more interest groups of workers (Kuhn, 1961). Such pressure may be exerted through the union or by the work group itself. In these cases, there may be threats of walkabouts, mass absenteeism, wildcat strikes, slowdowns, or working-to-rule (see Somers, 1956; MacDonald et al., 1956).

Kuhn (1961) refers to work-group pressures as fractional bargaining designed to gain special treatment of members of a particular employee group. His discussion of the "Hot Tread" case in a rubber plant illustrates the differences between the apparent and real causes of a fractional grievance. Thus, the amount of fractional bargaining is influenced by: (1) the reaction of the entire work group to a grievance, (2) the presence of union representatives as a second center of authority, and (3) the interests of different people and groups on both sides of the labor relationship who pursue their own goals. Kuhn then discusses the tactics of fractional bargaining, including costs, timing, and impacts on both the union and employer organizations. He makes clear that the use of fractional bargaining brings about certain intraorganizational and interorganizational problems.

What all of this suggests is that a thorough understanding of the grievance procedure requires recognition of both the *formal* and *informal* nature of the process. Therefore, we need to understand not only how the grievance procedure meets the objectives laid out for it both in theory and practice, but also the dynamics of the process. Kuhn's (1961) study of twenty different plants in nine industries provides some of this understanding, but his study was largely qualitative and it explored a limited set of grievance procedure dynamics.

STRENGTHS AND WEAKNESSES
OF THE GRIEVANCE PROCEDURE

The strengths and weaknesses of the grievance process have been frequently debated in the literature.

Strengths

Staudohar (1977) identifies the following strengths and benefits of the grievance procedure:

1. an orderly channel to reduce pressures and anxieties of employees;
2. a mechanism for equitable and just interpretation and application of negotiated terms;
3. a communication outlet to promote understanding of the negotiated agreement by both sides;
4. a built-in substitute for a test of economic strength that can provide ongoing consideration of agreement disputes without upsetting the flow work; and
5. a force against arbitrary, capricious, and discriminatory actions by management. (p. 6)

Lewin (1983) adds to this list of benefits:

Grievance procedures are commended not only for providing a peaceful means of resolving day-to-day workplace disputes and for enabling workers to participate in decisions that affect their work lives, but also for the benefits that they provide to management. These include a virtual guarantee of uninterrupted production during the life of the labor agreement, the use by management of union resources and personnel to police the labor agreement, and a systematic source of information about problem areas in the workplace—information that can be used for subsequent evaluation and corrective action. (pp. 127-128)

Briggs (1982a) identifies the following benefits of the grievance procedure: improving conflict management, communication, adjudication and due process, institutional strength enhancement, and personal objective management. Conflict management is perhaps the most widely recognized benefit of a grievance procedure. Without such a conflict resolution mechanism, workplace disputes in unionized settings presumably would be "resolved" through tests of economic strength. However, it is also possible, as Hirschman (1970) observes, that "employees who do not enjoy such a 'voice' opportunity might 'exit' the organization entirely, and in most instances the former is preferable to both employees and employers." (p. 49)

The adjudicatory and due process functions of unionized grievance procedures are served in most cases by specifying arbitration as the final step in the process. This has the advantage of increasing perceptions of fairness and equity and promoting the acceptability of grievance decisions.

Grievance procedures are also said to enhance institutional strength, for example by assisting unions in developing employee loyalty. Briggs (1984) and Kuhn (1961), as examples, believe that the union's major role in grievance processing is to help develop a bond of loyalty among bargaining unit employees. The procedures can also benefit both union and management personnel by assisting in the training and development of shop stewards and supervisors. Personal objectives also are furthered by grievance procedures. The creation of a vehicle for resolving union-management conflicts convinces union members that union leaders are doing their jobs, which, in turn, aids union leaders in getting reelected.

Weaknesses

Several weaknesses of grievance procedures are also mentioned in the literature. For example, Veglahn (1977) notes that:

> While grievance procedures should exist to provide a forum for solving problems, any grievance is disadvantageous to both parties. Management and workers have their attention diverted from their primary task while a solution is being sought. No winner results from decisions in the grievance procedure. A decision puts things into a state that would have been if the grievance had never occurred. The only thing that is different from the way things should have been in the first place is that someone is probably dissatisfied with the outcome. (p. 122)

Other disadvantages of grievance procedures are discussed by Dalton and Todor (1981): "Not only is the grievance process expensive but it is disruptive as well. Obviously, during the process, grievants are taken off the job to testify and managers must abandon their normal assignments, among a host of other disturbances" (p. 25).

A thorough summary of the disadvantages of grievance procedures to each party has been provided by Thomson and Murray (1976). For management, the major potential disadvantage of the grievance procedure concerns the limitation on management control when binding arbitration is the final step. A related concern is that the grievance procedure may be inflexible given the broad range of issues that can be raised through it. Unions are also concerned with the loss of control that may result when binding third-party arbitration is involved. However, for employees, the major disadvantages of the grievance procedure are delays in grievance processing and the cumbersomeness of the procedures, which may inhibit employees in pursuing grievances.

Probably the area within the grievance process most hotly contested by academicians and practitioners alike is the use of arbitration as the final decision step. Getman (1979) comments that, in some cases, arbitration may actually be detrimental:

> When labor relations are unsatisfactory, the existence of arbitration may actually exacerbate bad feeling. In such circumstances the jurisprudence of arbitration encourages management to enforce discipline for all offenses to avoid providing

arbitrators with a reason for mitigation. The union responds by filing numerous grievances that are regularly denied at the lower steps. The union is forced to go to arbitration frequently, which causes a backlog with concomitant delays in hearing and disposition. The hearing is pervaded with an atmosphere of hostility; it provides the parties with an additional opportunity to berate each other. Conflicts and wildcat strikes are provoked when management takes disciplinary action or denies a grievance, when arbitration is delayed, or when one of the parties considers an arbitrator's decision unacceptable. All of this makes the grievance machinery a cause of further tension. (p. 925)

Stessin (1977) also attacks the practicality of grievance arbitration:

Grievance attribution as it is structured in over 100,000 union contracts has lost many of its virtues, being neither economical nor quick, neither flexible nor informal. Evidence abounds that the system has succumbed to the rise of rigidity and is often ill-designed to serve as a quick means of settling disputes between workers and the boss. (p. 128)

Berenbeim (1980) concludes that management usually objects to arbitration primarily because of its costs and, secondly, because it is an invasion of management prerogatives. In nonunion enterprises, moreover, management is typically concerned about whether or not the use of arbitration in an appeals or grievancelike system will lead to union organizing. Though there is little experience to support this fear, according to Berenbeim, the unease persists.

Despite these disadvantages, however, arbitration is incorporated as the terminal step in almost all unionized grievance procedures, and support for this step remains strong in some quarters. As an example, 78 percent of the 235 officials of nineteen separate unions who were surveyed by Graham, Heshizer, and Johnson (1978) responded that arbitration was still the best method for resolving unsettled grievances during the life of the labor agreement. Thus, though there are advantages and disadvantages to grievance procedures in general and arbitration in particular, it seems likely that they will continue to exist for some time. What will be addressed next, therefore, is the question of whether expedited arbitration improves the functioning and effectiveness of grievance procedures.

EXPEDITED ARBITRATION

The time delays and costs of arbitration when used as the final step in the grievance procedure have been widely commented on and criticized in the literature (Landis, 1982). Graham, Heshizer, and Johnson (1978) found that high costs were a factor discouraging unions in their sample from proceeding to arbitration. Approximately one third (70) of the respondents said they had dropped grievances considered meritorious because of cost considerations. Data from the Federal Mediation and Conciliation Service (FMCS) showed that: "The average cost of arbitration in 1981 was $1,132, up from $1,290 in 1980. The average elapsed time between the requests for a FMCS panel and an award being rendered by an arbitrator was 151.09 days" (FMCS, 1981, pp. 37-39). Expedited arbitration has developed as a technique to respond to precisely these types of criticisms.

Experience with Expedited Arbitration

In an effort to solve some of the problems associated with conventional arbitration problems, an expedited arbitration procedure was adopted by the General Electric Company and the International Union of Electrical Workers (IUE) in 1971. The procedure called for the scheduling of hearings in all discharge and upgrading cases within 60 days; the elimination of detailed written opinions in discipline and discharge cases if questions of contract interpretation, arbitrability or due process were not involved; and the elimination of stenographic transcripts when the only issue was whether discipline or discharge was for just cause.

In August 1971, ten of the largest steel companies and the United Steelworkers Union also adopted an expedited procedure to help settle a large backlog of grievances. Expedited arbitration was used only for routine grievances and resulted in substantial savings of time and money. The parties involved were generally satisfied with the quality of the decisions resulting from the process. The procedure, called the Basic Steel Plan, will be described later in this chapter.

The U.S. Postal Service and its four largest unions agreed to begin expedited arbitration, effective January 1, 1974; it became a permanent part of the grievance system on July 1, 1975. Currently, the agreement limits the use of expedited arbitration to disciplinary cases involving 30-day suspension or less. Discharge cases or contract interpretation cases of a technical or policy-making nature are not considered under the expedited procedure.

The major difference between the U.S. Postal Service expedited arbitration system and the one adopted by the Steelworkers is in the selection of arbitrators. The Postal Service uses only experienced arbitrators from either the American Arbitration Association (AAA) or the FMCS roster. According to Cushman (1974), the parties reasoned that experienced arbitrators could more readily make effective use of a streamlined and speedy arbitration process tailored to the needs of the parties. Initially, the Postal Service established seven regional panels staffed with members of the AAA rosters, but since that time, 23 additional regional panels have been established with arbitrators from the FMCS. Under the Steel Plan, in contrast, twelve expedited arbitration panels were established in major steel-producing localities and these were staffed by more than 200 young arbitrators, mostly attorneys, who had little previous arbitration experience.

In addition to these examples, Stessin (1977) notes that since 1971, over 500 U.S. companies and unions have adopted expedited arbitration procedures.

Models of Expedited Arbitration

Grievance procedures that culminate in expedited arbitration vary in form from company to company. However, Hoellering (1972) identified several elements that are common to a majority of the procedures. These include:

1. Identification of the types of cases which should and could be arbitrated under expedited procedures.
2. Provision for an adequate number of experienced arbitrators who are able to meet contracted time limits and who are available for early hearing dates.
3. Prompt impartial administration to handle appointment of arbitrators (usually requiring knowledge of the arbitrators in the area and their availability), scheduling of hearings, arranging compensation of arbitrators, and the performance of other similar administrative details.
4. The cooperation of management, labor, and the arbitrators to make the expedited process work. (p. 325)

Rarely are all types of grievance issues considered appropriate for expedited arbitration. Most firms limit expedited arbitration to minor disciplinary grievances and occasionally to discharge cases. Most non-routine and complex grievances remain subject to traditional arbitration. Thus, where it exists, expedited arbitration does not supplant traditional arbitration, but instead, serves as a parallel track on the grievance route (Stessin, 1977). One reason for this duality of procedures is identified by Sandver, Blaine, and Woyar (1981): "The very nature of the expedited arbitration process limits the types of cases it can effectively deal with. In complex cases involving major policy questions or questions of contract interpretation, the parties' primary goal is *not* speed. The parties want a well considered, thoroughly researched and well-informed decision from the arbitrator, even if they have to wait a few months to get it" (p. 20). Obtaining an adequate number of arbitrators who are able to handle the expedited arbitration cases in a timely manner is also difficult. As noted earlier, the steel industry has dealt with this problem primarily by using young, relatively inexperienced lawyers as arbitrators since they are generally available on short notice compared to experienced arbitrators, who are likely to have full arbitration schedules. Most other parties, however, have not followed this practice.

The cooperation of *all* parties—labor, management, and the arbitrator —is crucial to the success of expedited arbitration. Seitz (1981) states that long time-spans between dates of grievance filing and dates of arbitration, time delays in scheduling of hearings, and delays in the conduct of arbitration hearings frustrate the effectiveness of grievance arbitration. His main point is that any or all parties could be guilty of causing delays in grievance arbitration, and he illustrates his point with an example:

> While writing a draft of this article on February 25, 1981, I received a telephone call asking me to serve as an arbitrator for a large employing unit and union. It dramatically illustrates what is said in the text. I inquired when the parties wished to hold the hearings and was prepared to suggest three open dates, for me, within the next two months. My caller informed me, however, that the parties have many arbitrations scheduled and wished the hearing to be held on January 8, 1982, eleven and a half months after notice of my designation! (p. 31)

In some cases, however, delay may actually be used by management or the union to gain some advantage or objective. Getman (1979) gives an example of a union employing such delaying tactics: "The existence of a grievance procedure provides a union with a technique for putting relatively inexpensive pressure on management. If there are a great number of grievances pending at one time, management personnel will be occupied with grievance resolution and will be distracted from other functions" (p. 923). From these comments, it is evident that at least some cooperation must exist between the parties in order for expedited arbitration to succeed.

Research on Expedited Arbitration

Prior to concluding this section on expedited arbitration, the research by Sandver, Blaine, and Woyar (1981), which evaluates expedited arbitration systems in five separate firms, deserves comment. To our knowledge, it is the only research that has been conducted on the effectiveness of expedited arbitration.

The authors examined the Basic Steel Plan, the Postal Service System, and the procedures at the Long Island Railroad, the Kelsey-Hayes Corporation, and the International Paper Company.

Basic Steel Plan. The Basic Steel Plan has changed little from 1971. It calls for the use of panels consisting primarily of new arbitrators and, if mutually agreed upon by the parties involved, provides for elimination of the fourth step in the traditional five-step grievance process. This plan also requires that:

1. the hearing be informal;
2. no briefs be filed or transcripts made;
3. there be no formal rules of evidence in the testimony;
4. each party's case be presented by a previously designated local representative;
5. the arbitrator has the obligation to assure that all necessary facts and considerations are presented in the hearing; and
6. the arbitrator renders an award within 48 hours from the close of the hearing.

The reason for stating the details of this plan is that the other plans in the Sandver-Blaine-Woyar study were all derived from it, though each of the other plans has certain unique characteristics.

U.S. Postal Service. The Postal Service adopted expedited arbitration in 1974, but as noted, its plan differs from the Basic Steel Plan primarily in that the Postal Service uses only experienced arbitrators. The authors reviewed 47 cases (27 expedited cases and 20 regular cases) and found that:

The average time necessary to render an award under the expedited system was six days; for cases heard in the regular arbitration system, this time lapse was 68.5 days. The length of the average expedited decision was 1.85 pages; in contrast, the average regular arbitration decision was 10.15 pages in length. The parties indicated in personal interviews that in 1979 their share of the total cost of an average regular arbitration case varied between $750 and $1500, while comparable costs for an expedited case ranged between $300 and $400. (Sandver, Blaine, and Woyar, 1981, p. 13)

Thus it can be concluded that the Postal Service System is effectively fulfilling its dual objectives of reducing the delay and costs of traditional arbitration. However, the impact of Postal Service expedited arbitration on the post-settlement behavior of the parties was not addressed in the study.

Long Islang Railroad. The Long Island Railroad (LIRR) and the United Transportation Union (UTU) adopted expedited arbitration in 1972 to handle disciplinary grievances. They decided to use only experienced arbitrators.

Sandver, et al. (1981) reviewed the 566 cases settled under expedited arbitration between the time the plan was initiated and the time it was dropped at the request of the union in 1978. In those cases, 111 hearings were held during the life of the expedited arbitration system and 265 written awards were rendered; the remaining cases were settled without arbitration. The average cost per case was $328 and the average time from hearing date to decision date was 20.9 days.

According to both union and management representatives at the Long Island Railroad, expedited arbitration did succeed in reducing the time lag but the union criticized the system's cost—which is apparently why it was dropped in 1978. The parties replaced it with an arbitration system provided by the government, which is slower but less expensive (for the parties) than the expedited procedure.

Kelsey-Hayes. In 1974 Kelsey-Hayes completely replaced its traditional arbitration system with an expedited system. Sandver, et al. (1981) studied all 95 cases processed under expedited arbitration from the plan's initiation to the time of their study in 1979. They found that the average arbitrator's fee under the new system was $181 per case, which was significantly below the national average of $900 per regular arbitration case that prevailed at that time. Consequently, expedited arbitration appeared to result in very significant cost savings at Kelsey-Hayes, but the time savings were far less dramatic, though still significant. The total time period from grievance filing to award was 180 days in the expedited procedure versus 223 days for a conventional arbitration case at Kelsey-Hayes. One hundred sixty-four of the 180 days elapsed between the time of grievance filing and the hearing date; only sixteen days were consumed, on average, between the hearing and the award. Also, "the labor and management representatives perceived very little difference between expedited and traditional arbitration with respect to the extent of legal formalisms used in conducting the hearing" (p. 16).

International Paper. International Paper uses expedited arbitration in conjunction with traditional arbitration and employs experienced arbitrators. Twenty-six sample expedited cases were randomly chosen by the authors for study. Interestingly, in this company the time lapse from grievance filing to award was 323.7 days, or quite a bit longer than the national average time lapse of 223 days for regular arbitration. Most of this lag (317.9) was due to prehearing delay. Thus Sandver, et al. (1981) concluded that: "As a result of this larger time lag in the prehearing phase, the overall time figures for the expedited procedure at the International Paper Company do not show any improvement over traditional arbitration insofar as the final resolution of grievances is concerned. In fact, the time is lengthened by a full 100 days" (p. 17). Cost reductions, however, were perceived by the parties as significant and, as in previous cases, union and management perceived few or no differences in results as between expedited and traditional arbitration.

Assessment. Expedited arbitration is being applied in a multitude of forms and with mixed results. In this small sample of cases, the procedure generally resulted in a reduction in time delays and costs. The authors concluded that "after viewing the evidence collected here, we predict that the use of expedited grievance arbitration systems will increase in future years" (p. 21). However, they expected the increase in the popularity of expedited arbitration to be rather slow for the following reasons:

1. Due to its very nature, expedited arbitration can only effectively deal with simple, routine cases.
2. The emphasis in expedited arbitration is on speed, thus limiting the time parties have to prepare their cases.
3. The expedited arbitration process prohibits briefs and transcripts. This in turn limits the information upon which the decision will be based. The arbitrator must rely on oral presentations, notes, and memory.
4. Finally, the greater the complexity of the case, the more far-reaching the consequences of the award. It could be disastrous to future cases if complex issues were resolved within 48 hours at the expense of careful study and reflection on the part of arbitrators. (pp. 22-23)

GRIEVANCE MEDIATION

Grievance mediation is another approach that has been advocated for improving the unionized grievance procedure. We noted in Chapter 1 that this process was common in labor-management relations prior to World War II. Gregory and Rooney (1980) define grievance mediation "as any effort on the part of a neutral person to assist two parties in reaching agreement on a grievance that is moving toward or is actually at impasse. The role of the neutral person, who is usually a state or federal mediator, is one of assistance and persuasion. He attempts to resolve the impasse through encouraging the parties to resolve the grievance voluntarily" (p. 503).

Grievance mediation may take the following forms: (1) as an alternate to grievance arbitration; (2) where the arbitrator uses mediation at some point in the arbitration proceedings (med-arb); (3) where mediation is formally recognized as a distinct step in the grievance procedure and is handled by someone other than the person who will serve as the arbitrator if the grievance can't be settled by the parties; and (4) where the parties agree to use it on an ad hoc basis (Gregory and Rooney, 1980).

Like expedited arbitration, grievance mediation's primary benefits are that it is less expensive than grievance arbitration and is likely to take less time. A third benefit is that, if it is successful, the parties do not lose control over the final resolution of the grievance. Bowers (1980) believes that grievance mediation is particularly attractive to small unions and employers who have limited financial resources. She also predicts that the financial constraints operating on many unions in the 1980s will enhance their receptivity to grievance mediation.

Users and Issues

Who has been using grievance mediation and for what types of issues? Bowers (1982) reported that the National Federation of Federal Employees, National Association of Counties, and at least one local of the American Federation of State, County, and Municipal Employees (AFSCME) had initiated grievance mediation efforts. Goldberg and Brett (1983) report the use of this procedure in the coal mining industry.

Bowers, Seeber, and Stallworth (1982) provide additional information on the use of grievance mediation, based on a study of state and federal mediation. First, they found that grievance mediation was most often used in Pacific states, followed by mid-Atlantic states, and North Central states. Second, state mediators were most commonly used in the public sector and in the food, health care, construction, and aerospace industries. Third, federal mediators most often conducted grievance mediation in the lumber, steel, printing, and automobile industries.

The mediators interviewed by the researchers believed that grievance mediation was most useful for issues of discipline, seniority, workrules, layoffs, and overtime. However, employment discrimination, fundamental management rights, union security, union jurisdictional disputes, dues check-off, pensions, and subcontracting were viewed by the mediators as unsuitable issues for grievance mediation.

Effectiveness of Grievance Mediation

Three studies have attempted to assess the success of grievance mediation. Gregory and Rooney (1980) initially undertook an informal poll of mediators who worked in the state of Michigan in the 1970s. The poll showed that state mediators reported success in resolving 83 percent of private sector grievance cases and 84 percent of public sector grievance cases through grievance mediation. Earlier federal mediators had reported a 99 percent success rate in closing private sector cases. The authors then sampled 60 grievance mediation cases closed in 1979 at the Detroit Office of the Michigan Employment Relations Commission; both public and private sector cases were included in the sample. The results showed that 58.3 percent of the grievances were settled by mediation and that only 16.6 percent of the chosen cases required arbitration to reach settlement.

Bowers, Seeber, and Stallworth (1982) asked a sample of state and federal mediators to identify factors related to successful grievance mediation. The respondents identified the following: low case loads, support by peers and supervisors in the agency for conducting grievance mediation, dissatisfaction of the parties with grievance arbitration, clarity in defining the grievance issue, restricting the authority of the mediator to the specified issue(s), the mediator supplying written recommendations only at the request of the parties, and joint sessions with the parties to clear grievance settlement recommendations.

The respondents also listed other, related factors that seemed to enhance the success of grievance mediation. In particular, the parties had to understand and accept grievance mediation as a process, accept the voluntary nature of resolving the grievance, and the mediator needed to have at least five years of mediation experience to handle grievance mediation effectively.

These two studies cited relied on responses from mediators to assess the effectiveness of grievance mediation. Studies by Brett and Goldberg (1983), Goldberg and Brett (1983b), and Goldberg (1982) represent a more sophisticated approach to this issue. Their results are based on experiments with grievance mediation in the Appalachian coal fields. Labor relations and grievance resolution procedures among coal companies located in four union districts in Virginia, Kentucky, Indiana, and Illinois were studied over two six-month periods, beginning in mid-1980. The researchers provide substantial details concerning the experimental design, rules for using grievance mediation, and data obtained in the studies.

What were their results? First, 89 percent of the grievances taken to mediation were resolved short of arbitration; thus, only 11 percent of the cases went to arbitration. Second, the grievances resolved through mediation took considerably less time to complete than those that culminated in arbitration awards. Third, the average mediation case cost $295, or much less than the average cost of $1,034 for arbitrating non-discharge grievances in the districts at that time. Note that these costs included only the third party's fees and expenses. Nevertheless, on an aggregate basis, Brett and Goldberg (1983) reported cost savings of mediation over arbitration of some $95,000 in these districts during the time periods studied. Finally, grievants, local union representatives, and local company operating personnel all evidenced overall satisfaction with grievance mediation—though on a few specific dimensions the majority of grievants were dissatisfied. When asked to compare mediation and arbitration, the parties showed a clear preference for mediation. Goldberg and Brett (1983a) also linked their findings to the results of earlier studies in the United States and Canada in which grievance mediation appeared to meet with high levels of success.

Thus, it appears that grievance mediation offers a potentially effective alternative to grievance arbitration, where enhanced effectiveness takes the forms of reduced time delays and reduced costs relative to grievance arbitration. Moreover, Goldberg and Brett (1981) argue that grievance mediation also improves the basic labor-management relationship.

JUSTICE AND DIGNITY

Another recent innovation in the grievance process was the inclusion of a "justice and dignity" clause in the 1981 labor agreements between the Steelworkers' Union and major can companies. Over time employer and union complaints about the human and financial costs associated with disciplinary suspensions and discharges in can industry work settings had accumulated rapidly. Further, some employers bristled when informed that arbitrators did not uphold discharges of employees and required the company to reinstate the employees with full back pay and benefits. Because it is not uncommon for six months or more to elapse between discharge and reinstatement, the cost of reinstatement can be significant. Union leaders complained that disciplinary suspensions or discharges left employees in limbo and without income during the period in which grievances were being processed. Employees understandably wanted to clear the record so that they could be reinstated at work, yet there was no assurance that the grievances would be resolved in favor of employees. Even if the employees were returned to work, the probability of continued employment was considered low. In sum, union leaders argued that, in such cases, employees absorbed the major costs associated with grievance processing.

Representatives of the United Steelworkers of America (USWA) and several major can companies developed language in their 1981 contracts to address this issue; specifically, a justice and dignity clause was added to the agreements. The language provides that a suspended or discharged employee will be kept on the job while the parties process the grievance. The only exceptions to this provision are threats to safety, theft, or concerted refusal to perform work. In such cases, the employer has the right to suspend or discharge the employee or employees involved.

What are the benefits of this provision? The employer gains by not being vulnerable to back-pay claims since the person has not lost any work time. The employee benefits by retaining his or her job rights until the issue is resolved. Further, in a broader sense, such action is consistent with the U.S. legal principle that a person is innocent until proven guilty. Cahn (1983) analyzed the first six arbitration cases that tested the applicability of the justice and dignity clause. However, he limited himself to drawing conclusions about the principles that arbitrators used to determine whether contract language should or should not apply to a given case, and he produced no data or analysis concerning the effectiveness or outcomes of these cases.

KEY STUDIES OF THE GRIEVANCE PROCEDURE

In this section, we briefly review some of the key studies of grievance procedures that are reported in the literature. For purpose of organization, the categorization scheme proposed by Dalton and Todor (1979) provides a useful starting point. They suggest that prior work on grievance procedures can be assigned to one of the following categories, based on the principal focus of the research:

1. Demographic differences between grievants and non-grievants.
2. Effects of union and management leadership patterns on grievance rates.
3. Organizational structure and the incidence of grievance activity.
4. Personality traits and grievance behavior.

To this list we add an additional category:

5. Outcome studies.

Demographic Differences Between Grievants and Non-Grievants

Eckerman (1948) conducted one of the earliest studies of grievance systems. His sample consisted of grievant and non-grievant members of two unions, a machine-shop union and a foundry union. All subjects were employed in a large Midwestern plant. The purposes of the study were to determine if significant differences existed between aggrieved and non-aggrieved employees, and to identify the type and disposition of grievances. Eckerman found that:

1. Most grievances were filed over pay and wage disputes.
2. Grievants had higher wages, more seniority, held more previous jobs, and started their employment at significantly lower wage rates than non-grievants. Grievants were also more likely to be married, be in debt, and have children than non-grievants.
3. No significant differences were found between grievants and non-grievants with respect to age or education.

Ash (1970) replicated some of Eckerman's research but, in addition, examined other demographic and grievance procedure characteristics. His sample was drawn from a large manufacturing firm that employed more than 10,000 production and maintenance workers. Among Ash's findings were that grievance activity did not fluctuate during the year (by month or season) and that grievance activity was unrelated to work accident rates. Contrary to Eckerman's findings, Ash concluded that grievants were younger, more likely to be veterans, and were more likely to be Caucasian (that is, non-minority) than non-grievants.

Sulkin and Pranis (1967) also examined various demographic characteristics that presumably differentiate grievants from non-grievants. They found significant relationships for only five of the fourteen independent variables studied. Specifically, grievants were more educated, more active in the union, more often late reporting to work, employed at lower hourly wage rates, and received lower pay increases than non-grievants.

A study by Price et al. (1976) compared three samples of grievants with a large sample of non-grievants. One grievant group consisted of individuals who had filed one or two grievances against their immediate supervisors, the second group consisted of individuals who had filed more than two grievances, and the third group was limited to individuals who had filed grievances over disciplinary actions taken by the company against them. Using a file of 4,000 grievances, the authors compared the three grievant groups with the non-grievant group on the basis of sex, seniority, and job classification. From this study, they concluded that the three grievant groups did not differ significantly in terms of the independent variables examined, but that the grievants were significantly more experienced and more skilled than the non-grievants.

Another demographic study was conducted by Kissler (1977) to determine if biographical differences exist between grievants and non-grievants in the public sector. The results contradicted the findings of Eckerman (1948) in that no significant relationships between age or education and grievance activity were discovered. The author also found no evidence that grievance activity was related to job tenure, income, or sex; however, grievance activity was positively related to work absence and minority group status of employees. These results appear to contradict the findings of Ronan (1963), Price et al., (1976), and Ash (1970), but this may be largely due to the use of different samples by the researchers.

Effects of Leadership Patterns on Grievance Rates

Fleishman and Harris (1962) investigated the relationship between supervisory and subordinate job behavior, using the constructs of consideration and structure. These leadership patterns were defined as follows:

Consideration included behavior indicating mutual trust, respect, and a certain warmth and rapport between the supervisor and his group. This does not mean that this dimension reflects a superficial "pat-on-the-back," "first-name-calling" kind of human relations behavior. This dimension appears to emphasize a deeper concern for group members' needs and includes such behavior as allowing subordinates more participation in decision making and encouraging more two-way communication.

Structure included behavior in which the supervisor organizes and defines group activities and his relation to the group. Thus, he defines the role he expects each member to assume, assigns tasks, plans ahead, establishes ways of getting things done, and pushes for production. This dimension seems to emphasize overt attempts to achieve organizational goals.

The results of this study showed a negative (though curvilinear) relationship between a foreman's "consideration score" and the number of grievances in his work group. In other words, increased consideration was associated with reduced grievance rates. Fleishman and Harris also found that increases in structure were associated with increases in the number of grievances filed. Taking account of differences in the strengths of the observed relationships, the authors concluded that grievances were most frequent where foremen were low in consideration regardless of their emphasis on structure.

Glassman and Belasco (1975) investigated grievance activity as a function of union leadership, rather than managerial style, and did so in the context of public schools. They concluded that a "large proportion of the rates of both grievance filing and appealing are explained by chairman-based variables" (p. 241). In particular, they noted that the initial filing of a grievance tended to be associated with the following:

1. A perception by teachers that they were excluded from decision-making processes.
2. Assignment of the grievant to a school with few minority teachers.
3. An absence of opposition from rival organizations.
4. The presence of an upwardly mobile grievance chairman.

Grievance processing beyond the initial stage, however, was associated with four somewhat different variables:

1. A grievance chairman who was single.
2. A grievance chairman who was female.
3. Short tenure at the present school.
4. A high concentration of minority students and teachers in the school.

The authors concluded that the grievance process in the public schools was frequently invoked as a vehicle to move beyond the local level of authority in an effort to foster organizational change. In other words, the grievances that were taken to higher levels were viewed by teachers and other members of the bargaining organizations as means to certain ends rather than as ends in and of themselves.

Dalton and Todor (1982b) studied the effects of union stewards on the grievance process. The intervention of the steward in the grievance process was found to be a far more significant determinant of grievance rates in the firm than the characteristics of the union members themselves. According to the authors, this relationship may be one reason why studies dealing with the characteristics of grievance filing by rank-and-file members typically do not explain more than 10 percent of the variance in grievance activity.

Organizational Structure and the Incidence of Grievance Activity

Weiss (1957) studied grievance filing as a function of the degree of centralization of organizational authority. His central hypothesis was that decentralized organizations would experience a significantly lower level of grievance activity than their more centralized counterparts. However, Weiss was unable to confirm this hypothesis in his empirical work.

A leading study on grievance initiation was conducted by Sayles (1958). He hypothesized that grievance rates would vary from group to group depending on the social system of the group, especially as that system was influenced by technology. In this conception, the social system determines work-group attitudes, actions, and thus, grievance behavior. Sayles's analysis was guided by the following fourfold categorization of work groups:

1. Apathetic: low skills, varied tasks, little interworker cooperation required, low level of grievance activity.

2. Erratic: some skills, performed similar tasks, some interworker cooperation required, medium level of grievance activity.

3. Strategic: semiskilled, jobs required individual judgment, individuals worked together but on separate operations, high level of grievance activity.

4. Conservative: highly skilled, independent and widely scattered tasks, medium level of grievance activity.

The research findings generally supported the hypotheses that the strategic group would be the heaviest user of the grievance procedure and the conservative group would use the procedure only when its status was threatened.

Ronan attempted to build on Sayles's findings by analyzing formal grievance activity in two plants of a single firm. However, one plant was relatively new and the other much older, which distorted the results because many grievances were engendered over the "newness" of the first plant. Further, Ronan collapsed Sayles's four categories into two so that it is perhaps not surprising that he found no significant differences in grievance filing between members of the two groups.

Nelson (1979) attempted to correct some of the errors in Ronan's study and to provide a fuller test of Sayles's hypotheses. Using a sample of 53 work groups in a single plant, he found that apathetic groups had the lowest rate of grievances, strategic groups had the highest rate, and the erratic and conservative groups had moderate or intermediate rates. These results supported the relationship between technology and grievance rates reported by Sayles.

A study by Muchinsky and Maassarani (1981) built on Ronan's work and sought to determine if more grievances are filed in new facilities where union and management personnel are relatively unaccustomed to dealing with each other. The authors were interested in determining if this finding also applied to the public sector given its relatively new union-management relationships. They sampled public service organizations in Iowa, and found that the inexperience of the parties was indeed associated with high rates of grievance filing and the denial of employee grievances.

Peach and Livernash (1974) compared pairs of high- and low-grievance departments in several steel companies in an attempt to highlight the variables contributing to quantitative and qualitative differences in grievance activity. Their sample was drawn from six plants, which ranged in size from 2,000 to more than 13,000 employees. The authors found that a high grievance rate was associated with an unfavorable task environment, aggressive and militant union leadership, and ineffective managerial decision making as indicated by leadership, organizational, and policy deficiencies. A low grievance rate was characterized by a favorable task environment that was both relatively stable and largely free from technological disturbances, and with effective management and organizational policies.

Following closely the work of Peach and Livernash, Muchinsky and Maassarani (1980) studied the impact of environmental factors on employee grievances in the public sector. The results of their study, based on two public service organizations in Iowa, were similar to those reported by Peach and Livernash. Thus, the authors concluded that the determinants of grievance activity are common to the public and private sectors. Obviously, however, a sample of but two public organizations severely limits the validity and generalizability of this conclusion.

Personality Traits and Grievance Behavior

Stagner (1956) was the first to use the Guilford-Martin Personnel Inventory to demonstrate that grievants have greater personal sensitivity than non-grievants. In a later study, Stagner (1962) demonstrated that when socioeconomic variables (for example, wages, fringe benefits, and working conditions) were controlled, personality variables became "meaningful" in interactions between union and management. For example, personality factors such as friendliness, ascendance, and masculinity were (according to Stagner) "plausibly" correlated with managers' concessionary behavior, satisfaction with the level of union influence, and amount of consultation undertaken with the union on shop matters. Stagner also concluded that the extent of union achievements, the amount of union pressure, and unionists' tendency toward legalism in dispute resolution were each "plausibly" correlated with at least one personality variable. Finally, Stagner found that shop environments characterized by a "low emotional tone" tended to have shop stewards who were highly sensitive and easily upset. Personality characteristics were judged to have especially large effects on grievance activity in this type of shop environment.

A study by Gandz (1979) investigated personality roles rather than personality traits. Gandz interviewed 80 Canadian managers to determine their perceived roles in grievance handling and resolution, and then allocated the data among the five following managerial roles: policeman, employer advocate, mediator, adjudicator, and advisor. Fully half of the industrial relations managers perceived themselves as adopting the mediator role.

Gandz concluded that no one role was optimal for every grievance situation, largely because three main types of grievance-related conflict exist in organizations: pseudo-conflict, common-problem conflict, and conflicts of interest. Gandz proposed that each type of conflict required a fundamentally different management role in order for grievances to be handled effectively. Gandz also identified four distinct industrial relations climates which must be considered in the resolution of workplace problems. These were open conflict, containment of aggression, a spirit of accommodation, and enthusiastic cooperation. He determined the dominant type of conflict present in a firm through analysis of conflict incidents, including grievances, work slowdowns, and absenteeism, and developed a matrix that identified contingencies or optimal matches of management roles with modes of conflict resolution.

Gandz and Whitehead (1982) reported a study linking organizational climate to grievance initiation and resolution using mail questionnaire responses from industrial relations executives distributed among companies in twenty major industries. A follow-up study was conducted among line managers and supervisors in a single firm. The overall finding was that a poor labor-management climate was associated with high levels of grievance activity for both disciplinary and nondisciplinary matters.

Outcome Studies

Gideon and Peterson (1979) compared two different types of grievance procedures in a single wood-products firm over a three year period. They examined company logs of grievance meetings and conducted interviews with key company labor relations staff and union representatives. One of the grievance procedures in this firm contained four steps and provided for binding arbitration when the parties were unable to resolve the dispute at lower grievance steps. All steps contained strict time limits for appeal and response. The second grievance procedure covered only logging employees who were represented by a separate local union. While this procedure also contained four steps, it did not culminate in arbitration. Rather, if the appeal committee provided for at the fourth step was unable to resolve the dispute, the union could take a strike vote and actually go on strike seven days after giving written notice to the employer.

Several broad conclusions were derived from a comparison of these two grievance systems. First, the appeal method contributed to a more volatile labor environment than the arbitration method. Second, the union using the appeal method greatly increased its chances of winning the grievance by moving to step three of the four-step grievance procedure while, under the arbitration method, the union's chances of winning were only moderately increased by moving to step three. Third, only about half as many grievances were taken to the arbitration stage of the first procedure as were taken to the appeal stage of the second procedure. Fourth, management won significantly more grievance cases under the arbitration method than under the appeal method.

Moore (1981) investigated the outcomes of 228 grievances according to type, duration, level of settlement, outcome, and adjudicability. He concluded that restrictions placed on the types of grievances eligible for adjudication created an undesirable and unnecessary hindrance to industrial justice.

In another study of the arbitration of employee grievances, LaVan, Carley, and Jowers (1980) compared arbitration decisions involving employees of nonprofit hospitals and nursing homes before and after 1974, the year in which these groups came under coverage of the Taft-Hartley Act. They found no significant differences in the outcomes of grievance decisions between the two periods.

Sulzner (1980) examined the outcomes of grievance procedures and arbitration in the federal government. Almost two-thirds of his sample of respondents perceived grievance procedures to have substantial impacts on personnel policies and practices. However, Sulzner also found that arbitration was rarely resorted to in the federal sector, at least during the 1970s.

Dalton and Todor (1981) examined the outcomes of seventeen different categories of grievances filed by members of a large West Coast union. Significant differences were observed by category. For example, grievances involving denial of sick benefits had positive outcomes for the employer about 80 percent of the time, whereas grievances concerning performance evaluation had positive outcomes for the union more than 85 percent of the time. The authors also found that grievance categories with the largest amount of filing activity were the ones with the highest proportions of positive outcomes—wins—for the employer.

Dalton and Todor (1982a) used the same data set to study the relationships among locus of control, job involvement, union involvement, and five specific behaviors of union stewards in a West Coast communications firm. The steward behaviors included counseling the employee to abandon the grievance process, settling the potential grievance through discussion with the employee's supervisor, filing a grievance at the request of a rank-and-file member, filing a grievance when a member showed no active interest in the grievance, and filing a grievance on behalf of the union when a union member was unwilling to do so. The researchers found that job involvement was not significantly related to any of the union steward behaviors, external locus of control was negatively related to all five behaviors, and union involvement was significantly related to the last two union steward behaviors.

A study by Graham and Heshizer (1979) analyzed the effects of contractual language on grievance activity. The researchers found that language that appeared to encourage settlement of grievances at lower steps of the procedure had no significant effects on actual levels of settlement specifically or the parties' behavior more broadly.

A more recent study by Knight (1986) reached different conclusions. Analyzing questionnaire responses from 330 union and management officials in four different industry settings, Knight found that the frequency of references to previous grievance settlements and arbitration decisions was positively related to subsequent grievance resolution for the sample as a whole. However, the results were statistically significant only for the management respondents despite the fact that the union officials involved in grievance handling made more frequent references to prior grievance settlements and arbitration decisions.

Knight's findings are all the more interesting when considered in relation to a study by Katz, Kochan, and Gobeille (1983). These authors investigated the relationships among industrial relations climate variables, economic performance, and Quality-of-Working Life (QWL) programs in eighteen plants of the General Motors Corporation. They found that grievance rates, which served as one climate measure, were significantly negatively correlated with product quality and direct labor efficiency. However, when changes in plant-level performance over two distinct time periods in samples of low- and high-QWL plants were analyzed, no consistent relationships with grievance activity were observed. Moreover, and as the authors of this study recognize, the causal

Table 2.1
A Summary of Studies of the Grievance Procedure

STUDY	INDEPENDENT VARIABLES	MODERATING VARIABLES	DEPENDENT VARIABLES	FINDINGS
Eckerman (1948)	Several demographic variables such as number of children, marital status, height and weight	Two different unions - a machine shop union and a foundry union	Grievant vs. non-grievant, type and disposition of grievances	1. Most grievances are over wage and pay issues 2. Grievants have larger pay raises, more seniority, more past jobs, started at a lower wage rate, are more likely to be married, in debt, and have children than non-grievants 3. Grievants and non-grievants are not significantly different with respect to height, weight, age, and educational attainment
Stagner (1956)	Degree of sensitivity of individuals	Working conditions	Number of grievances filed	Grievants are more sensitive than non-grievants and thus more likely to file grievances in the face of a given set of working conditions.
Weiss (1957)	Degree of centralization of authority		Number of grievances filed	Unable to substantiate hypothesis
Sayles (1958)	Technology	Skill level of employees Variation in tasks Inter-worker coordination required	Grievance rate	Hypotheses supported: 1. apathetic groups have low grievance rates 2. erratic groups have medium grievance rates 3. strategic groups have high grievance rates 4. conservative groups have medium grievance rates
Stagner (1962)	Personality variables		Degree of union achievement Amount of union pressure Tendency toward legalism	Certain personality characteristics have an impact on grievance activity

Table 2.1 (continued)

STUDY	INDEPENDENT VARIABLES	MODERATING VARIABLES	DEPENDENT VARIABLES	FINDINGS
Fleishman and Harris (1962)	Foreman behavior - consideration - structure		Grievance rate employee turnover rate	1. Relationship between foreman behavior and work group grievances is negative and curvilinear for consideration Structure is positively but curvilinearly related to grievance rate 2. Grievances occur most frequently among groups whose foremen are low in consideration regardless of the amount of emphasis on structure
Ronan (1963)	Sayles' four different types of groups differentiated by technology and skill level	Age differences between two plants - one new and one old	Grievance activity	1. No basic differences between two groups (Sayles' four groups were consolidated into two) 2. Findings distorted because "new" plant had many grievances filed due to its "newness"
Sulkin and Pranis (1967)	Numerous variables, including number of grievances, amount of union participation, sick days, absences, tardiness, hourly wage rate, number of pay increases, tenure, work force experience, age, education, sex, and race		Grievant vs. non-grievant	Grievants are more likely to have more education, be active in the union, be late more often, have lower hourly pay rates, and have fewer pay increases than non-grievants
Ash (1970)	Various demographic and grievance characteristics		Grievant vs. non-grievant grievance activity	1. Grievants are younger than non-grievants 2. Grievance activity does not fluctuate seasonally or by month of the year 3. Grievants are more likely to be veterans than non-grievants 4. Non-grievants are more likely to be women, married, have children, be aliens, and be rehired than grievants

STUDY	INDEPENDENT VARIABLES	MODERATING VARIABLES	DEPENDENT VARIABLES	FINDINGS
Jennings (1974a)	Blumer's interpersonal typology: codified, power, sympathetic		Foreman/steward relationship	1. Formal role requirements do not guide the parties in their interactions
Jennings (1974b)	Several demographic variables, including age, education, experience, structural variables such as number of employees and technology		Foremen perceptions of importance their organizations attach to grievance handling	Foremen do not place a high priority on grievance handling. Foremen do not have strongly homogeneous attitudes
Peach and Livernash (1974)	Size and character of the community, working conditions, and technology	Type of union leadership Type of management Union election year	Level of grievance activity	1. Grievance rates are higher in union election years 2. Unfavorable task environment, aggressive and militant union leadership, and ineffective managerial decision-making are related to high grievance rates 3. Low grievance rates caused by favorable task environment and few technological disturbances
Glassman and Belasco (1975)	Chairman based variables and demographic variables such as number of minorities, and opposition from rival organizations		Initial grievance filing activity Grievance appeal activity	Initial grievance filing is associated with: 1. perception by teachers that they are excluded from decision-making 2. assignment to schools with few minorities 3. absence of rival organization 4. presence of an upwardly mobile chairman Appeal activity is associated with: 1. a chairman who is single or female 2. short tenure at current school 3. high proportions of minority students and teachers in a school

Table 2.1 (continued)

STUDY	INDEPENDENT VARIABLES	MODERATING VARIABLES	DEPENDENT VARIABLES	FINDINGS
Begin (1978)	Level of settlement processing time		Faculty grievance	1. Increase in perceived fairness 2. Personnel procedures formalized 3. More lower level settlements 4. Increased processing time
Price, et al. (1976)	Forty different behavioral and demographic variables	Sex, seniority and job classification	Grievant vs. non-grievant Multigrievants vs. non-grievants Disciplinary grievants vs. non-grievants	An exploratory study; very few factors intercorrelated.
Walker and Robinson (1977)	Leadership style of supervisor - democratic or autocratic	Age, education, geographic area, tenure as foreman, and number of workers supervised	Grievance rate, types of grievance steps at which grievances are settled, number of grievances overturned by higher levels of management	1. Autocratic supervisors have fewer overall grievances, discipline related grievances, overtime related grievances, and harrassment grievances than democratic supervisors 2. Autocratic supervisors also have fewer grievances settled at lower levels and fewer decisions on grievances overturned by higher management than democratic supervisors 3. Autocratic supervisors are better contract administrators than democratic supervisors
Kissler (1977)	Grade, step, age, tenure, education, sick days, income, no. of promotions, union membership, sex, race	Blue-collar and white-collar occupations	Grievance activity	1. Grievance activity not related to tenure or age 2. Grievants have less union representation, more sick days, and more minority representation than non-grievants

STUDY	INDEPENDENT VARIABLES	MODERATING VARIABLES	DEPENDENT VARIABLES	FINDINGS
Graham, Heshizer and Johnson (1978)	No independent variables (survey)		Attitudes toward arbitration	A survey found: 1. 78% of respondents think arbitration is the best method of settling unresolved grievances 2. union members are unwilling to strike over grievances 3. costs of arbitration discourage unions from proceeding to arbitration
Gideon and Peterson (1979)	Arbitration method vs. appeal method		Overall grievance activity Level of grievance resolution Which side was favored Resolution pattern by levels Discipline/discharge activity	1. Appeal method produces a more volatile labor environment than the arbitration method 2. Timberland's union increased its chances of winning or at least getting a compromise by appealing to Step III 3. Arbitration method accounted for only about half as many grievances as the appeal method 4. Based on number of grievances won, management should prefer the arbitration method and the union the appeal method
Nelson (1979)	Sayles' work group classifications: apathetic, erratic, strategic, conservative		Level of grievance activity	Sayles' hypotheses hold: apathetic work groups had lowest grievance rate and strategic groups the highest. Erratic and conservative groups both had intermediate grievance levels.
Graham and Heshizer (1979)	Contractual language specifying low-level grievance resolution		Step in grievance procedure at which grievances are resolved	1. Grievances resolved more readily at the oral stage than the written stages 2. Low-level contract language did not affect the level of grievance resolution

Table 2.1 (continued)

STUDY	INDEPENDENT VARIABLES	MODERATING VARIABLES	DEPENDENT VARIABLES	FINDINGS
Brett and Goldberg (1979)	Frequency of wildcat strikes	Population of county, unemployment rate, occupational distribution, family income, quality of housing, schools and public services	No. of labor problems Levels at which problems are resolved Confidence of miners in non-local grievance steps Perceived value of a strike	1. No. of labor problems not related to strike activity 2. Local level of grievance resolution contributes to low strike level 3. Confidence in higher step grievance resolution not significant 4. Partial support for differing values at low and high strike mines of striking
LaVan, Carley, and Jowers (1980)	Before vs. after 1974 Taft-Hartley amendment		Differences in way grievances are handled, such as % of cases filed by union or individual employee, % of cases using expert witnesses, and % of cases involving union issues	1. No pre- and post-1974 differences for 11 of the 13 variables tested 2. Increased use of expert witnesses since 1974 in arbitration hearings 3. Tendency of arbitrators to award back-pay has increased

STUDY	INDEPENDENT VARIABLES	MODERATING VARIABLES	DEPENDENT VARIABLES	FINDINGS
Sulzner (1980)	- Representation of employees under negotiated grievance procedure - coverage of disciplinary actions - representation of employees under the negotiated arbitration procedure		Personnel policies and practices	1. Nearly 2/3 of respondents thought the grievance procedure impacted on personnel policies and practices 2. Little impact is associated with the size and scope of the grievance process, but does vary with the substance of grievances 3. Discipline grievances are more likely to be processed than promotion grievances
Muchinsky & Maassarani (1980)	Work environment in public sector agencies		Types of grievance	Results are similar to those of Peach and Livernash. Work environment does impact organizational behavior as reflected in number and types of grievances filed
Hayford and Pegnetter (1980)	Specific elements of due process		Comparison of unionized grievance procedure with civil service appeal systems in four states	The grievance procedure is the better of the two approaches because a. a broader scope of issues can be adjudicated b. greater assurance of competent employee representation at hearing c. mutual selection of the third party neutral d. employee perceptions of neutrality of the third party e. enhanced finality of adjudication
Dalton and Todor (1981)	Grievances by category		- % in each category - % won, compromised, withdrawn, abandoned, or lost by category - % positive outcome for union - % positive outcome for management	1. Certain categories of grievances are likely to have positive outcomes for unions and other categories for management 2. Categories in which grievances are most frequently filed are less likely to have a positive union outcome

Table 2.1 (continued)

STUDY	INDEPENDENT VARIABLES	MODERATING VARIABLES	DEPENDENT VARIABLES	FINDINGS
Muchinsky and Maassarani (1981)	Article grieved location of griev- ant	Department	Disposition of grievances - denied or upheld	1. Denial rate is much higher in the public sector than the private sector 2. Significant interaction between article grieved and grievance disposition in one department (DSS) but not in the other (DOT). DOT had small volume of grievances 3. Inexperience of departments resulted in large grievance denial rate by managers
Gandz and Whitehead (1982)	Organizational climate		Grievance initiation and resolution	Grievance rates higher where union-management relationship is poor as judged by line man- agers and industrial relations executives in sampled organizations
Moore (1981)	Adjudicable griev- ances vs. non- adjudicable grievances	Type of griev- ance: - pay - discipline - leave - special leave - miscellaneous	Disposition of griev- ance: - granted - denied - partially granted - abandoned - resolved - partially resolved first and intermedi- ate level of results final level of results past grievance results time delays	Restrictions placed on types of grievances eligible for adjudication create an undesir- able hindrance to industrial justice
Dalton and Todor (1982a)	Company commitment union commitment job satisfaction		Steward behavior	Differences in commitment of union stewards to the union and the company are strongly related to steward grievance handling behaviors

STUDY	INDEPENDENT VARIABLES	MODERATING VARIABLES	DEPENDENT VARIABLES	FINDINGS

Dalton and Todor (1982b)	Locus of control, job involvement, and union involvement		Behavior of union steward in responding to a potential or real grievance	1. Job involvement not significantly associated with any of the five possible steward grievance behaviors
				2. Union involvement significantly related to steward:
				  a. encouraging member to file when no interest shown by involved person
				  b. filing grievance over objections of involved member.
				3. External locus of control negatively related to all five steward grievance behaviors

Goldberg and Brett (1983a)	Number of third step grievances	Mediator's advisory opinion if arbitration was used	Grievance outcome, speed of settlement, cost, and satisfaction of parties	1. 89% of grievances settled through mediation 2. Mediation 3 months faster on average than arbitration 3. Mediation $739 cheaper on average than arbitration 4. All parties expressed high levels of satisfaction with mediation
Katz, Kochan and Gobeille (1983) and Katz, Kochan and Weber (1985)	Quality of working life (QWL) programs	Industrial relations performance, including grievance filing rates	Product quality and direct labor efficiency	1. Industrial relations performance significantly positively associated with product quality and direct labor efficiency 2. QWL program not consistently related to changes in industrial relations performance or economic performance
Freeman and Medoff (1984)	Unionism, capital/labor ratios, and other variables	Grievance and arbitration clauses, percent of workers who filed grievances	Job tenure and job quits	Grievance procedure coverage significantly negatively associated with job quits and positively associated with job tenure

Table 2.1 (continued)

STUDY	INDEPENDENT VARIABLES	MODERATING VARIABLES	DEPENDENT VARIABLES	FINDINGS
Norsworthy and Zabala (1985)	Grievances filed per worker, unresolved grievances per worker, and worker behavior index		Total factor productivity, total unit cost, and production worker productivity	Grievances filed per worker significantly negatively correlated with total factor productivity and production worker production, and positively correlated with total unit co
Knight (1986)	Reference to previous grievance settlements and arbitration decisions	Types of grievances, organization level	Grievance resolution	1. References to previous grievance settlements significantly positively related t management perceptions of subsequent grievance resolution 2. union officials made more frequent references than management officials to previous grievance settlements and arbitration decisions
Ichniowski (1986)	Grievance filing rates, arbitration decisions	Plant dummies, production process dummies, and controls for factor inputs	Tons of paper produced per month per plant	1. Grievance filing rates significantly negatively associated with plant productivity 2. plant productivity significantly lower in one nonunion plant than in nine unionized plants

tended to adopt a historical and institutional approach. There has been relatively little input from the behavioral and social sciences, although some attempts at building models of workplace behavior are now beginning to emerge. (pp. 2-3)

Lewin's (1983) critique of the grievance literature included the following observations:

Despite its widespread use and putative benefits, the grievance procedure has received surprisingly little study, especially in the contemporary period. The best known works in the field, such as those of Kuhn (1961) and Slichter, Healy and Livernash (1960) are two decades old, and the data on which they are based are even older. This is unfortunate because important changes have recently occurred in American industrial relations, including the growth of unionism among government employees and in the health and hospital sectors; a steady if not spectacular rise in the unionization of women, white-collar and professional workers; and major changes in production processes, work rules and productivity incentives in the construction, newspaper, garment, supermarket, meatpacking and steel industries, among others. (p. 128)

More recently, Gordon and Miller (1984) offered five specific criticisms of the grievance procedure literature. First, there are no common standards for determining grievance rates. Second, it is not possible to equate grievance activity across private firms and nonprofit and public employers because of the different "formulas" and measures used by researchers. Third, the various studies provide no common standard or measure by which to judge whether grievance activity in a particular organization is high, medium, or low. Fourth, there are no common grievance classification schemes in the relevant literature. Fifth, the multiplicity of factors that potentially affect grievance activity has been given insufficient attention by researchers.

What may underlie most if not all of these criticisms is that published work on the grievance procedure remains largely atheoretical. Certainly no general theory of the grievance process has yet emerged, and few attempts have been made to develop such a theory. Consistent with this lack of theoretical focus, most research designs employed to study grievance procedures have been simplistic. Typically, a small group of independent variables and one or two dependent variables are examined; intervening variables or interaction effects are rarely studied. Relatedly, questionnaires and company records have often been used in grievance procedure studies, while in-depth interviews, experimental designs, and multimethod studies· have been rarely undertaken. This has led to a heavy reliance on descriptive statistics and correlational analyses. Finally, because grievance procedure studies have used widely varying samples and research settings, the validity and reliability of the conclusions contained in the grievance literature are open to serious question.

SUMMARY

In this literature review, we summarized extant research in the area of grievance procedures. The structure, mechanics, and functions of the grievance procedure in unionized settings were reviewed first, and this was followed by an assessment of the strengths and weaknesses of grievance procedures. Next, we reviewed two techniques that have developed in response to criticisms of conventional grievance procedures, namely, expedited arbitration and grievance mediation. Then, the leading studies of the grievance procedure were summarized and their independent, moderating, and dependent variables were identified. Last, we briefly examined some of the received criticisms of grievance procedure research and added some of our own.

In conclusion, we agree with the observations about the grievance procedure made some 25 years ago by McKersie and Shropshire (1962): "It is the day-to-day administration of a contract that determines how well the objectives of the contract are realized. And it is the day-to-day administration that most influences the development of a constructive relationship between the contracting parties" (p. 135). Because we agree with this view, we also believe that new, improved research on contemporary grievance procedures should be undertaken. This book is intended to provide one such contribution.

3
The Study Design

A variety of research designs for studying grievance procedures could be formulated. For example, it is possible to conduct experimental studies of grievance procedure effectiveness in which student subjects play grievant, supervisor-manager, and even arbitrator roles in laboratory settings. Similarly, quasi-experimental designs, in which "real world" grievance handlers and arbitrators are asked to deal with and rule on hypothetical grievances, could be constructed.

In general, experimental and quasi-experimental designs are not widely used by industrial relations researchers, although they have occasionally been used to study the collective bargaining process and apparently are enjoying a modest resurgence of interest among some scholars.[1] The major reason for this lack of use is that experimental and quasi-experimental research designs have a large component of artificiality. Subjects who play roles in laboratory and laboratory-like settings are unlikely to be influenced by the constraints and pressures—variables—that affect real world grievances and grievance handling. More pointedly, the reality of ongoing employment relationships and ongoing labor and management institutions is exceptionally difficult to replicate—if it can be replicated at all—in experimental and quasi-experimental settings.[2]

Observation and participant-observation research designs, which have a long if relatively minor tradition in industrial relations research, could also be used to study grievance procedures. That is, one could observe the processes of grievance filing and grievance handling in one or more specific settings over a period of time and thereby attempt to analyze the dynamics of grievance handling or derive measures of grievance process effectiveness. There is no denying that observation and participant-observation research designs often provide a richness of detail and a depth of insight that cannot be matched by other designs.[3] However, apart from their considerable logistical difficulties, the major limitation of such designs concerns generalizability. In some respects the observational method of research is the ultimate case study and, thus, one never knows how representative such a case may be.

In light of the difficulties and limitations of experimental and observational research designs, a multistage field study was determined to be the most appropriate design for examining grievance procedures in this research.[4] The three main components of the design were a large-scale mail survey of management and union officials in four industries and sectors; structured interviews with samples of management and union officials in each of these same industries and sectors; and content analysis of grievance files in one steel company, one retail trade firm, one local hospital and one local public school district. These will be more fully described later in this chapter.

CONCEPTS AND MEASURES: GRIEVANCE PROCEDURE EFFECTIVENESS (DEPENDENT VARIABLE I)

The systems model of the grievance procedure outlined in Chapter 1 provides the analytical framework for the empirical examination of grievance procedures undertaken in this study. The major dependent variable in the study is grievance procedure effectiveness; recall that effectiveness is a multidimensional concept and, consequently, the relevant effectiveness dimensions must be operationalized and measured. However, several questions arise concerning the conceptualization and measurement of the effectiveness of the grievance process.

Unlike the notion of efficiency, which in the context of employment can be operationalized via the application of economic concepts of marginal cost and marginal revenue, the notion of effectiveness requires a more "political" set of concepts to be made operational.[5] That is, the uses of the grievance process and the results of the process as perceived by the parties involved in it become salient in determining the effectiveness of the process. Consequently, sets of objective (behavioral) and attitudinal measures of grievance procedure effectiveness were required to be formulated and operationalized.

The objective measures include the grievance rate (per 100 employees); the level of grievance settlement within the multilevel structure of the grievance procedure; the speed of grievance settlement, measured in days to settlement; and the arbitration rate (per 100 employees). The attitudinal measures include management and union officials' perceptions of the importance of issues treated by the grievance procedure and the equity of grievance handling and settlement.[6]

Taking up these measures in greater detail, the grievance rate has been widely used in studies of grievance procedure functioning, but the meaning to be attached to this measure remains both elusive and controversial.[7] A low grievance rate, which at first glance might be taken to indicate an effectively functioning grievance procedure, may result from management domination of employees or from employee fear of management reprisals for filing grievances. A high grievance rate may result from union domination of the employment relationship or from a desire to achieve gains through the grievance procedure that couldn't be obtained through collective bargaining. Further, workplace disputes between labor and management may be settled informally and therefore never reach the formal grievance procedure, or they may be subject to a policy that every dispute no matter how minor must be resolved through the procedure; low and high grievance rates would result, respectively. Nevertheless, from a research standpoint it would hardly be acceptable to ignore the grievance rate, therefore in this study it shall be treated as one among several measures of grievance procedure effectiveness. Specifically, labor-management relationships characterized by intermediate rates of grievance filing will be judged to have more effective grievance procedures than labor-management relationships characterized by either very low or very high rates of grievance filing. In all cases, the rates are based on grievances per 100 employees.

Most grievance procedures provide several levels or steps for the resolution of workplace disputes.[8] A grievance that is taken to the upper steps of the procedure increasingly moves away from the direct parties to the dispute, as it is processed by representatives of the two sides. While this representation function provides certain benefits to the direct parties to the dispute, it also generates substantially increased costs of grievance processing. From an effectiveness standpoint, moreover, a grievance settlement is more likely to receive the acceptance and commitment of the direct partners to the dispute if they have had a hand in fashioning the settlement. Therefore, the effectiveness of the grievance process will be regarded as inversely related to the level of grievance settlement.

Similar comments apply to the speed of grievance settlement. The jurisprudential principle that justice delayed is justice denied is applicable to grievance processing, for grievance settlements fashioned only after lengthy processes have played themselves out are unlikely to be effective or salient to the parties. In other words, the delay itself overshadows the specifics of the grievance settlement. Thus, the effectiveness of the grievance process will be regarded as inversely related to the speed of grievance settlement.[9]

Arbitration is the terminal step of almost all grievance procedures contained in collective bargaining contracts in the United States. In conventional grievance procedures, the arbitration step is invoked only after the exhaustion of all preceding steps, and its use entails both indirect and direct costs, with a portion of the latter being shared equally by the parties to the dispute. As a relatively costly procedure, arbitration is intended to be only rarely invoked, presumably on matters of special importance to both sides. A grievance procedure that features a high rate of arbitration is likely to reflect ineffective grievance handling. Therefore, the effectiveness of the grievance process will be regarded as inversely related to the arbitration rate, where that rate is based on arbitrations per 100 employees.

In part because of the slowness of some grievance procedures and in part because of the high costs of conventional grievance arbitration, expedited grievance procedures have recently been instituted in some industries and sectors.[10] An expedited procedure may call for skipping some grievance steps; more stringent time limits on the parties to formulate responses to the other side at each step; the dispensation of certain administrative requirements, such as a complete written record of the grievance hearing; or various combinations thereof. While expedited procedures might well be taken as a measure of grievance procedure effectiveness, they are very likely to affect other effectiveness measures, for example, the speed of settlement. Consequently, expedited grievance procedures are treated as an independent variable in this study, and are discussed in the next section.

Concerning attitudinal measures of grievance procedure effectiveness (the construction of which represents an attempt to go beyond previous research on this subject), the first of these is the importance of the issues taken up through the grievance procedure, as judged by labor and management officials who are parties to the procedure. The specific measure of effectiveness combines the importance ratings of labor and management rather than treating them separately. Grievance procedure effectiveness is expected to be positively related to the combined rating of grievance issue importance.

The second attitudinal measure of grievance procedure effectiveness is the parties' perceived equity of grievance handling and settlement.[11] Where labor and management both perceive the greivance procedure to provide highly equitable grievance handling and settlement, the procedure is regarded as highly effective. Where one party considers grievance handling to be highly equitable and the other party considers it to be highly inequitable, the grievance procedure is considered to be moderately effective (the same is true where both parties rate grievance handling as neither particularly equitable nor inequitable). Where both parties judge grievance handling to be highly inequitable, the grievance procedure is considered to have low effectiveness.

INDEPENDENT VARIABLES AND HYPOTHESES

The systems model of the grievance process presented in Chapter 1 identifies several sets of independent variables that are expected to influence grievance procedure effectiveness. Among these are management and union organizational characteristics and grievance policies as well as characteristics of the labor-management relationship and the grievance process. Because there is not a well-developed theory of the grievance process, it is arguable that formal hypotheses about grievance procedure effectiveness should be formulated. The approach taken here is to specify formal hypotheses about the relationships between certain independent variables and grievances process effectiveness where such specifications are warranted by prior empirical research, deductive logic, or (pragmatically) data availability. Hypothesis testing helps to clarify and narrow the empirical analysis and also permits the avoidance (or at least the dampening) of the ad hoc treatment of data that prevails in the literature on this subject. Note that hypotheses are specified for one or more (but not all) variables within the particular sets of independent variables shown in Figure 1.1.

In terms of employer and union characteristics, *size of bargaining unit* is expected to be positively related to the grievance rate, the arbitration rate, the level of settlement, and the importance of issues raised through the grievance procedure, and negatively related to speed of settlement. These hypotheses are based on the notion that the interests and potential grievances of employees are more closely attended to in small organizations than in large ones.[12] Personal contacts with peers and supervisors and opportunities for employees to voice issues and work-related concerns appear to be greater in small organizations than in large ones. Similarly, the opportunities for supervisors and managers to respond to employee concerns seem to be greater and the costs of such responses seem to be lower in small organizations than in large ones.

Relatedly, *occupational diversity of the bargaining unit* is expected to be positively related to the grievance rate, the arbitration rate, and the level of settlement, and negatively related to the speed of settlement. Occupational and union membership diversity may result in a lack of attention being paid to the specific work-related concerns of particular subgroups in the employer and union organizations. Such subgroups may have to vie for attention and are likely to use the grievance procedure more and press grievances further through the procedure than a work group or union composed of a single occupational specialty.[13]

Centralization of decision making in the management organization *and* in the union organization are predicted to be positively related to grievance rates, arbitration rates, and the level of settlement and negatively related to the speed of settlement. In general, the more centralized the decision-making process of an organization, the farther removed are organizational leaders from the day-to-day workplace concerns of employees.[14] This is true—or expected to be true—of employer organizations whether in the private, public, or nonprofit sectors and of union organizations having single occupation or multioccupational memberships.

Voluntary turnover of employees in the bargaining unit is expected to be negatively related to grievance rates, arbitration rates, the level of settlement, and the perceived importance of issues raised in the grievance procedure. These hypotheses are based on the view that turnover or exit is an alternative to grievance filing or the exercise of voice in the employment relationship.[15] Employee groups whose members rarely leave their employers are more likely than employee groups whose members frequently leave their employers to be active in grievance filing and to regard the grievance procedure as a mechanism for addressing important work-related concerns.

Management or union organizational policies of *committing all grievances to writing* or *taking certain types or classes of grievances as far as possible through the grievance procedure* are expected to be positively related to grievance rates, arbitration rates, and level of settlement and negatively related to the speed of settlement and perceived equity of settlement. The literature shows that management and union organizations vary markedly in terms of policies toward grievances.[16] Some organizations avoid written grievances as a matter of policy, others require that virtually all grievances be reduced to writing if they are to be recognized at all, and still others have less extreme policies. Hence we pose the aforementioned hypotheses concerning "written commitment" and "complete pursuit" of grievances.

Concerning labor-management relationship characteristics, the more *adversarial the relationship* the more likely are grievance rates, arbitration rates, and levels of settlement to be high, speed of settlement to be slow, and perceived equity of settlement to be low. In a bargaining context, adversarial labor relations may result in strikes, slowdowns, lockouts, or other expressions of militancy. In the period(s) between contract negotiations, the nature of the relationship between labor and management may be most clearly reflected in grievance issues and grievance handling.[17] This is the basis for positing specific relationships between labor-management relationship characteristics and measures of grievance procedure effectiveness.

The *length of the collective bargaining relationship* between the parties might be expected to be positively related to grievance procedure effectiveness as a whole. A portion of the literature suggests that as the parties gain experience in dealing with each other, the labor relationship matures and conflicts are dealt with relatively directly and swiftly.[18]

However, these notions have rarely been empirically verified, and so we offer no a priori predictions about the relationship between the length of time that the parties have bargained with each other and specific measures of grievance procedure effectiveness. Nevertheless, we do expect to find significantly higher grievance rates and levels of grievance settlement and a significantly lower speed of grievance settlement in the period immediately preceding the negotiation of a new collection agreement, compared to other periods.

Supervisor and union steward knowledge of the grievance procedure are both expected to be negatively related to the grievance rate, the arbitration rate, and the level of settlement and positively related to the speed of settlement, the importance of issues raised in the grievance procedure, and the perceived equity of grievance settlement. A substantial literature attests to the critical role played by supervisors and stewards in enforcing work rules, interpreting the labor agreement, and serving as buffers between the employee and the work organization.[19] We interpret this literature to mean that supervisory and steward knowledge of the grievance procedure will be positively related to grievance procedure effectiveness as a whole.

The *average cost of grievance handling* is expected to be negatively related to grievance rates, arbitration rates, and level of settlement, and positively related to the speed of settlement and the importance of issues raised in the grievance procedure. In essence, these hypotheses reflect the view that the "demand" for grievances will be inversely related to the costs of grievance processing. No prediction is offered with respect to the relationship between grievance processing costs and perceived equity of grievance settlement.

Among characteristics of the grievance procedure, per se, the degree of structure in the procedure and the presence (or absence) of expedited procedures are particularly noteworthy for purposes of this study. Specifically, *the more structured the procedure* the more likely are grievance rates, arbitration rates, and levels of settlements to be high, the speed of settlement to be low, and the importance of issues raised via the procedure to be high. These hypotheses stem from the view that a highly structured grievance procedure tends to legitimize grievance filing—that is, to generate a demand for grievances—but also signifies that grievances should be sufficiently important to warrant the attention of representatives of the management and union organizations.[20]

Where *provisions for expedited grievance processing* are present, they are expected to be positively associated with grievance rates, arbitration rates, and perceived equity of settlement and negatively associated with level of settlement and speed of settlement. Compared to conventional grievance procedures, expedited procedures "promise" settlements that are relatively swift and relatively close to their sources of origin. At the same time, they are likely to enhance the demand for grievances and arbitration. It is unclear whether expedited procedures affect the importance of grievances actually filed, but they are likely to bring about a greater perceived equity of settlement than would prevail under conventional procedures.

Table 3.1 summarizes the expected relationships between the independent variables discussed here and the individual measures of grievance procedure effectiveness.

LONGITUDINAL CHANGES

What of the environmental variables affecting grievance procedure effectiveness? The single most important of these, in our judgment, is the economic environment, which is difficult to operationalize in a cross-sectional, survey-based study. However, data were obtained for a three-year period, 1980-1982, during which a major economic recession occurred. What hypotheses about the effects of recession on grievance processing and effectiveness may be offered?

On the one hand, a substantial literature shows that unionization, strikes, and other forms of worker militancy are closely and positively correlated with the business cycle, that is, they rise during expansions and decline during recessions.[21] If grievance filing is considered a form of militancy, then the incidence of grievances should also fall during a recession. On the other hand, voluntary turnover also declines during recessions, involuntary turnover increases, downward pressure is exerted on pay and benefits (or on rates of pay and benefit increases), and workrules are tightened or adhered to more closely.[22] These factors suggest that grievance activity will rise during a recession.

Combining these two contrasting perspectives suggests that the effect of economic recession on grievance filing and effectiveness is indeterminate, a priori, and must be determined empirically. Nevertheless, the adjustments to internal labor markets made by employers during periods of recession seem to us to be particularly compelling, and they lead to the following hypotheses:

- Grievance rates will decline over the 1980-1982 period across the four industries and sectors.
- Levels of settlement will increase over the 1980-1982 period across the four industries and sectors.
- Speed of settlement will decline over the 1980-1982 period across the four industries and sectors.
- Arbitration rates will increase over the 1980-1982 period across the four industries and sectors.

Table 3.1

Predicted Relationships between Independent
Variables and Measures of Grievance Procedure Effectiveness

Dependent Variable*

Independent Variable	Grievance Rate	Level of Settlement	Speed of Settlement	Arbitration Rate	Perceived Importance of Issues	Perceived Equity of Settlement
Size of bargaining unit	+	+	-	+	+	NS
Occupational diversity of bargaining unit	+	+	-	+	NS	NS
Centralization of decision making	+	+	-	+	NS	NS
Voluntary turnover	-	-	NS	-	-	NS
Committing grievances to writing	+	+	-	+	NS	-
Taking certain grievances as far as possible	+	+	-	+	NS	-
Adversarial labor relations	+	+	-	+	NS	-
Length of bargaining relationship	+	+	-	NS	NS	NS

Table 3.1 (continued)

Dependent Variable*

Independent Variable	Grievance Rate	Level of Settlement	Speed of Settlement	Arbitration Rate	Perceived Importance of Issues	Perceived Equity of Settlement
Supervisor knowledge of grievance procedure	-	-	+	-	+	+
Union steward knowledge of grievance procedure	-	-	+	-	+	+
Average cost of grievance handling	-	-	+	-	+	NS
Grievance procedure structure	+	+	-	+	+	NS
Expedited grievance	+	-	-	+	NS	+

* = positive relationship
- = negative relationship
NS = not specified

- The perceived importance of issues raised in the grievance process will increase over the 1980-1982 period across the four industries and sectors.
- The perceived equity of grievance settlement will decline over the 1980-1982 period across the four industries and sectors.

Interindustry and Intersectoral Differences

Should grievance activity and grievance effectiveness vary significantly across the four industries and sectors? This will, of course, be determined empirically, but there are reasons for believing, a priori, that interindustry and intersectoral differences will be observed.

Consider that among the industries and sectors chosen for study, unionization occurred earliest in steel manufacturing, which is also characterized by relatively high capital intensity, difficult working conditions, and a work force that is almost exclusively male. Unionization emerged relatively recently in retail trade and especially in local schools and nonprofit hospitals; trade and services are typically less capital intensive than durable-goods manufacturing; and the work force is heavily female in retail trade and even more so in hospitals and schools, where the focus of this research is on nurses and teachers, respectively.

These industrial and sectoral characteristics suggest the following hypotheses:

- Grievance rates and arbitration rates will be higher in steel than in the three other industries and sectors.
- The level of settlement will be higher in steel than in the three other industries and sectors.
- The speed of settlement will be highest in nonprofit hospitals and lowest in steel.
- The perceived importance of issues raised in the grievance process will be higher in steel and local schools than in retail department stores and nonprofit hospitals.
- The perceived equity of grievance settlement will be highest in steel and lowest in nonprofit hospitals.

RESEARCH SETTINGS AND SITES

Four industries and sectors drawn from the private, public and nonprofit segments of the U.S. economy were chosen to provide the research settings for this study; they are steel manufacturing, retail department stores, nonprofit hospitals, and local public schools. Some labor relations characteristics of these industries and sectors are given below.

Steel manufacturing (private sector) has a largely semiskilled blue collar work force that is overwhelmingly male and heavily unionized. Production workers are represented by the United Steelworkers of America (USWA), and collective bargaining has been present in the industry since the mid-1930s.[23] Early on, bargaining was conducted on a company-by-company basis but later it became highly centralized so that, by the mid-1950s, multiemployer bargaining predominated in the steel industry. In the 1970s individual steel companies began to drop out of the Steel Companies' Coordinating Committee, the industry's multi-employer bargaining arm, and by the mid-1980s multiemployer bargaining was abandoned altogether. Recognize however that even when multiemployer bargaining was at its height, separate labor agreements were concluded between individual companies and the USWA.

These agreements have long provided for multistep grievance procedures that culminate in arbitration.[24] Generally, permanent arbitrators have been appointed by the union and each major company for the life of the contract. Expedited arbitration was introduced into the industry in the early 1970s and can be invoked for a wide variety of grievances, including written reprimands and short-term suspensions. However, grievances involving long-term suspensions, discharges, concerted activity, and multiple grievances arising out of the same event are subject to conventional arbitration.

Retail department stores (private sector) operate in a highly competitive environment and for sales and clerical jobs employ a heavily white-collar, largely female work force. The industry is moderately unionized by the Retail, Wholesale and Department Store Union (RWDSU) and, to a lesser extent, by the United Food and Commercial Workers Union (UFCW). Collective bargaining, which has a relatively short history in the industry, is conducted on a company-by-company basis, and multi-employer bargaining, which exists in other parts of the retail trade sector, such as supermarkets, has not been attempted in this industry.[25] Labor agreements are generally concluded between a company and, say, the RWDSU for all store locations; in most cases, these agreements include multistep grievance procedures. Provisions for grievance arbitration are present in almost all of these agreements, but expedited arbitration is rare in the industry. Note that department stores also bargain with maintenance personnel, typically represented by the Service Employees International Union, and with truck drivers and delivery personnel, who are represented by the Teamsters' Union. The present study is limited to grievance activity involving only members of the RWDSU and the UFCW.

Nonprofit hospitals (nonprofit sector) constitute one of three major types of hospitals that operate in the United States, the others being proprietary and public hospitals. Collective bargaining in nonprofit hospitals emerged on a large scale in the mid-1960s, especially in urban areas of the country. Overall, about one-quarter of all hospital employees are represented by labor unions and employee associations.[26] Hospital orderlies, attendants, and sometimes maintenance personnel are represented by several different unions, such as the Service Employees' International Union, the Laborers' International Union, and the National Hospital Union. In some hospitals interns and residents are organized and belong to the Physicians' National Housestaff Association or to independent unaffiliated unions. Nursing personnel, who are overwhelmingly female, are heavily organized and are represented by the American Nurses Association (ANA). Only the grievance procedures contained in nurses' labor contracts with nonprofit hospital employers are included in this study. Bargaining in the nonprofit hospital sector is often conducted on a multiemployer basis but, as in steel manufacturing, separate agreements are concluded between each hospital and organized nurses. Grievance procedures contained in these agreements are multi-step and usually include arbitration provisions, but the use of expedited arbitration is rare.

Local public schools (public sector) witnessed the rapid growth of teacher unionism in the 1960s, and collective bargaining is now widespread in this sector.[27] Teachers, who are predominantly female, constitute about 40 percent of all state and local government employees in the United States, and noninstructional personnel employed by public schools account for about another 10 percent. Organized teachers are represented by the National Education Association (NEA) and the American Federation of Teachers (AFT); the two organizations compete for members and representation status in many parts of the country. Collective bargaining in local public schools is typically conducted between representatives of individual school districts and local unions affiliated with the NEA or the AFT. However, regional- and state-level union representatives often participate in local school negotiations. Labor agreements in the schools contain multistep grievance procedures and in most cases arbitration constitutes the last step of the procedure. Expedited grievance procedures have not made much headway in local public schools.

Taken together, these research settings provide a rich mix of industries and services, technologies, workers, management and labor organizations, and collective bargaining relationships for studying the modern grievance process. They will permit us to examine the variations among several independent variables that are expected to affect the functioning and effectiveness of the grievance process.

SAMPLE SELECTION

The process of selecting respondent managers and union officials for inclusion in this study was as follows. In steel manufacturing, 35 corporations headquartered in the United States were randomly selected from Standard and Poor's *Registry of Corporations*. A letter was then sent to the top industrial relations official in each company asking if the company had one or more collective bargaining agreements with the USWA and, if it did, whether or not the company would be willing to cooperate in the study (a brief description of the study was included with the letter). Simultaneously, letters were sent to the president and research director of the USWA asking which of the 35 steel companies the union had collective agreements with and whether or not the union would be willing to cooperate in the study (again, a brief description of the study was included with the letter). The union officials as well as management officials in 28 of the steel companies agreed to cooperate in the study. A copy of the collective bargaining agreement between each cooperating company and the USWA was then obtained.

Next, each of the top industrial relations officials in the cooperating companies was asked to identify up to ten line managers and industrial relations staff members throughout the company who had had grievance-handling responsibility for workers represented by the USWA and who had been employed with the company continuously between 1980 and 1982—the period for which grievance data were requested. Once these managers were identified, each of them was contacted, given a brief description of the study, asked to participate in the study, and told that the company was cooperating in the study. They were then asked to identify the union official(s) or representative(s) with whom they dealt most often on grievance matters. These procedures yielded 162 steel industry managers and professionals and 155 USWA officials, stewards, and representatives who were involved in grievance handling. A questionnaire (described later in this chapter) was then sent to all but eight of the managers and eight of the USWA officials (all of whom were told that the company and the union were cooperating in the study). Those excluded from the survey were contacted and asked to participate in structured interviews. Four of the steel industry managers and five of the USWA officials agreed to do so and were subsequently interviewed.

In the retail department store industry, 50 firms were randomly chosen from a national registry and letters were sent to officials of the RWDSU and the UFCW asking which of the firms each of these unions had negotiated collective bargaining agreements with and whether or not they would be willing to cooperate in the study (a brief description of the study was included with the letters). Thirty-six of the firms had at least one collective bargaining agreement with the RWDSU or the UFCW, and letters were sent to the top industrial relations or personnel management official in each firm requesting the firm's cooperation in the study (a brief description of the study was included with the letter). Positive responses were received from representatives of 21 of these firms. Each of these officials was then asked to identify up to ten industrial relations managers, personnel managers, or other managers throughout the firm who had had grievance-handling responsibility for workers represented by the RWDSU or the UFCW, or both, and who had been employed with the firm continuously between 1980 and 1982. These individuals were then contacted, given a brief description of the study, asked to participate in the study, and told that the firm was cooperating in the study. They were also requested to identify the union official(s) or representative(s) with whom they dealt most often on grievance matters. These procedures yielded 141 retail department store managers and 145 union officials. A questionnaire was then sent to all but eight of the managers and eight of the union officials (the latter were told that their union, the RWDSU or the UFCW, was cooperating in the study). Those excluded from the survey were contacted and asked to participate in structured interviews. Four of the retail store managers and four of the union officials agreed to do so and were subsequently interviewed.

In the nonprofit hospital sector, letters were initially sent to the top officials of the American Hospital Association (AHA) and the American Nurses Association soliciting their cooperation in the study (a brief description of the study was included with the letters). The AHA agreed to provide a list of all nonprofit hospitals that belong to the association. Twenty-five hospitals were randomly selected from the list and letters were sent to the executive director and top labor relations manager or personnel manager of each hospital asking if a collective bargaining agreement was maintained with the ANA and, if so, whether or not the hospital would cooperate with the study. Twelve of the 22 hospitals that had such agreements agreed to cooperate in the study, and the top labor relations official or personnel official in each hospital was asked to identify up to ten management personnel who had had grievance-handling responsibility for nurses represented by the ANA and who had been employed with the hospital continuously between 1980 and 1982. These personnel were then contacted, provided a brief description of the study, asked to participate in the study, and told that the hospital was cooperating in the study. They were then asked to identify the union official(s) or representative(s) with whom they dealt most often on grievance matters. These procedures yielded 107 hospital managers and 98 ANA officials and representatives who were involved in grievance handling. A questionnaire was then sent to all but six of the managers and six of the ANA officials (the latter were told that the ANA was cooperating in the study). Those excluded from the survey were contacted and asked to participate in structured interviews. Three of the hospital managers and four of the ANA officials agreed to do so and were subsequently interviewed.

In the local school sector, letters were sent to top officials of the

National Education Association (NEA) and the American Federation of Teachers (AFT) soliciting their cooperation in the study and asking for lists of the top NEA and AFT officials in six states—New York, New Jersey, Michigan, Illinois, California, and Washington (a brief description of the study was included with the letters). These officials were then contacted, asked to cooperate in the study, and requested to provide a list of the three largest school districts in each state with which they maintained collective bargaining agreements. The superintendents of these districts were then contacted, furnished a brief description of the study, asked if they maintained a collective bargaining agreement with the NEA or the AFT, and, if so, requested to cooperate in the study. Sixteen of the school district superintendents indicated a willingness to cooperate, and they were subsequently asked to identify up to ten administrative and management officials who had had grievance-handling responsibility for teachers represented by the NEA or AFT and who had been employed with the district continuously between 1980 and 1982. Each of these officials was then contacted, provided a brief description of the study, asked to participate in the study and told that the school district was cooperating in the study. They were then asked to identify the union official(s) or representative(s) with whom they dealt most often on grievance matters. These procedures yielded 128 school administrators and managers and 116 NEA and AFT officials and representatives who were involved in grievance handling. A questionnaire was then sent to all but eight of the school officials and eight of the union officials (the latter were told that their labor organization, the NEA or AFT was cooperating in the study). Those excluded from the survey were contacted and asked to participate in structured interviews. Six of the school officials and six of the union officials agreed to do so and were subsequently interviewed.

Table 3.2 summarizes the samples of respondents who were asked to provide data in connection with the questionnaire and interview phases of this study.

DATA SOURCES AND DATA COLLECTION

Several data sources were used in this study. To conduct the large-scale mail survey, a questionnaire was designed to elicit information about background characteristics of the industry or sector; characteristics of the union and management organizations; the nature and composition of the collective bargaining relationship; the functions and structure of the grievance process; the extent of grievance activity over a three-year period (1980-1982); perceptions about grievance use, importance, equity, and resolution; union and management strategies and policies concerning grievance processing and resolution; the frequency

Table 3.2
Questionnaire and Interview Sample Sizes,
by Industry/Sector

Industry/Sector

Category of Respondent	Steel Manufacturing		Retail Department Stores		Nonprofit Hospitals		Local Public Schools	
	Questionnaire sample	Interview sample	Questionnaire sample	Interview sample	Questionnaire sample	Interview sample	Questionnaire sample	Interview sample
Management Officials	162	8	141	8	107	6	128	8
Union Officials	155	8	145	8	98	6	116	8
Total	317	16	286	16	205	12	244	16

and outcomes of arbitration; the use of expedited grievance procedures; the incidence of and variation in grievances by issue; the use of special grievance handling techniques, such as brainstorming; and the evaluation of grievance process effectiveness.

It was originally thought that one questionnaire could be used and would be responded to by knowledgeable union and management officials across the four industries and sectors. However, a pretesting process (described below) clearly indicated that the questionaire needed to be tailored to the industry and category of the respondent. Therefore, eight separate questionnaires were designed and administered (one for the union officials and one for the management officials in each industry and secteor).

Before actually administering the questionnaire to the samples of respondents, a pretest was conducted. This was done by sending sets of the questionnaires to four academic colleagues, four union officials, and four management officials. Each reviewer was asked to read the questionnaires carefully, identify unclear or overly general questions and those that should be discarded, and make suggestions for improvement of the instruments. The reviewers were also asked to make judgments about the fit of the questionnaires to each of the research settings included in the study. A question was discarded when this action was recommended by two or more of the reviewers. Approximately 40 percent of the questions were revised on the basis of reviewers' recommendations, and five questions were added to the instruments as a result of the review process. The final versions of the questionnaires were then mailed to the samples of respondents, together with the appropriate cover letters and prelabeled, prepaid return envelopes. Respondents were requested to return the questionnaires within 30 days. Follow-up letters were sent to nonrespondents 45 days after the original mailing. Thirty days later, remaining nonrespondents were contacted by telephone and asked to return the completed questionnaires. Copies of the management questionnaire for the steel industry and the union questionnaire for the nonprofit hospital sector are included in Appendix 1.

A second data source for this study consisted of structured interviews conducted with 36 union and management officials in the four industries and sectors. The primary reason for obtaining interview data was to supplement and enrich the quantitative analysis of questionnaire data. The interviews permitted the researchers to (1) deepen their understanding of the dynamics of grievance procesisng, (2) obtain insights into possible causal relationships in grievance processing, and (3) supplement the analysis of the parties' perceptions of the importance of grievance issues and the equity of grievance settlement.

A substantially modified form of the questionnaire was constructed and used as the interview schedule. These interviews were conducted in the field, specifically in the offices of the various management and union officials, and averaged approximately two hours each. An interviewee's responses to structured or forced-choice questions were placed or noted on the interview schedule by the researcher; responses to less structured and open-ended questions were briefly noted during the interview and were more fully written up shortly after the interview was concluded. Copies of the management interview schedule for the retail trade industry and the union interview schedule for local public schools are included in Appendix 2.

A third data source consisted of grievance processing records and files maintained by one employer in each of the four industries and sectors. Access to the records was obtained after lengthy discussion and negotiation with management and union officials. Security of the documents and preservation of the confidentiality of the individuals involved in grievance issues and processing were of major concern to both management and union officials. A set of safeguards for the grievance files and certain procedures for ensuring confidentiality of the participants were established to the parties' satisfaction, and the grievance records were then made available to the researchers. The content analysis that was subsequently conducted provided further qualitative insights into grievance handling, but its main importance was in permitting the researchers to gain understanding of the post-grievance settlement behavior of the parties to grievances. The research design for this portion of the study is discussed below.

POST-GRIEVANCE SETTLEMENT BEHAVIOR (DEPENDENT VARIABLE II)

As noted earlier, the vast bulk of the literature on the grievance process focuses on grievance settlement and treats such settlement as a dependent variable. However, it is possible to regard grievance settlement as an intervening variable and to ask how such settlement affects the subsequent behavior of employees, supervisors, and managers. Do grievance settlements affect employee job performance, attendance, turnover, or promotions? Do grievance settlements affect supervisors' or managers' job performance, attendance, turnover, or promotions? Does management use grievance-handling and settlement information to assess and perhaps alter job content, supervision, and employee relations policy and practices?

In an attempt to answer these and other related questions, longitudinal analysis of selected grievance records was undertaken in this study. One steel firm, one retail department store, one nonprofit hospital, and one local school district, together with their respective unions, cooperated in this portion of the study. The research process was as follows.

First, the grievance files were examined to develop familiarity with their format, content, and comprehensiveness. The files covered the 1977-1983 period in the case of the steel firm, the 1978-1983 period in the case of the retail department store, the 1979-1983 period in the case of the nonprofit hospital, and the 1977-1983 period in the case of the local school district. Second, personnel files were examined to develop familiarity with their format, content, and comprehensiveness. Performance measurement, work attendance, job change, and turnover data were singled out for special attention.

Third, alphabetized lists of employees who did and did not file grievances in 1982 were prepared, based on the grievance and personnel files in each of the four organizations (or selected subdivisions and locations thereof). The head industrial relations or human resource official in each organization reviewed the respective lists for accuracy. Using the lists as the relevant populations, random samples of grievance filers and nonfilers were then drawn.

Fourth, personnel data were matched with each grievance filer and nonfiler. These included selected demographic characteristics (for example, age, sex, race, education, and years of work experience) and certain work history data. The latter were obtained for the 1980-1983 period, except for employees who began employment after 1980 and those whose employment ended before 1983. For each employee, then, annual measures of job performance (typically a supervisor's rating), work attendance, promotions, and turnover were obtained. The turnover data were disaggregated by type, and included quits, retirements, layoffs, and discharges. In cases of missing or incomplete data, the industrial relations and human resource officials sometimes provided supplemental information.

Fifth, grievances actually filed in 1982 were categorized by type (using an eightfold categorization scheme devised after examining all grievance filers), speed of settlement (in days), level of settlement (ranging from one, typically informal discussion, to five, typically arbitration), and favorability of settlement (to the employee or the employer).[28] The last of these characteristics was determined by the researchers after reading grievance files and arbitration decisions, and the variable was coded zero if the settlement was in favor of the employee and one if the settlement was in favor of the employer. Where favorability of settlement was unclear, a judgment was reached after discussions with management and union officials who were knowledgeable about the particular grievance in question. In this regard, special account was taken of grievance arbitration (and lower-level settlements) that resulted in the reinstatement of or award of back pay to discharged employees.

Sixth, each of the employers was asked to provide a list of first-line supervisors who were employed in 1982. Data were then collected on the incidents of grievances that involved each supervisor. As before, the grievances were categorized by type, speed of settlement, level of settlement, and favorability of settlement. Also as before, personnel-file data were matched to each supervisor. This included demographic characteristics as well as performance, work attendance, job change, and separation data for the 1980-1983 period (or less if the supervisor became employed after 1980 or separated before 1983).

Seventh, the top industrial relations or human resource officials in each organization were interviewed about changes in management personnel over the 1980-1983 period. The objective here was to identify, albeit qualitatively, the role of workplace conflict, as expressed through grievance filing and settlement, in decisions about management personnel changes. Content analysis of company documents and personnel records was performed to supplement the interview data, and this enabled us to construct a detailed history of management changes in each organization over the 1980-1983 period. Where feasible, grievance data, including type of grievance, speed of settlement, level of settlement, and favorability of settlement, were assembled for each manager or managerial position in the organizations studied. Also where feasible, personnel-file data were matched with each manager; these included demographic, job performance, job change, and turnover data.

These procedures yielded a data base that enabled us to conduct a longitudinal analysis of the consequences of grievance settlement. The samples included 1,524 grievance filers and 1,444 nonfilers over the entire 1980-1983 period; 745 grievance filers and 698 nonfilers during 1982; and 264 supervisors-managers of grievance filers and 252 supervisors-managers of nonfilers in 1982. For research purposes the nongrievance filers were treated as a control group (the characteristics of grievance filers and nonfilers are discussed in Chapter 6), and one portion of the analysis will focus on the main intergroup differences within each and across the four organizations studied. Of particular interest is the extent to which grievance filing and the characteristics of grievance settlement—speed, level, and favorability—affect employee job performance and continuity of employment.

While several specific dimensions of these relationships will be examined in Chapter 6, the major hypothesis to be investigated in this portion of the study is that grievance filing and certain characteristics of grievance settlement have positive effects on employee performance and negative effects on employee turnover. In this regard, the grievance procedure is viewed as the main mechanism through which organized workers exercise "voice," and voice is viewed as an alternative to "exit," (Hirschman, 1970; Freeman and Medoff, 1984; Ichniowski and Lewin, 1988). Thus, the grievance filers in this study should have higher measured job performance or performance ratings and lower quit rates in the post-grievance filing period—that is, in 1983—than nonfilers (adjusting for pre-grievance-filing job performance and turnover)—that is, in 1981. Moreover, we expect these differences to be accentuated by speedy settlements, lower-level settlements, and settlements decided in favor of employees.

Concerning supervisors and managers, the major issue of concern in this study is whether and how job performance, job mobility, and turnover are affected by the incidence of grievance filing and the consequences of grievance settlement. While we chose not to specify a priori hypotheses in this regard, the empirical analysis will be devoted to such questions as the following: Are supervisors and managers against whom grievances are filed less likely to be promoted and more likely to leave or be separated from their jobs than supervisors who have few or no grievances filed against them? Do supervisors and managers with low grievance rates or high rates of grievance settlement in favor of the employer have different performance, promotion, and turnover experiences than managers with high grievance rates or low rates of grievance settlement in favor of the employer? These and the related questions to be taken up in this study reflect our concern for gaining a better understanding of the internal organizational dynamics and behavioral consequences of grievance activity and settlement than has heretofore been obtained.

NOTES

1. See, for example, Magenau (1983), Neale and Bazerman (1983), and Delaney, Sockell, and Brockner (1988).

2. For a fuller discussion of the external validity limitations of experimental and quasi-experimental research designs, see Campbell and Stanley (1963).

3. For examples of such research, see Roy (1952), Dalton (1959), and Sayles (1958).

4. See Schatzman and Strauss (1973) and Kerlinger (1973) for discussions of the benefits and limitations of field research.

5. Government organizations are frequently judged according to their effectiveness in meeting one or another public policy goal, in contrast to the market-based efficiency criteria that are typically used to assess private organizations. See, for example, Mogulof (1971). For applications of effectiveness concepts and measures to public and private organizations, see Hall (1980).

6. Note that the objective or behavioral measures used here are largely based upon the research literature reviewed in Chapter 2. The attitudinal measures have generally not been employed by previous researchers.

7. See Slichter, Healy, and Livernash (1960).

8. See Thomson and Murray (1976).

9. Of course it may be argued that the outcome of a grievance case is as at least as important to one or the other party as the speed of settlement. The issue of grievance procedure outcomes, including post-settlement outcomes, will be examined in Chapter 6.

10. See Stessin (1977).

11. For some preliminary results from measuring this variable, see Lewin (1984).

12. Note that union "success" in representation elections is inversely related to the size of the bargaining unit. See Heneman and Sandver (1983).

13. See Slichter, Healy, and Livernash (1960) and Kuhn (1961).

14. See Donaldson and Warner (1974).

15. See Hirschman (1970) and Freeman and Medoff (1984).

16. See Ash (1970) and Slichter, Healy, and Livernash (1960).

17. For relevant examples supporting this proposition, see Kuhn (1961).

18. See Kerr (1955).

19. See Kuhn (1961).

20. This is not to deny that apparently under grievance procedures with varying degrees of structure, most grievances are settled at the initial informal discussion stage. See Chamberlain and Kuhn (1986) for further discussion of this point.

21. See, for example, Ashenfelter and Pencavel (1969).

22. See Flanagan, Smith, and Ehrenberg (1984).

23. See Stieber (1980) for a detailed treatment of labor relations in this industry.

24. See Peach and Livernash (1974).

25. There are few scholarly treatments of labor relations in retail department stores. For selected information, see Bloom, Perry, and Fletcher (1972).

26. See Miller (1980) for a detailed account of labor relations in the hospital sector.

27. See Doherty (1980) for an account of labor relations in local public education.

28. The eight major categories are pay and work, benefits, working conditions, performance and mobility, discipline, discrimination, management rights, and supervisory relations. Twenty-seven subcategories of grievance issues will also be examined in Chapter 6.

4

Grievance Procedure Effectiveness: Aggregate Analysis

This chapter presents our analyses of grievance procedure character-istics, functioning, and effectiveness based largely on survey data. Both behavioral and perceptual data are considered, and specific hypotheses that were set out in Chapter 3 are empirically tested. Particular attention is given to the measurement and quantitative analysis of the determinants of grievance procedure effectiveness.

DESCRIPTIVE STATISTICS

Table 4.1 provides data on responses to the mail questionnaires. The combination of the original mailings and two follow-up procedures yielded response rates of between 53 and 64 percent for the manage-ment and union officials in the four industries and sectors. Approxi-mately 58 percent of the management officials and 57 percent of the union officials in the total sample responded to the questionnaires.

Table 4.2 presents descriptive statistics for the major behavioral vari-ables of interest in the study. Over the 1980-1982 period, the grievance rate per 100 employees was highest in steel manufacturing, 14.7, and lowest in retail department stores, 7.5. The grievance rate varied by about tenfold among individual steel manufacturing firms, by about ninefold among retail department stores, by sixfold among nonprofit hospitals, and fivefold among local public schools.

On average, the level of grievance settlement over the 1980-1982 period was lowest in hospitals, followed closely by retail department stores, then by local schools and steel manufacturing firms. However, grievance settlements were achieved more slowly in hospitals than in

Table 4.1
Questionnaire Responses, by
Industry/Sector

	Steel manufacturing	Retail department stores	Nonprofit hospitals	Local public schools
Managers				
Sample Size	162	141	107	128
Responses to Original Survey	57	44	39	43
Responses to follow up #1	26	18	16	17
Responses to follow up #2	19	13	8	11
Total Responses	102	75	63	71
Response Rate (%)	63.0%	53.2%	58.9%	55.5%
Union Officials				
Sample Size	155	145	98	116
Responses to Original Survey	40	39	30	42
Responses to follow up #1	22	23	20	19
Responses to follow up #2	18	17	12	13
Total Responses	80	79	62	74
Response Rate (%)	53.3%	54.5%	63.3%	64.%

Table 4.2
Descriptive Statistics concerning Grievance Activity and Settlement, by Industry/Sector, 1980-1982

	Steel		Department Stores		Hospitals		Schools	
	Mean	Range	Mean	Range	Mean	Range	Mean	Range
Grievance Rate (per 100 employees,) Annual Average								
1980-82	14.7	2.4-22.6	7.5	2.0-18.7	9.4	3.8-23.7	7.9	4.6-22.6
1980	16.4	2.8-24.7	8.4	2.5-21.4	9.7	4.0-24.4	8.3	4.9-24.6
1981	13.9	2.5-21.3	7.6	2.1-18.2	8.9	3.3-21.6	7.8	4.3-22.2
1982	11.8	2.0-20.5	6.8	1.6-17.4	9.5	4.2-24.9	7.3	3.9-20.7
Level of Settlement (1 = low, 5 = high) Annual Average,								
1980-82	2.6	1.2-4.4	1.8	1.0-4.2	1.6	1.2-4.3	2.1	1.5-4.5
1980	2.3	1.0-4.5	1.7	1.0-4.3	1.7	1.3-4.5	2.2	1.6-4.5
1981	2.8	1.4-4.4	1.5	1.2-4.0	1.4	1.0-3.9	2.0	1.3-4.3
1982	2.6	1.2-4.3	1.9	1.1-4.1	1.9	1.3-4.4	1.9	1.4-4.6
Speed of Settlement (in days) Annual Average,								
1980-82	12.8	2.5-41.6	12.2	4.4-52.4	13.7	7.5-56.0	13.4	11.5-51.4
1980	12.4	2.3-40.4	12.1	4.2-51.6	13.9	7.7-57.5	13.7	11.9-52.8
1981	13.1	2.8-43.2	11.9	4.0-53.2	13.3	7.0-52.6	13.4	11.2-51.2
1982	12.9	2.5-39.8	12.4	4.7-52.8	13.8	7.6-57.2	13.0	10.9-50.6
Arbitration Rate (per 100 employees) Annual Average,								
1980-82	2.4	0.2-8.3	0.7	0.0-7.8	1.1	0.4-6.8	0.9	0.6-12.5
1980	2.7	0.3-9.1	0.6	0.1-8.0	1.3	0.2-7.3	1.0	0.7-13.4
1981	2.2	0.1-8.1	0.5	0.0-7.6	0.8	0.1-6.2	0.7	0.5-10.3
1982	2.0	0.2-7.7	0.8	0.1-7.7	1.2	0.4-7.0	0.9	0.6-13.6

local schools, steel manufacturing, and especially retail department stores. Note, too, that in some hospitals, local schools, and retail trade establishments the average speed of grievance settlement exceeded 50 days.

The arbitration rate per 100 employees during 1980-1982 was highest in steel manufacturing and lowest in retail department stores. The single highest arbitration rate, 13.6, occurred in a local school district, the lowest, zero, in a retail department store. Arbitration rates ranged from a little above zero for some organizations in each of the four industries and sectors to highs of about 7.0 in individual hospitals, 8.0 in individual retail department stores and steel manufacturing firms, and 13.5 in certain local public school districts.

The data in Table 4.2 also show that, in general, grievance activity declined annually over the 1980-1982 period, thus providing preliminary support for the hypothesis posited in Chapter 3. In steel manufacturing, for example, the mean grievance rate per 100 employees declined from 16.4 in 1980 to 11.8 in 1982 for the firms included in this study. Declines in grievance rates over the 1980-1982 period were also recorded in department stores and local schools. The one exception to this pattern was the nonprofit hospital sector, where the grievance rate fell from 9.7 to 8.9 per 100 employees between 1980 and 1981, but rose to 9.5 per 100 employees in 1982. Arbitration rates per 100 employees in steel manufacturing firms declined progressively over the 1980-1982 period. In the three other industries and sectors, however, arbitration rates initially declined but then increased. Levels and speed of grievance settlement in the four industries and sectors displayed no particular patterns between 1980 and 1982, except in local schools where both declined.

Table 4.3 presents descriptive data concerning the major attitudinal/perceptual variables of interest in this study. These data show that the perceived importance of issues raised in the grievance procedure was highest in steel manufacturing, lowest in retail department stores, and consistently higher among union than among management respondents. Union-management differences in perceptions of the importance of issues raised in the grievance procedure were largest in hospitals and retail department stores. Note that the range of (combined) importance scores more than doubled (and, in the case of department stores, more than tripled) from the lowest to the highest score.

The data in Table 4.3 show that, on a combined union official–management official response basis, the perceived equity of grievance settlement was slightly above the midpoint of the rating scale (3.0) in steel manufacturing and local school districts and slightly below the midpoint in retail department stores and nonprofit hospitals. In two instances, namely, nonprofit hospitals and local schools, management respondents had a higher perceived equity of settlement, on average, than union respondents, whereas the opposite relationship prevailed in steel manu-

Table 4.3
Descriptive Statistics concerning Perceptions
of Grievance Activity and Settlement,
by Industry/Sector

	Steel		Department Stores		Hospitals		Schools	
	Mean	Range	Mean	Range	Mean	Range	Mean	Range
Perceived Importance of Issues Raised (1 = low, 5 = high)								
Management Respondents	3.6	1.6-4.7	2.7	0.8-4.3	3.1	1.1-4.2	3.1	1.4-4.5
Union Respondents	3.9	2.2-4.8	3.2	1.6-4.7	3.7	2.5-4.8	3.4	1.8-4.6
Combined Responses	3.7	1.7-4.7	3.0	1.0-4.5	3.4	1.7-4.4	3.3	1.6-4.6
Perceived Equity of Grievance Settlement (1 = low, 5 = high)								
Management Respondents	3.0	1.6-4.3	2.6	1.4-4.1	3.2	1.8-4.6	3.4	1.9-4.5
Union Respondents	3.4	2.0-4.6	3.0	1.8-4.2	2.5	1.2-4.2	3.2	1.7-4.6
Combined Responses	3.2	1.8-4.4	2.8	1.6-4.1	2.8	1.5-4.3	3.3	1.8-4.4

facturing and retail department stores. The range of perceived equity of grievance settlement scores more than doubled from the low to the high score in each of the four industries and sectors.

RELATIONSHIPS AMONG DEPENDENT VARIABLES

Table 4.4 presents the intercorrelation matrix among the dependent variables. As expected and as has been found in other studies (Anderson, 1979; Briggs, 1984), the speed of grievance settlement is significantly positively correlated with the level of grievance settlement across the four industries and sectors.[1] Also as predicted, the greater the arbitration rate, the higher the level of grievance settlement and the slower the speed of settlement.

The perceived importance of issues raised in the grievance procedure— a variable for which no theroetically grounded hypotheses were posed—is significantly positively correlated with the arbitration rate at the $p = <$ .01 level. This finding suggests that, apart from "wins and losses" in or the perceived equity of grievance settlement, the perceived importance

Table 4.4
Zero-Order Correlation Matrix for Grievance Procedure Effectiveness Measures

Measure	Grievance Rate	Level of Settlement	Speed of Settlement	Arbitration Rate	Perceived Importance of Issues	Perceived Equity of Settlement
Grievance Rate	1.00					
Level of Settlement	.16	1.00				
Speed of Settlement	.11	.39**	1.00			
Arbitration Rate	.09	.22*	.28*	1.00		
Perceived Importance of Issues	-.07	.14	.11	.42**	1.00	
Perceived Equity of Settlement	-.13	-.31**	-.34**	.08	.29*	1.00

* = Significant at p = < .05

** = Significant at p = < .01

of grievance issues is strongly affected by the settlement of grievances at the final step of the procedure. Such reasoning is perhaps partially "confirmed" by the positive (though insignificant) correlations of perceived importance of grievance issues with the level and speed of grievance settlement, and by the negative (though insignificant) correlation of perceived importance of grievance issues with the grievance rate.

The perceived equity of grievance settlement declines significantly as the level of settlement rises, the speed of settlement declines, and the perceived importance of grievance issues rises. The first two findings are important, if unsurprising, because they provide empirical support for the oft-voiced contention that (industrial) justice delayed is (industrial) justice denied. The third finding, which addresses a relationship not addressed in previous studies, suggests that perceptions of equity are strongly influenced by perceptions of issue importance; that is, the more important the issue raised in the grievance process, the more likely settlement of the issue is to be perceived as inequitable. Note also that, while statistically insignificant, perceived equity of grievance settlement is negatively associated with the grievance rate. This suggests that as the grievance procedure becomes more heavily used, grievance settlements will be perceived to be inequitable, on average.

INDEPENDENT VARIABLES:
MEASUREMENT AND ANALYSIS

The independent variables listed in Table 4.5 are those for which formal hypotheses were specified in Chapter 3. Some of these variables, such as voluntary turnover and size of the bargaining unit, are measured continuously; other variables, such as policies to commit grievances to writing and the occupational diversity of the bargaining unit, are measured by single-item scales; and still other variables, such as centralization of the management and union organizations, are measured by multiple-item indices.

For the last group of variables, factor analysis was employed. Varimax rotation was chosen because of its orthogonal treatment of variables. A minimum factor loading of .40 was specified to ensure high factor reliability, and alpha coefficients were computed to test for the reliability of factors. For this purpose, unit weights rather than factor-loading weights were used; this is consistent with scoring procedures typically applied to the (Likert) type of scales employed here.[2] Table 4.6 presents the Alpha coefficient reliability estimates for these scales. All of the coefficients are above .50, with a range of .54 to .82 and an average Alpha coefficient of .65. This indicates that for each factor the item scales are measuring the same concept.

Table 4.5
Independent Variables and Measures

	Variable Measure
Management Characteristics	
° Centralization of Decision Making	Multiple Item Index
° Committing Grievance to Writing	Single Item Scale
° Policy of Taking Certain Grievances Through Procedure	Multiple Item Index
° Voluntary Employee Turnover	Continuous
Union Characteristics	
° Size of Bargaining Unit	Continuous
° Occupational Diversity of Bargaining Unit	Single Item Scale
° Centralization of Decision Making	Multiple Item Index
° Committing Grievances to Writing	Single Item Scale
° Policy of Taking Certain Grievances through Procedure	Multiple Item Index
Labor-Management Relations Characteristics	
° Adversarial Labor Relations	Multiple Item Index
° Length of Bargaining Relationship	Continuous
° Cost of Grievance Handling	Continuous
° Supervisor Knowledge of Grievance Procedure	Multiple Item Index
° Steward Knowledge of Grievance Procedure	Multiple Item Index
Grievance Procedure Characteristics	
° Grievance Procedure Structure	Multiple Item Index
° Expedited Grievance Handling	Multiple Item Index

Table 4.6
Alpha Coefficient Reliability Estimates

Factor	Number of Items	Alpha Coefficient
Management Characteristics		
° Centralization of Decision Making	4	.66
° Taking Certain Grievances Through the Procedure	3	.58
Union Characteristics		
° Centralization of Decision Making	4	.60
° Taking Certain Grievances Through the Procedure	3	.54
Labor-Management Relations Characteristics		
° Adversarial Labor Relations	4	.74
° Supervisor Knowledge of Grievance Procedure	4	.63
° Steward Knowledge of Grievance Procedure	4	.68
Grievance Procedure Characteristics		
° Grievance Procedure Structure	3	.58
° Expedited Grievance Handling	4	.82

Correlation Analysis

The relationships between the independent and dependent variables were initially examined via correlation analysis. The procedure was to derive zero-order correlation coefficients for each of the sixteen independent and six dependent variables; these are shown in Table 4.7.

With respect to management characteristics, a policy of taking certain grievances as far as possible through the procedure was significantly negatively associated with the speed of grievance settlement and significantly positively associated with the level of grievance settlement, the arbitration rate, the perceived importance of issues raised in the grievance procedure, and the equity of grievance settlement. A policy of committing all grievances to writing was strongly positively associated with the grievance rate ($p = < .01$) and the perceived importance of issues raised in the grievance procedure. Centralization of management decision making was significantly related to only one dependent variable, namely, the level of grievance settlement; that is, the more centralized management decision making, the higher the level of grievance settlement. As predicted, voluntary employment turnover was significantly negatively associated with both grievance rates and arbitration rates. However, and contrary to hypothesized relationships, this variable was not significantly associated with the level of grievance settlement or the perceived importance of issues raised in the grievance procedure.

Concerning union characteristics, the size of the bargaining unit was significantly positively correlated with three of the four behavioral-type dependent variables, namely, the grievance rate, level of settlement, and the speed of settlement. A policy of committing all grievances to writing was significantly positively associated with the grievance rate, level of settlement, speed of settlement, and the perceived importance of issues raised in the grievance procedure. A policy of taking certain grievances as far as possible through the procedure was positively associated with the grievance rate, the speed of settlement, the arbitration rate, and the perceived equity of grievance settlement. By and large, occupational diversity of the bargaining unit and centralization of union decision making were not significantly correlated with the dependent variables.

Of the labor-management relations characteristics, adversarial labor relations and supervisor knowledge of the grievance procedure were most strongly and consistently related to measures of grievance procedure effectiveness. The more adversarial the labor-management relationship, the higher the grievance rate, the arbitration rate, and the level of settlement, the slower the settlement, and the lower the perceived equity of grievance settlement. Supervisor knowledge of the grievance procedure was significantly negatively associated with grievance rates, arbitration rates, level of settlement, and speed of settlement and was

Table 4.7
Zero-Order Correlation Coefficients

Independent Variable	Dependent Variable					
	Grievance Rate	Level of Settlement (In Steps)	Speed of Settlement (In Days)	Arbitration Rate	Importance of Issue	Equity of Settlement
Management Characteristics						
° Centralization of Decision Making	.08	.18*	-.09	-.10	.04	.07
° Committing Grievances to Writing	.37*	.11	.08	.06	.15*	.09
° Taking Certain Grievances through Procedure	.12	.17*	.19*	.18*	.22*	.18*
° Voluntary Employee Turnover	-.22*	.07	.13	-.23*	.09	.05
Union Characteristics						
° Size of Bargaining Unit	.38*	.19*	.17*	.12	-.10	-.06
° Occupational Diversity of Bargaining Unit	.06	.03	-.05	-.07	-.03	-.04
° Centralization of Decision Making	.12	-.08	-.17*	.08	.12	.13
° Committing Grievances to Writing	.26**	.15*	.18*	.07	.19*	.09
° Policy of Taking Certain Grievances through Procedure	.16*	.12	.20*	.19*	.11	.21*

Table 4.7 (continued)

Independent Variable	Dependent Variable					
	Grievance Rate	Level of Settlement (In Steps)	Speed of Settlement (In Days)	Arbitration Rate	Importance of Issue	Equity of Settlement
Labor Management Relations <u>Charactersitics</u>						
° Adversarial Labor Relations	.30**	.24**	.19*	.21*	.10	-.23*
° Length of Bargaining Relationship	-.04	-.02	-.04	.08	.17*	.15*
° Cost of Grievance Handling	-.11	-.18*	-.11	-.15*	.08	-.17*
° Supervisor Knowledge of Grievance Procedure	-.15*	-.16*	-.19*	-.21*	.18*	.07
° Steward Knowledge of Grievance Procedure	.17*	-.18*	-.13	.11	.23**	.11
<u>Grievance Procedure Characteristics</u>						
° Grievance Procedure Structure	.20*	.10	.12	.09	.11	.10
° Expedited Grievance Handling	.16*	.33**	-.37**	.34**	.07	.29**

* = significant at $p = <.05$
** = significant at $p = <.01$

positively associated with the perceived importance of issues raised in the grievance process. Union steward knowledge of the grievance procedure was significantly related to some measures of grievance procedure effectiveness, specifically the grievance rate (positive), level of settlement (negative), and perceived importance of issues raised in the procedure (positive). Note that supervisor knowledge of the grievance procedure and union knowlede of the grievance procedure have opposite effects on the grievance rate (but not the arbitration rate). As predicted, the cost of grievance handling was negatively associated with the level of settlement and the arbitration rate. Further, the cost of grievance handling was negatively related to the perceived equity of grievance settlement. The length of the bargaining relationship was not significantly related to any of the behavioral-type dependent variables, but was significantly positively related to both the perceived importance of issues raised in the grievance procedure and the perceived equity of grievance settlement.

As to grievance procedure characteristics, the degree of structure (formality) of the procedure was significantly related to the grievance rate but not to other dependent variables. In contrast, the presence of expedited grievance-handling procedures was significantly related to all but one of the measures of grievance procedure effectiveness. Specifically and as predicted, expedited grievance procedures were positively related to the grievance rate, the arbitration rate, and the perceived equity of grievance settlement, and negatively related to the speed of settlement. In fact, all but one of the (significant) coefficients on the expedited procedure variable were significant at the $p = < .01$ level.

Regression Analysis—Full Model

To identify more precisely the determinants of grievance procedure effectiveness, regression analyses of the survey data were performed. The initial regressions included the full set of independent variables previously identified; the results are shown in Table 4.8.[3]

In general, the findings are consistent with those of the correlation analysis and, in most instances, confirm the original hypotheses. A management policy of committing grievances to writing, the size of the bargaining unit, union policies of committing grievances to writing and taking certain grievances as far as possible through the procedure, adversarial labor relations, union steward knowledge of the grievance procedure, the degree of grievance procedure structure, and provisions for expedited grievance handling were all significantly positively associated with the grievance rate. Voluntary employee turnover and supervisor knowledge of the grievance procedure were, as predicted, significantly negatively associated with the grievance rate. Centralization of

Table 4.8
Regression Coefficients for the Full Model
of Grievance Procedure Effectiveness

Independent Variable	Dependent Variable					
	Grievance Rate	Level of Settlement (In Steps)	Speed of Settlement (In Days)	Arbitration Rate	Importance of Issue	Equity of Settlement
Management Characteristics						
° Centralization of Decision Making	.05	.16*	-.05	-.07	.01	.04
° Committing Grievances to Writing	.31**	.09	.04	.10	.17*	.07
° Taking Certain Grievances Through the Procedure	.10	.19*	.22*	.20*	.25**	.19*
° Voluntary Employee Turnover	-.20*	.10	.11	-.18*	.06	.03
Union Characteristics						
° Size of Bargaining Unit	.31**	.17*	.19*	.13	-.07	-.07
° Occupational Diversity of Bargaining Unit	.03	.06	-.08	-.03	-.04	-.02
° Centralization of Decision Making	.13	-.04	.11	.09	.09	.10

| | Dependent Variable | | | | | |
Independent Variable	Grievance Rate	Level of Settlement (In Steps)	Speed of Settlement (In Days)	Arbitration Rate	Importance of Issue	Equity of Settlement
Union Characteristics (continued)						
° Committing Grievances to Writing	.21*	.17*	.16*	.04	.21*	.07
° Taking Certain Grievances Through the Procedure	.18*	.16*	.21*	.17*	.10	.20*
Labor-Management Relations Characteristics						
° Adversarial Labor Relations	.33**	.27**	.21*	.23*	.08	-.19*
° Length of Bargaining Relationship	-.07	.01	-.06	-.05	.19*	.17*
° Cost of Grievance Handling	-.08	-.21*	-.12	-.16*	.04	-.20*
° Supervisor Knowledge of Grievance Procedure	-.18*	-.22*	-.20*	-.23*	.20*	.08
° Steward Knowledge of Grievance Procedure	.16*	-.16*	-.11	.09	.25**	.09

99

Table 4.8 (continued)

Independent Variable	Grievance Rate	Level of Settlement (In Steps)	Speed of Settlement (In Days)	Arbitration Rate	Importance of Issue	Equity of Settlement
				Dependent Variable		
Grievance Procedure Characteristics						
° Grievance Procedure Structure	.18*	.08	.09	.05	.10	.06
° Expedited Grievance Handling	.19*	.28**	-.34**	.37**	.02	.31**
R^2	.53	.46	.41	.52	.38	.34

* = significant at $p = <.05$
** = significant at $p = <.01$

decision making in the management and union organizations, a management policy of taking certain grievances as far as possible through the procedure, occupational diversity of the bargaining unit, and the cost of grievance handling were not, as had been hypothesized, significantly related to the grievance rate, nor was the length of the bargaining relationship, for which no a priori hypothesis was specified. Union steward knowledge of the grievance procedure was significantly positively associated with the grievance rate, whereas the opposite relationship had been predicted.

Column two of Table 4.8 shows that certain management and union characteristics were associated with higher-level grievance settlements. These include centralization of the management organization, management and union policies to take certain grievances as far as possible through the procedure, a union policy to commit certain grievances to writing, and the size of the bargaining unit. Several labor-management relationship characteristics were significantly negatively correlated with the level of settlement, including the cost of grievance handling and supervisor and steward knowledge of the grievance procedure. However, the variables having the strongest (positive) relationships with the level of grievance settlement were adversarial labor relations and provisions for expedited arbitration. The latter finding is somewhat misleading because expedited procedures often call for skipping certain steps in the grievance procedure, and the scoring method used for this variable did not result in a reduced level score when, for example, a particular grievance procedure provided for moving directly from the first to the last step. However, no such technical problem exists with respect to the adversarial labor relations variable; the more adversarial the relationship, the higher the level of grievance settlement.

For the most part, the variables that were significantly related to the level of grievance settlement were also significantly related to the speed of settlement, as shown in column three of Table 4.8. A union policy of requiring grievances to be put in writing, union and management policies of taking certain grievances as far as possible through the procedure, the size of the bargaining unit, and adversarial labor relations all acted to increase the time required to settle grievances (the positive signs on the coefficients of these variables mean more days to settlement). Supervisor knowledge of the grievance procedure and provisions for expedited arbitration acted to reduce the time required to settle grievances, with the coefficient on the latter variable being significant at the $p = < .01$ level. Note that the cost of grievance handling and union steward knowledge of the grievance procedure had the expected (negative) signs, but were not significantly associated with the speed of grievance settlement.

As predicted, management and union policies to take grievances as far through the procedure as possible were positively associated with the arbitration rate, as were adversarial labor relations and provisions for expedited grievance handling (column four of Table 4.8). Voluntary employee turnover, the cost of grievance handling, and supervisor knowledge of the grievance procedure were significantly negatively associated with the arbitration rate. Though they had the expected signs, the coefficients on several other variables (for example, size of the bargaining unit) were not significantly related to the arbitration rate. A few variables (for example, centralization of management decision making and union steward knowledge of the grievance procedure) had signs on the coefficients which were the opposite of those predicted, but these, too, were insignificantly related to the arbitration rate.

Turning to the regression results for the attitudinal/perceptual-type dependent variables, column five of Table 4.8 shows that management and union policies to commit grievances to writing, a management policy to take certain grievances as far through the procedure as possible, the length of the bargaining relationship, and supervisor and steward knowledge of the grievance procedure were all significantly positively related to the perceived importance of issues raised through the grievance procedure. The results for the supervisor and union steward knowledge variables were as predicted, while no formal hypotheses were offered with respect to the other (significant) independent variables. Contrary to predictions, the coefficients on the size of bargaining unit, voluntary employee turnover, cost of grievance handling, and grievance procedure structure variables were insignificantly related to the perceived importance of issues raised through the grievance procedure.

The regression results also show that management and union policies to take certain grievances as far through the procedure as possible, the length of the bargaining relationship, and provisions for expedited griev-ance processing had significant positive effects on the perceived equity of grievance settlement (column six, Table 4.8). The opposite effects were associated with the adversarial labor relations and cost of grievance-handling variables. *In toto,* these results confirm the original hypotheses with respect to the adversarial labor relations, length of the bargaining relationship, and expedited grievance-handling variables, but were opposite of the predictions for the management and union character-istics variables (no hypothesis was offered about the relationship between grievance-handling cost and perceived equity of grievance settlement).

Regression Analysis—Modified Model

In both the correlation and regression analyses, some of the indepen-dent variables were seldom if ever significantly associated with measures of grievance procedure effectiveness. These include the centralization of decision making in the management and union organizations, occupational diversity of the bargaining unit, and the structure of the grievance procedure. Consequently, a modified regression analysis was performed that excluded these variables; the results are shown in Table 4.9.

Note first that the modified model appears to be better specified than the full model, as indicated by the significant coefficients on most of the variables and only slight declines in the R^2s from those reported in Table 4.8. Second, the individual coefficients on the independent variables with respect to each of the measures of grievance procedure effectiveness are generally (though slightly) larger than in the case of the full model, and all of the variables that were significant in the full model remain so in the modified model. Third, and as was true of the full model, the independent variables account for relatively more of the variance among the behavioral-type dependent variables than among the attitudinal/perceptual-type dependent variables. Fourth, provisions for expedited grievance processing, supervisor knowledge of the grievance procedure, adversarial labor relations, and management and union policies to take certain grievances as far as possible through the procedure remain the strongest and most consistent predictors of grievance procedure effectiveness. Fifth, some independent variables (for example, voluntary employee turnover) continue to be significant determinants of behavioral- but not attitudinal-type dependent variables, while the opposite is true of some other independent variables (for example, length of the bargaining relationship).

Regression Analysis—Decomposed Dependent Variables

Because there is no dominant theory of grievance procedure effectiveness and because the independent variables in this analysis have differential effects on individual measures of grievance procedure effectiveness, it is important to consider whether separate models of grievance procedure effectiveness should be specified, depending upon the effectiveness measure in question. To address this issue, separate regression equations were estimated for three sets of dependent variables: (1) the grievance rate and the arbitration rate, (2) the level of settlement and the speed of settlement, and (3) the perceived importance of issues raised through the grievance procedure and perceived equity of grievance settlement. The results are shown in Tables 4.10, 4.11, and 4.12, respectively.

The coefficients in Table 4.10 show that voluntary employee turnover and supervisor knowledge of the grievance procedure are significantly negatively correlated with both grievance and arbitration rates, while a

Table 4.9
Regression Coefficients for the Modified
Model of Grievance Procedure Effectiveness

Independent Variable	Dependent Variable					
	Grievance Rate	Level of Settlement (In Steps)	Speed of Settlement (In Days)	Arbitration Rate	Importance of Issue	Equity of Settlement
Management Characteristics						
° Committing Grievances to Writing	.33**	.11	.07	.09	.20*	.10
° Taking Certain Grievances through the Procedure	.12	.23*	.25*	.24*	.28**	.21*
° Voluntary Employee Turnover	-.24*	.12	.09	-.22*	.08	.07
Union Characteristics						
° Size of Bargaining Unit	.34**	.19*	.23*	.11	-.05	-.08
° Committing Grievances to Writing	.20*	.18*	.19*	.07	.23*	.09
° Taking Certain Grievances through the Procedure	.19*	.17*	.24*	.20*	.11	.23*

	Dependent Variable					
Independent Variable	Grievance Rate	Level of Settlement (In Steps)	Speed of Settlement (In Days)	Arbitration Rate	Importance of Issue	Equity of Settlement
Labor-Management Relations Characteristics						
° Adversarial Labor Relations	.36**	.30*	.22*	.27**	.09	-.23*
° Length of Bargaining Relationship	-.04	.04	-.02	-.06	.22*	.20*
° Cost of Grievance Handling	-.07	-.23*	-.10	-.18*	.06	-.24*
° Supervisor Knowledge of Grievance Procedure	-.21*	-.24*	-.22*	-.25*	.22*	.10
° Steward Knowledge of Grievance Procedure	.18*	-.19*	-.13	.11	.27**	.06
GRIEVANCE PROCEDURE CHARACTERISTICS						
° Expedited Grievance Handling	.20*	.32**	-.38**	.41**	.05	.35**
R^2	.51	.44	.40	.50	.36	.33

* = significant at $p = <.05$
** = significant at $p = <.01$

Table 4.10
Regression Coefficients on Grievance
and Arbitration Rates

	Dependent Variable			
Independent Variable	Grievance Rate	Arbitration Rate	Grievance Rate	Arbitration Rate
Management Characteristics				
° Committing Grievances to Writing			.23*	.12
° Taking Certain Grievances Through the Procedure			.13	.22*
° Voluntary Employee Turnover	-.27**	-.22*	-.26**	-.20*
Union Characteristics				
° Size of Bargaining Unit			.34**	.10
° Committing Grievances to Writing			.24*	.09
° Taking Certain Grievvances Through the Procedure	.22*	.20*	.20*	.18*
Labor-Management Relations Characteristics				
° Adversarial Labor Relations	.37**	.28**	.33**	.25*
° Cost of Grievance Handling			-.09	-.18*
° Supervisor Knowledge of Grievance Procedure	-.21*	-.25*	-.20*	-.22*
° Steward Knowledge of Grievance Procedure			.18*	.11

Table 4.10 (continued)

Independent Variable	Dependent Variable			
	Grievance Rate	Arbitration Rate	Grievance Rate	Arbitration Rate
Grievance Procedure Characteristics				
° Grievance Procedure Structure			.19*	.08
° Expedited Grievance Handling	.23*	.44**	.21*	.36**
R²	.63	.59	.68	.66

* = significant at p = <.05
** = significant at p = <.01

union policy of taking grievances as far as possible through the procedure, adversarial labor relations, and provisions for expedited arbitration are significantly positively related to grievance and arbitration
rates. Adding other variables to the model (columns three and four)
increases the R^2s, and suggests that certain management, union, labor
relations, and grievance procedure characteristics help to explain the
variance in grievance procedure effectiveness across the four industries
and sectors.

The regression coefficients in Table 4.11 indicate that management
and union policies of taking certain grievances as far as possible through
the grievance procedure, the size of the bargaining unit, a union policy of
committing all grievances to writing, and adversarial labor relations are
significantly positively related to the level and speed of grievance
settlements. Supervisor knowledge of grievance procedures acts to
reduce the level of and time to grievance settlement, while provisions for
expedited grievance procedures have positive and negative effects,
respectively, on the level and speed of grievance settlement. Other
variables (shown in columns three and four of Table 4.11) add to the
explanatory power of the equations, but not materially.

The coefficients in Table 4.12 show that a management policy of
taking grievances as far as possible through the procedure and the length
of the bargaining relationship are significantly positively related to the
perceived importance of issues raised through the grievance procedure
and the perceived equity of grievance settlement. The explanatory
power of the equations for these measures of grievance procedure effec-

Table 4.11
Regression Coefficients on Level
and Speed of Settlement

Independent Variable	DEPENDENT VARIABLE			
	Level of Settlement (In Steps)	Speed of Settlement (In Days)	Level of Settlement (In Steps)	Speed of Settlement (In Days)
Management Characteristics				
° Centralization of Decision Making			.18*	-.01
° Taking Certain Grievances Through the Procedure	.21*	.24*	.20*	.23*
Union Characteristics				
° Size of Bargaining Unit	.20*	.25*	.18*	.22*
° Committing Grievances to Writing	.19*	.19*	.18*	.19*
° Taking Certain Grievances Through the Procedure	.18*	.23*	.17*	.21*
Labor-Management Relations Characteristics				
° Adversarial Labor Relations	.30**	.25*	.27**	.22*
° Cost of Grievance Handling			-.22*	-.13
° Supervisor Knowledge of Grievance Procedure	-.25*	-.23*	-.23*	-.21*
° Steward Knowledge of Grievance Procedure			.19*	.11
Grievance Procedure Characteristics				
° Expedited Grievance Handling	.31**	-.38**	.29**	-.35**
R²	.52	.49	.54	.51

* = significant at p = <.05
** = significant at p = <.01

Table 4.12
Regression Coefficients on Importance of Grievance Issues and Equity of Grievance Settlement

Independent Variable	Dependent Variable			
	Importance of Issue	Equity of Settlement	Importance of Issue	Equity of Settlement
Management Characteristics				
° Committing Grievances to Writing			.20*	.10
° Taking Certain Grievances through the Procedure	.29**	.22*	.27**	.20*
Union Characteristics				
° Committing Grievances to Writing			.23*	.09
° Taking Certain Grievances through the Procedure			.12	.23*
Labor-Management Relations Characteristics				
° Adversarial Labor Relations			.11	-.22*
° Length of Bargaining Relationship	.24*	.20*	.22*	.18*
° Cost of Grievance Handling			.07	-.22*
° Supervisor Knowledge of Grievance Procedure			.23*	.10
° Steward Knowledge of Grievance Procedure			.26*	.09
Grievance Procedure Characteristics				
° Expedited Grievance Handling			.06	.35**
R^2	.26	.23	.37	.31

* = significant at $p = <.05$
** = significant at $p = <.01$

tiveness is enhanced markedly, however, by the inclusion of certain other management, union, and labor relations characteristics (see columns three and four of Table 4.12).

In sum, the decomposed regression analysis suggests that there is an empirical basis for developing separate theoretical models of the determinants of particular measures of grievance procedure effectiveness. Voluntary employee turnover, for example, is significantly (positively) related to grievance and arbitration rates, but not to other measures of grievance procedure effectiveness. In another instance, the size of the bargaining unit and the length of the bargaining relationship appear to be significantly (positively) related to the level and speed of grievance settlement, but not to other measures of grievance process effectiveness. However, additional independent variables, such as provisions for expedited grievance handling and supervisor knowledge of the grievance procedure, appear to have significant effects on most if not all measures of grievance procedure effectiveness. Given these findings, it is appropriate to consider whether a simplified explanation of grievance procedure effectiveness can be developed by constructing an overall effectiveness index that combines what heretofore have been treated as separate dependent variables.

Regression Analysis—Aggregated Dependent Variable

To construct a single or aggregate measure of grievance procedure effectiveness, ten point, nine interval scales were constructed for the grievance rate, arbitration rate, level of settlement, and speed of settlement. The scales were applied to the responses from the completed questionnaires and the resultant scores were summed. In the cases of perceived importance of issues filed through the grievance procedure and perceived equity of grievance settlement, which were originally scored on five point, four interval scales, management and union respondents' scores from each individual labor relationship represented in the sample were combined, and the sum of ten minus the combined score was then added to the sum of the scores on the behavioral-type variables. In other words, if management and union respondents' combined score on the perceived importance of issues filed through the grievance procedure was seven (four for the management respondent, three for the union respondent), then ten minus seven, or three, was added to the sum of the scores on the behavioral variables. The same was done for the perceived equity of grievance settlement scores.

This procedure was required because high scores on the behavioral-type variables—the grievance rate, arbitration rate, level of settlement, and speed of settlement—reflect ineffective grievance handling, whereas high scores on the attitudinal type variables—the perceived importance of issues raised through the grievance procedure and the perceived equity of grievance settlement—reflect effective grievance handling. The results of testing this aggregate model of grievance procedure effectiveness are shown in Table 4.13.

The table lists coefficients for all of the independent variables that were originally specified. Column one excludes variables that were not significant in any of the earlier tests of separate dependent variables, while column two excludes these as well as variables that were significant in only one of the six earlier equations. The results indicate that two management characteristics, three union characteristics, two labor-management relationship characteristics, and one grievance procedure characteristic were significantly associated with the overall index of grievance procedure effectiveness. Management and union policies of committing all grievances to writing are (both) significantly positively related to the overall index. Keeping in mind the scoring procedure used to construct the index, these findings mean that policies to commit all grievances to writing are associated with less effective grievance procedures. The same interpretation can be placed on the coefficients on management and union policies to take certain grievances as far as possible through the procedure, size of the bargaining unit, and adversarial labor relations. In contrast, the coefficient on supervisor knowledge of the grievance procedure has a negative sign, implying that it is associated with more effective grievance procedures. Provisions for expedited grievance processing are significantly positively associated with the overall effectiveness index; however, certain characteristics of this variable suggest considerable caution in interpreting the statistical results. Recall that, by its nature, expedited grievance processing leads to high-level settlements and correspondingly high arbitration rates, but also to speedy grievance settlements.

The limitations of aggregating separate measures of grievance procedure effectiveness are perhaps reflected in the variables that were not significantly related to the overall effectiveness index. For example, voluntary employee turnover is negatively but insignificantly related to the overall index, yet earlier results showed that this variable was associated with significantly lower grievance and arbitration rates. Similarly, the length of the bargaining relationship is not significantly related to the overall index of grievance procedure effectiveness, yet earlier this variable was shown to be significantly positively associated with the perceived importance of issues filed through the grievance procedure and the perceived equity of grievance settlement. The fact that, in previous empirical testing, centralization of management decision making was significantly positively related to the level of grievance settlement (Table 4.8), and the additional fact that the degree of grievance procedure structure was significantly positively related to the arbitration rate (Table 4.8), are "lost" in the aggregate results

Table 4.13
Regression Coefficients on Aggregate Grievance
Procedure Effectiveness Measures

Independent Variable	Dependent Variable Overall Grievance Procedure Effectiveness Index		
	Full Model	Modified Model #1	Modified Model #2
Management Characteristics			
° Centralization of Decision Making	.05	.07	-
° Committing Grievances to Writing	.17*	.18*	.19*
° Taking Certain Grievances through the Procedure	.23*	.23*	.24*
° Voluntary Employee Turnover	-.06	-.07	-.07
Union Characteristics			
° Size of Bargaining Unit	.16*	.17*	.17*
° Occupational Diversity of Bargaining Unit	.01	-	-
° Centralization of Decision Making	.08	-	-
° Committing Grievances to Writing	.17*	.18*	.18*
° Taking Certain Grievances through the Procedure	.18*	.19*	.19*
Labor-Management Relations Characteristics			
° Adversarial Labor Relations	.25*	.24*	.25*

Table 4.13 (continued)

Independent Variable	Dependent Variable Overall Grievance Procedure Effectiveness Index		
	Full Model	Modified Model #1	Modified Model #2
Labor-Management Relations Characteristics (Continued)			
° Length of Bargaining Relationship	.13	.12	.12
° Cost of Grievance Handling	.11	.12	.12
° Supervisor Knowledge of Grievance Procedure	-.21*	-.22*	-.21*
° Steward Knowledge of Grievance Procedure	.14	.13	.13
Grievance Procedure Characteristics			
° Grievance Procedure Structure	.10	.11	-
° Expedited Grievance Handling	.23*	.23*	.24*
R^2	.29	.27	.26

* = significant at $p = <.05$
** = significant at $p = <.01$

presented in Table 4.13. We conclude, therefore, that the use of an overall measure of grievance procedure effectiveness, while intuitively appealing, has more empirical weaknesses than strengths, especially when compared to the use of separate or paired-effectiveness measures (see Tables 4.8, 4.10, 4.11, and 4.12).

GRIEVANCE ACTIVITY
AND COLLECTIVE BARGAINING

How, if at all, is grievance activity related to contract negotiations? From one perspective, grievance activity can be expected to increase in the period immediately preceding the (re)negotiation of a new contract. Such activity might signal the union's concern over specific contractual issues or a more general attempt to influence management's judgment about the union's power. Further, in focusing on new contract negotiations, management may be less attentive to issues that generate grievances than it would be at other times, thus adding a management "weakness" to a "union strength" explanation of enhanced grievance activity prior to bargaining.[4]

From another perspective, however, the union may focus so intently on contract negotiations that some of its resources are directed toward this activity and away from grievance handling. Similarly, management may decide to be especially attentive to grievances in the period immediately preceding negotiations in order to demonstrate a strong commitment to peaceful industrial relations or to indicate that resources devoted to grievance handling will not be drawn off and used for collective bargaining purposes. In sum, no a priori hypotheses about the relation between grievance activity and collective negotiations are posited here. However, it is possible to test for this relationship using the survey data obtained in this study.

The union and management respondents were asked to indicate the inclusive dates of their most recent labor agreement (within the 1980-1982 period). The data were then separated by year of agreement, with 1981 singled out for analysis. Recall that grievance data were provided for three years, 1980-1982. For employers with labor agreements ending (and beginning) in 1981 ($n = 82$), grievance activity was examined for the preceding year (1980), the year of the agreement (1981), and the first year following the agreement (1982). Figure 4.1 presents plots of the means and standard deviations of the grievance rate and the arbitration rate over the three years for this subsample of respondents ($n = 64$).

Clearly, grievance activity, as measured by grievance and arbitration rates, was markedly higher in the year in which contract negotiations took place than in the preceding or following year. More than 12.5 grievances per 100 employees were filed in 1981 for the sample of employers and unions having new contract negotiations in 1981, compared to 10.7 grievances per 100 employees in 1980 and 9.7 grievances per 100 employees in 1982. Arbitration rates displayed a similar pattern, with 2.0 arbitrations per 100 employees occurring in 1981, compared to 1.6 in 1980 and 1.4 in 1982. Further supporting the finding of enhanced grievance activity prior to collective negotiations are the data in Table 4.14. The upper portion of the table shows that employers with collective agreements reached in 1982 had higher grievance rates in that year than in the two immediately preceding years. The lower portion of the table shows that employers with collective agreements reached in 1980 had higher grievance and arbitration rates in that year than in the two subsequent years.

To test further for the relationship between grievance activity and contract negotiations, a dummy variable representing collective agreements negotiated in 1981 (yes = 1, no = 0) was entered into the basic

Figure 4.1

Grievance and Arbitration Rates for a Subsample
of Employers with Collective Bargaining
Agreements Negotiated in 1981

($n=82$)

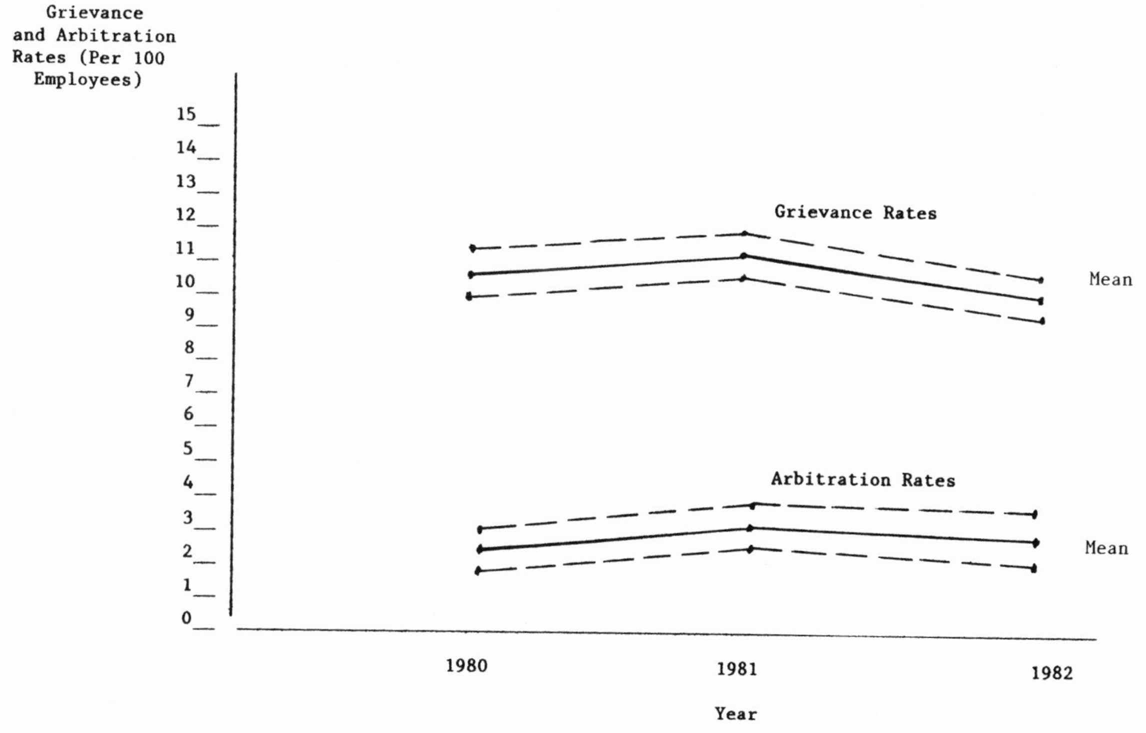

Grievance
and Arbitration
Rates (Per 100
Employees)

Table 4.14
Grievance and Arbitration Rates, by Year
of Contract Negotiations
(per 100 employees)

Year	Employers and Unions with Agreements Negotiated in 1982	
	Grievance Rate	Arbitration Rate
1980	10.4	1.6
1981	9.9	1.4
1982	11.1	1.9

Year	Employers and Unions with Agreements Negotiated in 1980	
	Grievance Rate	Arbitration Rate
1980	11.6	1.8
1981	9.5	1.2
1982	10.3	1.4

estimating equations for grievance rates and arbitration rates. The coefficients on the collective agreement variable were positive and significant in both equations ($p = < .01$ in the case of arbitration rates), thus confirming that grievance activity increases as the time for contract negotiations (or renegotiations) approaches. These results confirm the hypothesis specified in Chapter 3.

INDUSTRY/SECTOR VARIATION IN GRIEVANCE PROCEDURE EFFECTIVENESS

To this point, little has been said about industry and sectoral differences in grievance procedure effectiveness. While this issue will be more fully taken up in Chapter 5, Table 4.15 presents some initial evidence in this regard. The table shows regression coefficients derived from tests of the six grievance procedure effectiveness equations in which the four industries and sectors included in this study were entered as dummy variables. Methodologically, the procedure was to exclude steel as the base-line industry and to measure the effects of the other industries and sectors on the dependent variables in relation to steel. Only the coefficients on the industry/sector variables are shown in Table 4.15 (the industry/sector variable is treated as an environmental characteristic.)

Table 4.15
Measures of Grievance Procedure Effectiveness,
by Industry/Sector

Independent Variable	Dependent Variable					
	Grievance Rate	Level of Settlement (In Steps)	Speed of Settlement (In Days)	Arbitration Rate	Importance of Issue	Equity of Settlement
Environmental Characteristics						
° Retail Department Stores	-.21*	-.17*	-.08	-.27**	-.16*	-.15*
° Nonprofit Hospitals	-.11	-.21*	.30**	-.21*	-.07	-.16*
° Local Public Schools	-.24*	-.12	.23*	-.24*	-.06	.06
R^2	.56	.49	.44	.54	.41	.38

* = significant at $p = <.05$
** = significant at $p = <.01$

Clearly, grievance rates are significantly higher in steel manufacturing than in retail department stores, nonprofit hospitals, and local public schools. The level of grievance settlement is also significantly higher in steel than in retail department stores and nonprofit hospitals, but not local schools. Grievance settlements are significantly speedier in steel than in nonprofit hospitals and local schools—most likely because of the widespread provisions for expedited arbitration in the steel industry— while the arbitration rate is significantly higher in steel than in the three other industries and sectors.

The perceived importance of issues filed through the grievance procedure is significantly lower in retail department stores than in the three other industries and sectors. Further, the perceived equity of grievance settlement is significantly lower in retail department stores and nonprofit hospitals than in steel manufacturing and local public schools. Although further understanding of these findings awaits more detailed empirical analysis, these regression results imply that there is considerable industry/sector variation in specific measures of grievance procedure effectiveness.

SUMMARY AND CONCLUSIONS

Several characteristics of the management and union organizations, labor-management relations, and grievance procedure structure have been shown to be significantly related to various measures of grievance procedure effectiveness. The most consistent and strongest findings pertain to adversarial labor relations and expedited grievance processing. The more adversarial the labor relationship, as judged by the parties themselves, the higher are grievance rates, arbitration rates, and the level of grievance settlement, the slower is the speed of settlement, and the lower are management and union officials' perceptions of the equity of grievance settlement. Expedited grievance procedures are associated with higher grievance and arbitration rates and levels of settlement, but appear to reduce significantly the time required to settle grievances and to raise significantly the parties' perceptions of the equity of grievance settlement.

Management and union policies to take certain grievances as far as possible through the procedure act to increase the level of grievance settlement and the arbitration rate and to slow the speed of grievance settlement. The union policy (but not the management policy) in this regard appears to increase significantly the grievance rate, while the management policy (but not the union policy) is associated with a higher perceived importance of issues filed through the grievance procedure. A union policy of committing all grievances to writing significantly increases the arbitration rate, the level of grievance settlement, and the perceived importance of issues filed through the grievance procedure, while also acting to slow the speed of grievance settlement. However, a management policy to commit all grievances to writing has significant (positive) effects only on the grievance rate and the perceived importance of issues treated through the grievance procedure.

The knowledge of the grievance procedure possessed by supervisors and stewards has some common but also some dissimilar effects on (measures of) grievance procedure effectiveness. Both supervisor and steward knowledge serve to reduce the level of grievance settlement and increase the perceived importance of issues filed through the grievance procedure. However, supervisor knowledge, but not steward knowledge, is associated with faster grievance settlements and lower arbitration rates. Perhaps most important, supervisor knowledge is associated with lower grievance rates, while steward knowledge is associated with higher grievance rates.

This last finding is consistent with what we know about unionized grievance procedures from the scholarly literature and with interview comments obtained in this study. The literature indicates that one function of a supervisor is periodically to explain the employer's workplace and employee relations policies and practices to employees (Gandz, 1979; Jennings, 1974b). When this function is actually fulfilled, it should serve to reduce grievances over certain issues. One responsibility of a union steward is to be sufficiently knowledgeable about the employer's workplace and employee relations policies and practices to know when violations occur and if they are covered by the collective bargaining agreement and the grievance procedure (Dalton and Todor, 1982a; Graham, Heshizer, and Johnson, 1978). When this responsibility is actually fulfilled, grievances may well increase. Consequently, neither an especially high or an especially low grievance rate should result when supervisors and stewards are both very knowledgeable about the employer's workplace and employee relations policies and practices.

A mid-level hospital administrator with substantial grievance-handling experience who was interviewed during this study commented as follows:

Grievance activity in this hospital varies dramatically by department. The reason for this is that we have some supervisors who know the rules cold and others who hardly know them at all. We've also got some nurses' representatives who know these rules better than any of us, and other representatives who don't seem to know where the emergency room is! What this means is that we have some departments with astronomical grievance rates, and others where a grievance is very rare. I think we do best when the supervisor and the union representative know the rules and can explain them to nurses and to each other. In those cases, we get grievances, sure, but I can be pretty certain they're not frivolous or politically motivated.

Similarly, a union official from the RCIA offered the following observations:

I've gone around the block many times on grievance issues and I can tell you that a key factor in all of this is how much knowledge of rules and procedures the supervisor's got. If he doesn't know much, he just can't respond well to complaints and a lot of minor grievances start to work their way up through the system. If he is knowledgeable, then a lot of these issues can be settled before they even get written down. However, the area union representative is also a big factor here. A rep[resentative] who knows the rules knows how to pick and choose which grievances to act on, but a rep[resentative] who doesn't know the rules tends to send everything up. In any of these stores, you've got to have some legitimate grievances, but it shouldn't get out of hand. If the supervisors and the rep[resentative]s don't know the rules, either give them some training or get them out of there—at least that's what I'd do.

Again, these comments help us understand why moderate or intermediate grievance rates are likely to exist where both supervisor and steward knowledge of the grievance procedure (and perhaps organizational rules more broadly) are high.

Turning to other findings, the size of the bargaining unit is significantly related to three measures of grievance procedure effectiveness. Specifically, the larger the unit, the higher are grievance rates and the level of grievance settlement and the slower is the speed of settlement. Voluntary employee turnover is significantly negatively associated with only two measures of grievance-handling effectiveness, namely, grievance rates and arbitration rates. However, these findings are particularly important because they confirm the theoretical proposition that higher employee turnover, or exit, is an alternative to grievance filing, or voice, in the employment relationship.[5]

This point was commented on frequently by the management and union officials interviewed for this study. For example, a public school administrator observed the following:

You know you don't get grievances from the really dissatisfied teachers. Sure they may file them once in a while or float a trial balloon, but in my experience the truly aggrieved teacher decides to leave the school or maybe even the profession. Remember that I work in a district that's had lots of teacher turnover; from what I've seen most of that has to do with dissatisfaction with the school. Ironically, those who aren't so turned off stay with us and they tend to file grievances. In a way, maybe we should have more grievances if it helped us to hold onto some of our good teachers.

An AFT official with substantial grievance-handling experience commented on the same issue:

Well, it's a strange thing. I talk with teachers who've become disillusioned and I try to tell them that they should take their concerns to the school, not leave the school. Hell, that's why we've got grievance procedures. Even if they file grievances, it may be just because I urged them to do it. But then they drop them even if I say that the arbitrator is likely to rule in their favor. They just seem to throw up their hands and decide to go elsewhere. The folks who stay, they file grievances and use the arbitration procedure, as they should. The problem for the school is you lose a lot of good teachers.

Both officials seem to be making an argument for the stronger use of the grievance-type voice mechanism (at least in the schools), but the main benefit of these comments is to help us better understand why in this study voluntary turnover is negatively associated with both grievance and arbitration rates.

In this study the cost of grievance handling was significantly associated with faster grievance settlement and a lower arbitration rate, but also with a lower perceived equity of grievance settlement. A highly structured grievance procedure was significantly associated with higher grievance rates, but not with other effectiveness measures. The length of the bargaining relationship between the parties was not significantly related to any behavioral measures of grievance procedure effectiveness, but was positively associated with the perceived importance of issues filed through the grievance procedure as well as the perceived equity of grievance settlement. Finally, occupational diversity of the bargaining unit and the extent of centralization of the management and union organizations were insignificantly related to all measures of grievance procedure effectiveness.

Perhaps the main conclusion to be drawn from these findings is that although several variables are commonly significant (and others are commonly insignificant) for explaining grievance procedure effectiveness, any such explanation is quite sensitive to the measure or measures of effectiveness employed. Thus, it may well be best to accept the fact that effectiveness has several dimensions and to suppress any effort to devise a single overriding construct or measure of grievance procedure effectiveness. This conclusion will be reconsidered after additional analyses of industry and sectoral variation in grievance activity and grievance-handling effectiveness are presented in Chapter 5.

NOTES

1. Note that the speed of grievance settlement is measured in days to settlement. Therefore, a larger absolute value for this variable or a positive correlation between this variable and any other variable represents slower grievance settlements.

2. See Kerlinger (1973).

3. Note that several statistical tests showed that the independent variables measured separate dimensions of grievance procedure effectiveness and were not significantly intercorrelated.

4. See, for example, Chamberlain and Kuhn (1986) and Kuhn (1961).

5. See Ichniowski and Lewin (1987).

5

Grievance Procedure Effectiveness: Disaggregate Analysis

How does grievance procedure effectiveness vary among the four industries and sectors included in this study? Some preliminary evidence on this matter was presented in Chapter 4, but we now undertake a more detailed examination of grievance procedure effectiveness through a disaggregated analysis of survey and interview data.

RELATIONSHIPS WITH BEHAVIORAL VARIABLES

Tables 5.1 through 5.6 present regression coefficients for the six measures of grievance procedure effectiveness by industry and sector. Recall that the grievance rate over the 1980-1982 period was higher in steel manufacturing than in retail department stores, nonprofit hospitals, and local public schools. Table 5.1 shows that, despite this difference, several factors commonly affect the grievance rate in the four industries and sectors. A management policy of committing grievances to writing, the size of the bargaining unit, and adversarial labor relations are strongly positively related to the grievance rate in each industry and sector. Union policies of committing all grievances to writing and taking certain grievances as far as possible through the procedure, union steward knowledge of the grievance procedure, and voluntary employee turnover are significantly related to the grievance rate in three out of four cases, with the turnover coefficients having negative signs and the coefficients on the other variables having positive signs.

Several other variables that were significantly related to the grievance rate in the aggregate analysis presented in Chapter 4 are shown in Table 5.1 to be differentially related to the grievance rate by industry and

Table 5.1
Regression Coefficients on the Grievance Rate, by Industry/Sector

Independent Variable	Industry/Sector			
	Steel Manufacturing	Retail Department Stores	Nonprofit Hospitals	Local Public Schools
Management Characteristics				
· Centralization of decision making	.09	.03	.07	.04
· Committing grievances to writing	.34**	.27*	.36**	.24*
· Taking certain grievances through the procedure	.08	.12	.16*	.07
· Voluntary employee turnover	-.22*	-.17*	-.24*	-.13
Union Characteristics				
· Size of bargaining unit	.33**	.21*	.36**	.38**
· Occupational diversity of bargaining unit	.03	.08	.01	.07
· Centralization of decision making	.16*	.10	.13	.04
· Committing grievances to writing	.23*	.21*	.25*	.13
· Taking certain grievances through the procedure	.22*	.14	.19*	.18*
Labor-Management Relations Characteristics				
· Adversarial labor relations	.37**	.23*	.39**	.34**
· Length of bargaining relationship	-.04	-.09	-.10	-.02

Table 5.1 (continued)

Independent Variable	Industry/Sector			
	Steel Manufacturing	Retail Department Stores	Nonprofit Hospitals	Local Public Schools
Labor-Management Relations Characteristics (continued)				
· Cost of grievance handling	-.11	-.03	-.06	-.04
· Supervisor knowledge of grievance procedure	-.13	-.22*	-.24*	-.14
· Steward knowledge of grievance procedure	.11	.16*	.19*	.17*
Grievance Procedure Characteristics				
· Grievance procedure structure	.09	.25*	.26*	.11
· Expedited grievance handling	.26*	.13	.25*	.13

*Significant at p = <.05
**Significant at p = <.01

sector. Of particular interest, eight independent variables are significantly related to the grievance rate in the two private industries included in this study—steel and retail trade—while eleven variables are significantly related to the grievance rate in nonprofit hospitals, but only five in local public schools. This suggests that, across the four industries and sectors, grievances are motivated by certain common, but also certain distinctive, factors.

Indeed, the same can be said about the other measures of grievance procedure effectivensss. Table 5.2 shows that the size of the bargaining unit, supervisor knowledge of the grievance procedure, adversarial labor relations, and expedited grievance procedure provisions are commonly related to the level of grievance settlement, but that centralization of management decision making and the cost of grievance handling have significant effects on the level of grievance settlement in only two of the four industries and sectors (retail stores and hospitals). Management and union policies to take certain grievances as far as possible through the procedure, a union policy to commit all grievances to writing, and

Table 5.2
Regression Coefficients on the Level of Grievance
Settlement, by Industry/Sector

Independent Variable	Industry/Sector			
	Steel Manufacturing	Retail Department Stores	Nonprofit Hospitals	Local Public Schools

Management Characteristics

Independent Variable	Steel Manufacturing	Retail Department Stores	Nonprofit Hospitals	Local Public Schools
· Centralization of decision making	.12	.17*	.21*	.14
· Committing grievances to writing	.10	.07	.06	.11
· Taking certain grievances through the procedure	.12	.18*	.26*	.21*
· Voluntary employee turnover	.07	.11	.10	.06

Union Characteristics

Independent Variable	Steel Manufacturing	Retail Department Stores	Nonprofit Hospitals	Local Public Schools
· Size of bargaining unit	.15*	.15*	.18*	.16*
· Occupational diversity of bargaining unit	.03	.11	.02	.03
· Centralization of decision making	-.07	-.06	-.02	-.04
· Committing grievances to writing	.17*	.13	.20*	.18*
· Taking certain grievances through the procedure	.15*	.12	.20*	.17*

Labor-Management Relations Characteristics

Independent Variable	Steel Manufacturing	Retail Department Stores	Nonprofit Hospitals	Local Public Schools
· Adversarial labor relations	.28**	.24*	.30**	.28**
· Length of bargaining relationship	.03	-.02	.01	.06

Table 5.2 (continued)

Independent Variable	Industry/Sector			
	Steel Manufacturing	Retail Department Stores	Nonprofit Hospitals	Local Public Schools
Labor-Management Relations Characteristics (continued)				
· Cost of grievance handling	-.38**	-.13	-.18*	-.13
· Supervisor knowledge of grievance procedure	-.17*	-.21*	-.16*	-.29**
· Steward knowledge of grievance procedure	-.15*	-.11	-.19*	-.23*
Grievance Procedure Characteristics				
· Grievance procedure structure	.15*	.03	.06	.11
· Expedited grievance handling	.39**	.21*	.29**	.25*
R^2	.51	.41	.44	.48

*Significant at p = <.05
**Significant at p = <.01

union steward knowledge of the grievance procedure are significantly related to the level of grievance settlement in three of four cases. Conversely, the structure of the grievance procedure is significantly related to the level of grievance settlement in only one case (steel manufacturing).

Concerning the speed of grievance settlement, expedited grievance processing and supervisor knowledge of the grievance procedure significantly reduce the time to settlement across the four industries and sectors, as shown in Table 5.3, while adversarial labor relations significantly increase it.[1] The size of the bargaining unit, management and union policies to take certain grievances as far as possible through the procedure, and a union policy to commit all grievances to writing significantly increase the time required to settle grievances in three of the four industries. Centralization of management decision making slows griev-

Table 5.3
Regression Coefficients on the Speed of Grievance
Settlement, by Industry/Sector

Independent Variable	Steel Manufacturing	Retail Department Stores	Nonprofit Hospitals	Local Public Schools
		Industry/Sector		
Management Characteristics				
· Centralization of decision making	-.03	-.08	.16*	-.04
· Committing grievances to writing	.06	.02	.04	.03
· Taking certain grievances through the procedure	.24*	.14	.25*	.17*
· Voluntary employee turnover	.13	.07	.09	.06
Union Characteristics				
· Size of bargaining unit	.18*	.11	.23*	.21*
· Occupational diversity of bargaining unit	-.02	.15*	-.06	-.04
· Centralization of decision making	.10	.12	.07	.09
· Committing grievances to writing	.13	.18*	.20*	.17*
· Taking certain grievances through the procedure	.23*	.14	.24*	.18*
Labor-Management Relations Characteristics				
· Adversarial labor relations	.17*	.19*	.29**	.27**
· Length of bargaining relationship	-.04	.01	-.06	-.07

Table 5.3 (continued)

Independent Variable	Industry/Sector			
	Steel Manufacturing	Retail Department Stores	Nonprofit Hospitals	Local Public Schools
Labor-Management Relations Characteristics (continued)				
· Cost of grievance handling	-.17*	-.09	-.12	-.10
· Supervisor knowledge of grievance procedure	-.19*	-.16*	-.15*	-.27**
· Steward knowledge of grievance procedure	-.09	-.08	-.15*	.02
Grievance Procedure Characteristics				
· Grievance procedure structure	.06	.15*	.03	.05
· Expedited grievance handling	-.39**	-.21*	-.27**	-.24*
R^2	.46	.37	.42	.44

*Significant at p = <.05
**Significant at p = <.01

ance settlement in nonprofit hospitals, while union steward knowledge of the grievance procedure speeds up grievance settlement; occupational diversity of the bargaining unit and the degree of grievance procedure structure significantly increase the time to grievance settlement in retail department stores; the cost of grievance handling is associated with faster grievance settlement in steel manufacturing.

The regression results in Table 5.4 show that adversarial labor relations *and* provisions for expedited grievance handling are both significantly positively correlated with arbitration rates across the four industries and sectors. The coefficients on the former variable suggest that industrial conflict pushes grievance settlement to the final step of the procedure, whereas expedited grievance processing provides a mechanism for the parties to settle their differences without having to proceed laboriously through each step of the grievance procedure—a mechanism that the parties clearly use rather than avoid (see the last row of coefficients in Table 5.4).

Table 5.4
Regression Coefficients on the Arbitration
Rate, by Industry/Sector

Independent Variable	Industry/Sector			
	Steel Manufacturing	Retail Department Stores	Nonprofit Hospitals	Local Public Schools
Management Characteristics				
· Centralization of decision making	-.16*	.04	.03	-.03
· Committing grievances to writing	.08	.06	.05	.08
· Taking certain grievances through the procedure	.13	.17*	.29**	.23*
· Voluntary employee turnover	-.17*	-.19*	-.20*	-.13
Union Characteristics				
· Size of bargaining unit	.16*	.10	.17*	.09
· Occupational diversity of bargaining unit	.01	-.06	-.03	.02
· Centralization of decision making	.10	.12	.07	.11
· Committing grievances to writing	.03	.04	.06	.05
· Taking certain grievances through the procedure	.20*	.08	.18*	.14
Labor-Management Relations Characteristics				
· Adversarial labor relations	.26**	.22*	.27**	.25*
· Length of bargaining relationship	-.07	-.02	-.05	-.04

Table 5.4 (continued)

Independent Variable	Industry/Sector			
	Steel Manufacturing	Retail Department Stores	Nonprofit Hospitals	Local Public Schools
Labor-Management Relations Characteristics (continued)				
· Cost of grievance handling	-.07	-.02	-.05	-.04
· Supervisor knowledge of grievance procedure	-.14	-.22*	-.28**	-.23*
· Steward knowledge of grievance procedure	.10	.06	.13	.11
Grievance Procedure Characteristics				
· Grievance procedure structure	.11	.02	.04	.06
· Expedited grievance handling	.44**	.29**	.36**	.33**
R²	.56	.52	.62	.55

*Significant at p = <.05
**Significant at p = <.01

A management policy to take certain grievances as far as possible through the procedure is significantly positively associated with the arbitration rate in three of the four industries and sectors, while voluntary employee turnover and supervisor knowledge of the grievance procedure are significantly negatively correlated with the arbitration rate in three of four cases. In steel manufacturing and nonprofit hospitals, the size of the bargaining unit and a union policy to take certain grievances as far as possible through the procedure are significantly positively associated with the arbitration rate. The centralization of management decision making is associated with a lower arbitration rate in steel, but not in the three other industries and sectors.

RELATIONSHIPS WITH ATTITUDINAL VARIABLES

Turning to the results for the attitudinal-type dependent variables, four independent variables—a management policy to take certain grievances as far as possible through the procedure, a union policy to commit all grievances to writing, the length of the bargaining relationship, and union steward knowledge of the grievance procedure—are positively associated with the perceived importance of issues raised through the grievance procedure in all four industries and sectors (Table 5.5). Supervisor knowledge of the grievance process is significantly positively related to perceived grievance issue importance in three cases (steel, hospitals, and schools). Fully ten of the independent variables are not significantly related to perceived grievance issue importance in any industry or sector.

As to the perceived equity of grievance settlement, statistically significant regression coefficients were attained across the four industries and sectors for two variables, namely, a management policy to take certain grievances as far as possible through the procedure and the presence of expedited grievance procedures (Table 5.6). In three of four cases, the cost of grievance handling and adversarial labor relations are significantly negatively correlated with perceived equity of grievance settlement. Also in three of four cases, significant positive coefficients were attained for a union policy to take certain grievances as far as possible through the procedure. Eight independent variables are not significantly correlated with the perceived equity of grievance settlement across the four industries and sectors.

To summarize and more readily grasp the similarities and differences among the industry-specific findings, Table 5.7 shows the distribution of significant regression coefficients on the independent variables for each measure of grievance procedure effectiveness. Clearly, adversarial labor relations, provisions for expedited grievance processing, a management policy of taking certain grievances as far through the procedure as possible, and supervisor knowledge of the grievance procedure are the most "important" variables in this analysis in that they most commonly affect grievance filing, processing, and settlement across the four industries and sectors. Even in these cases, however, some notable industry differences are observed. Thus, adversarial labor relations reduce the perceived equity of grievance settlement in steel, hospitals, and schools but not in retail stores; expedited grievance processing increases the grievance rate in steel and hospitals, but not in retail stores and local schools; a management policy to take certain grievances as far as possible through the procedure significantly increases the grievance rate in hospitals but not in steel, retail stores, or schools; and supervisor knowledge of the grievance procedure increases the perceived importance

Table 5.5
Regression Coefficients on the Perceived Importance of Grievance Issues, by Industry/Sector

Independent Variable	Industry/Sector			
	Steel Manufacturing	Retail Department Stores	Nonprofit Hospitals	Local Public Schools
Management Characteristics				
· Centralization of decision making	.04	-.03	.01	.06
· Committing grievances to writing	.13	.18*	.19*	.12
· Taking certain grievances through the procedure	.26**	.22*	.30**	.28**
· Voluntary employee turnover	.08	.04	.03	.07
Union Characteristics				
· Size of bargaining unit	-.04	-.10	.02	-.04
· Occupational diversity of bargaining unit	.01	-.07	-.09	-.05
· Centralization of decision making	.10	.04	.08	.11
· Committing grievances to writing	.18*	.26**	.22*	.27**
· Taking certain grievances through the procedure	.08	.02	.05	.15*
Labor-Management Relations Characteristics				
· Adversarial labor relations	.11	.06	.07	.11
· Length of bargaining relationship	.20*	.16*	.17*	.26**

Table 5.5 (continued)

Independent Variable	Industry/Sector			
	Steel Manufacturing	Retail Department Stores	Nonprofit Hospitals	Local Public Schools
Labor-Management Relations Characteristics (continued)				
· Cost of grievance handling	.05	.06	.02	.06
· Supervisor knowledge of grievance procedure	.22*	.14	.17*	.24*
· Steward knowledge of grievance procedure	.29**	.21*	.23*	.30**
Grievance Procedure Characteristics				
· Grievance procedure structure	.08	.12	.06	.07
· Expedited grievance handling	.01	.02	.04	.02
R^2	.42	.35	.36	.40

*Significant at p = <.05
**Significant at p = <.01

of grievance issues in retail stores but not in steel, hospitals, or schools.

Table 5.7 also reinforces an earlier finding that while they are relatively unimportant in terms of the frequency with which significant correlation coefficients were obtained, some independent variables have significant effects on one or another measure of grievance procedure effectiveness in all four industries and sectors. For example, in steel, retail stores, and schools, the perceived importance of issues raised in the grievance procedure increases with the length of the bargaining relationship. In another example, the grievance rate increases in each industry/sector with the extent to which management maintains a policy of committing all grievances to writing.

Industry/sector differences in grievance procedure effectiveness and determinants of effectiveness are also evident from the overall frequency of significant regression coefficients. Across the six effective-

Table 5.6
Regression Coefficients on the Perceived Equity
of Grievance Settlement, by Industry/Sector

Independent Variable	Industry/Sector			
	Steel Manufacturing	Retail Department Stores	Nonprofit Hospitals	Local Public Schools
Management Characteristics				
· Centralization of decision making	.06	.02	.03	.07
· Committing grievances to writing	.09	.05	.07	.08
· Taking certain grievances through the procedure	.20*	.17*	.21*	.22*
· Voluntary employee turnover	.01	.06	.05	.02
Union Characteristics				
· Size of bargaining unit	-.06	-.02	-.15*	.04
· Occupational diversity of bargaining unit	-.02	-.15*	.02	-.05
· Centralization of decision making	.07	.09	.12	.10
· Committing grievances to writing	.05	.10	.09	.08
· Taking certain grievances through the procedure	.21*	.14	.17*	.23*
Labor-Management Relations Characteristics				
· Adversarial labor relations	-.20*	-.12	-.27**	-.24*
· Length of bargaining relationship	.19*	.14	.14	.22*

Table 5.6 (continued)

Independent Variable	Industry/Sector			
	Steel Manufacturing	Retail Department Stores	Nonprofit Hospitals	Local Public Schools
Labor-Management Relations Characteristics (continued)				
· Cost of grievance handling	-.26**	-.17*	-.09	-.19*
· Supervisor knowledge of grievance procedure	.11	.06	.07	.10
· Steward knowledge of grievance procedure	.07	.09	.10	.06
Grievance Procedure Characteristics				
· Grievance procedure structure	.05	.06	.08	.02
· Expedited grievance handling	.43**	.18*	.32**	.35**
R^2	.32	.29	.34	.36

*Significant at the $p = <.05$
**Significant at the $p = <.01$

ness measures, the independent variables had statistically significant regression coefficients 49 times in nonprofit hospitals, 43 times in steel manufacturing, 36 times in local schools, and 34 times in retail stores. Further, no single independent variable was statistically significant in all cases (that is, 6×4 or 24 times), and no variable was statistically insignificant in all cases (although the centralization of union decision making was significant only once, namely, in the case of the grievance rate in steel manufacturing). In light of these findings, can more be learned about industry/sector differences in grievance procedure effectiveness and determinants of effectiveness? This question is taken up in the next sections.

Table 5.7
Distribution of Significant Regression Coefficients on Independent Variables for Six Measures of Grievance Procedure Effectiveness, All Industries/Sectors†

Independent Variable	Dependent Variable						Frequency of Significant Regression Coefficients
	Grievance Rate	Level of Settlement (In Steps)	Speed of Settlement (In Days)	Arbitration Rate	Importance of Issue	Equity of Settlement	
Management Characteristics							
· Centralization of decision making	0	+RS,NH	+NH	-SM	0	0	4
· Committing grievances to writing	+ ALL	0	0	0	+RS,NH	0	6
· Taking certain grievances through the procedure	+NH	+RS,NH,LS	+SM,NH,LS	+RS,NH,LS	+ALL	+ALL	18
· Voluntary employee turnover	-SM,RS,NH	0	0	-SM,RS,NH	0	0	6
Union Characteristics							
· Size of bargaining unit	+ALL	+ALL	+SM,NH,LS	+SM,NH	0	-NH	14
· Occupational diversity of unit	0	0	+RS	0	0	-RS	2
· Centralization of decision making	+SM	0	0	0	0	0	1

Table 5.7 (continued)

| | Dependent Variable | | | | | | Frequency of Significant Regression Coefficients |
Independent Variable	Grievance Rate	Level of Settlement (In Steps)	Speed of Settlement (In Days)	Arbitration Rate	Importance of Issue	Equity of Settlement	
Union Characteristics (cont.)							
· Committing grievances to writing	+SM,RS,NH	+SM,NH,LS	+RS,NH,LS	0	+ALL	0	13
· Taking certain grievances through the procedure	+SM,NH,LS	+SM,NH,LS	+SM,NH,LS	+SM,NH	+LS	+SM,NH,LS	15
Labor-Management Relations Characteristics							
· Adversarial labor relations	+ALL	+ALL	+ALL	+ALL	0	-SM,NH,LS	19
· Length of bargaining relationship	0	0	0	0	+ALL	+SM,LS	6
· Cost of grievance handling	0	-SM,NH	-SM	-SM,NH	0	-SM,RS,LS	8
· Supervisor knowledge of procedure	-RS,NH	-ALL	-ALL	-ALL	-SM,NH,LS	0	17
· Steward knowledge of procedure	+RS,NH,LS	-SM,NH,LS	-NH	0	+ALL	0	11

Independent Variable	Dependent Variable						Frequency of Significant Regression Coefficients
	Grievance Rate	Level of Settlement	Speed of Settlement	Arbitration Rate	Importance of Issue	Equity of Settlement	
Grievance Procedure Characteristics							
· Grievance procedure structure	+RS,NH	+SM	+RS	0	0	0	4
· Expedited grievance processing	+SM,NH	+ALL	-ALL	+ALL	0	+ALL	18

† = industry designation: steel manufacturing (SM), retail department stores (RS), nonprofit hospitals (NH), local public schools (LS)

GRIEVANCE ISSUES AND ACTIVITY

Recall from Chapter 4 (Table 4.2) that grievance rates varied by industry and sector, with steel, hospitals, schools, and retail stores arrayed in descending order of grievance activity. How do these industries/sectors differ with respect to specific grievance issues? Table 5.8 provides data relevant to this question.[2]

Grievance Rates

In steel manufacturing, employee discipline, health and safety, working conditions, and management rights were the major grievance issues, on average, during the 1980-1982 period, as measured by filing rates per 100 employees. Together, these four categories accounted for almost 44 percent of all grievances filed in the nineteen companies that provided complete grievance data. Issues of job grading/work standards, pay, overtime assignments, discrimination, and subcontracting accounted for another 24 percent of grievances filed during the period.

In retail department stores, where the overall grievance rate among the respondent firms (n = 16) was less than half the rate in steel manufacturing, working conditions, work assignment, transfers, pay, discipline, and management rights were the leading grievance issues, together accounting for fully 50 percent of all grievances filed between 1980 and 1982. The work assignment and transfer grievances reflect labor-management conflict over store locations to which employees are assigned, and over the specific departments and areas of assignment (for example, appliances, children's clothes, furniture) within the stores. Issues of promotion and discrimination accounted for another 10 percent of grievances filed in retail department stores over the 1980-1982 period.

In nonprofit hospitals, where the grievance rate averaged slightly over 10 percent during the 1980-1982 period in the ten hospitals that provided complete grievance data, the major grievance issues were discipline, working conditions, work load, work assignment, health and safety, and management rights. Together these six issues accounted for almost 47 percent of all grievances filed. In the hospital context, the work load issue is specifically one of patient load, and the frequency of grievance filing over this issue reflects differences between nurses and hospital administrators over the number and type of patients that nurses must serve. The work assignment issue reflects disagreements over departmental and area assignment, rather than over the type of work to be performed. Issues of pay, performance evaluation, promotion, and discrimination accounted for another 21 percent of grievances filed in the hospitals during the 1980-1982 period.

In local public schools, working conditions, work assignment, health and safety, discipline, transfer, management rights, and work load were

Table 5.8
Frequency and Rate of Grievance Filing,
by Issue and Industry/Sector†

	Industry/Sector				
Grievance Issue	Steel Manufacturing	Retail Department Stores	Nonprofit Hospitals	Local Public Schools	All Industries/ Sectors
Pay	.8(4.9)	.6(7.7)	.5(4.8)	.2(2.6)	.5(4.7)
Job Grading/Work Standards	.9(5.5)	.3(3.8)	.3(2.9)	.2(2.6)	.4(3.8)
Technological Change	.4(2.5)	.2(2.6)	.4(3.9)	.1(1.3)	.3(2.8)
Work Assignment	.6(3.7)	.7(9.0)	.7(6.8)	.7(9.1)	.7(6.6)
Overtime	.8(4.9)	.2(2.6)	.3(2.9)	0(0)	.4(3.8)
Working Conditions	1.5(9.2)	.8(10.3)	.9(8.7)	.8(10.4)	1.0(9.4)
Discipline	2.3(14.1)	.6(7.7)	1.0(9.7)	.6(7.8)	1.1(10.4)
Performance Evaluation	.2(1.2)	.2(2.6)	.6(5.8)	.5(6.5)	.4(3.8)
Layoff	.4(2.5)	.1(1.3)	.2(1.9)	.2(2.6)	.2(1.9)
Recall	.3(1.8)	0(0)	0(0)	0(0)	.1(0.9)
Leave Time	.3(1.8)	.2(2.6)	.3(2.9)	.1(1.3)	.2(1.9)
Health and Safety	1.9(11.7)	.2(2.6)	.7(6.8)	.7(9.1)	.9(8.5)
Transfer	.3(1.8)	.6(7.7)	.4(3.9)	.6(7.8)	.4(3.8)

Table 5.8 (continued)

Grievance Issue	Steel Manufacturing	Retail Department Stores	Industry/Sector Nonprofit Hospitals	Local Public Schools	All Industries/ Sectors
Promotion	.3(1.8)	.4(5.1)	.6(5.8)	.4(5.2)	.4(3.8)
Work Hours	.4(2.5)	.5(6.4)	.3(2.9)	.2(2.6)	.4(3.8)
Discrimination	.7(4.3)	.4(5.1)	.5(4.8)	.4(5.2)	.5(4.7)
Productivity	.4(2.5)	.1(1.3)	.1(1.0)	.2(2.6)	.2(1.9)
Fringe Benefits	.3(1.8)	.2(2.6)	.2(1.9)	.1(1.3)	.2(1.9)
Union Security	.2(1.2)	1(1.3)	.1(1.0)	.2(2.6)	.2(1.9)
Management Rights	1.4(8.6)	.6(7.7)	.7(6.8)	.6(7.8)	.8(7.5)
Vacation/Holidays	.3(1.8)	.5(6.4)	.2(1.9)	.1(1.3)	.3(2.8)
Seniority	.4(2.5)	.2(2.6)	.2(1.9)	.1(1.3)	.2(1.9)
Strikes/Lockouts	.3(1.8)	0(0)	.3(2.9)	.1(1.3)	.2(1.9)
Work Load	.2(1.2)	.1(1.3)	.8(7.8)	.6(7.8)	.4(3.8)
Subcontracting	.7(4.3)	0(0)	0(0)	0(0)	.2(1.9)
TOTALS	16.3(100.0%)	7.8(100.0%)	10.3(100.0%)	7.7(100.0%)	10.6(100.0%)

†Grievance filing rates are per 100 employees, annual average 1980-82. Numbers in parentheses are percentages of grievances filed.

the major grievance issues, accounting for almost 60 percent of all grievances occurring between 1980 and 1982 in the twelve school districts
that supplied complete grievance data. Perhaps because these districts
are relatively large and located in urban areas, working conditions,
safety, transfer, and class size were relatively heavily represented
among teacher grievance issues. The management-rights issues have
largely to do with textbook choice, curriculum composition, recess and
lunchtime assignments, and use of substitute teachers. Another 17 percent of teacher grievances were filed over issues of performance evaluation, promotion, and discrimination.

In toto, the data in Table 5.8 suggest that certain grievance issues,
such as working conditions and discipline, are commonly important in
the four industries and sectors, while other issues vary in importance
among the industries and sectors. Thus, work assignment is a major
grievance issue in retail stores and local schools, where the presence of
multiple locations and facilities means that some employees receive less
than their preferred assignments. Health and safety issues loom large in
steel and schools, with danger and injury stemming largely from heavy
equipment usage and difficult work in steel manufacturing, and from
student and occasionally third-party assaults in local schools. Work load
is a major grievance issue in hospitals and schools, where the appropriate patient load per nurse and class size per teacher, respectively, are
matters over which employees and managers-administrators often dis-
agree. Performance evaluation is a moderately important issue in
hospitals and schools, but not in steel or retail stores; pay is a more
important grievance issue in retail stores than in the three other
industries and sectors; and subcontracting is a matter of some concern
in steel but not elsewhere.

Are different types of grievance issues differentially affected by the
independent variables that were previously shown to be significant determinants of aggregate grievance rates in each industry and sector (see
Table 5.1)? To address this question, grievances were decomposed into
those dealing with (1) discipline and management rights; (2) health and
safety, working conditions, work assignment, work load, and transfer;
(3) performance evaluation, promotion, discrimination, and pay; and
(4) all others, and the regressions were rerun both on an aggregate basis
and separately by industry and sector.

The regression results (which, for space reasons, are not presented
here) suggest the following conclusions. First, the "commonly important" independent variables with respect to aggregate grievance rates,
namely, management and union policies of committing grievances to
writing, voluntary employee turnover, the size of the bargaining unit, a
union policy of taking certain grievances as far as possible through the
procedure, adversarial labor relations, and union steward knowledge of

the grievance procedure generally remain significant across the major categories of grievances. However, turnover is not significantly related to category (2) grievances (health and safety, and so on), the size of the bargaining unit is most strongly related to grievance rates in categories (3) and (4) above, and adversarial labor relations are most strongly related to grievances in categories (1) and (2) above.

Second, certain variables that were occasionally significant in the aggregate grievance-data analysis (Table 5.1) are significantly related to certain categories of grievances. As examples, a management policy to take certain grievances as far as possible through the procedure is significantly related to category (2) grievances, which occur relatively frequently in nonprofit hospitals, and the centralization of union decision making is significantly related to category (1) grievances, which occur relatively frequently in steel manufacturing. These findings help to explain why these independent variables were only occasionally significant in the aggregate grievance-rate analysis presented earlier.

Third, supervisor knowledge of the grievance procedure is most strongly negatively associated with category (3) grievances. Since these grievances occur relatively more frequently in retail stores and nonprofit hospitals than in steel manufacturing and local schools, we are better able to understand the aggregate regression coefficients on the supervisor-knowledge variable presented in Table 5.1. It appears that supervisors are relatively more proficient in explaining management policy about performance evaluation, promotion, discrimination, and pay issues than about other types of job-related issues, and this has the effect of reducing grievance filing over category (3) issues.

Fourth, the presence of expedited grievance provisions is most strongly related to category (1) grievances, that is, discipline and management rights. Since these types of issues are relatively more prominent—more commonly grieved—in steel and hospitals than in retail stores and schools, the regression coefficients on the expedited grievance procedure variable that were reported in Table 5.1 are now better understood.

Arbitration Rates

The differences between steel and the three other industries/sectors with respect to arbitration rates are even larger than the differences in grievance rates. Table 5.9 shows the average annual frequency of arbitrations by issue and industry/sector for the 1980-1982 period.

Discipline issues reached the arbitration stage of the grievance procedure more frequently than any other issue, and this was true in all cases except the local schools. In fact, across the entire sample of employers, discipline issues accounted for well over one-quarter of all arbitrated issues during the 1980-1982 period, and they also accounted

Table 5.9
Frequency and Rate of Arbitration,
by Issue and Industry/Sector†

Grievance Issue	Steel Manufacturing	Retail Department Stores	Industry/Sector Nonprofit Hospitals	Local Public Schools	All Industries/ Sectors
Discipline	.6(22.2)	.3(30.0)	.3(21.4)	.3(25.0)	.5(26.3)
Management Rights	.4(14.8)	.1(10.0)	.2(14.3)	.1(8.3)	.3(15.8)
Health and Safety	.4(14.8)	0(0)	.1(7.1)	.2(16.7)	.3(15.8)
Work Load	0(0)	0(0)	.2(14.3)	.1(8.3)	.1(5.3)
Work Assignment	.1(3.7)	.2(20.0)	.2(14.3)	.1(8.3)	.1(5.3)
Working Conditions	.3(11.1)	.1(10.0)	.1(7.1)	.1(8.3)	.2(10.5)
Transfer	.1(3.7)	.1(10.0)	.1(7.1)	.1(8.3)	.1(5.3)
Discrimination	.3(11.1)	0(0)	.1(7.1)	.1(8.3)	.1(5.3)
Pay	.2(7.4)	.1(10.0)	0(0)	0(0)	.1(5.3)
Performance Evaluation	0(0)	0(0)	0(0)	.8(8.3)	0(0)
Promotion	0(0)	0(0)	.1(7.1)	0(0)	0(0)
Other	.3(11.1)	.1(10.0)	0(0)	0(0)	.1(5.3)
TOTAL	2.7(100.0%)	1.0(100.0%)	1.4(100.0%)	1.2(100.0%)	1.9(100.0%)

†Arbitration rates are per 100 employees, annual average 1980-82. Numbers in parentheses are percentages of arbitrations held.

for higher proportions of arbitrations in retail stores and local schools than in steel and hospitals (see row 1 of Table 5.9). Management rights and health and safety issues accounted for almost 30 percent of all arbitrations in steel, 25 percent in local schools, about 21 percent in hospitals, and 10 percent in retail stores.

To determine if the independent variables differentially affected specific types of arbitrated grievance issues, the significant variables in the aggregate industry-specific arbitration rate analysis (see Table 5.4) were separately regressed on the following grievance categories: (1) discipline; (2) management rights and health and safety; (3) work load, work assignment, working conditions, and transfer; and (4) discrimination, pay, performance evaluation, promotion, and other issues.

The main findings of this analysis (which, again, for space reasons are summarized rather than fully presented here) indicate, first, that the centralization of management decision making significantly reduces the arbitration rate in the case of disciplinary grievances. Since the incidence of arbitrations over disciplinary issues is twice as large in steel as in the other industries and sectors, the significant negative coefficient on this variable reported in Table 5.4 for steel manufacturing alone is now more understandable. Second, the size of the bargaining unit, which was initially found to be associated with higher arbitration rates in steel and hospitals, is shown in the disaggregated analysis to be significantly positively associated with nondisciplinary grievance arbitrations—categories (2), (3), and (4) above. Since nondisciplinary grievance arbitrations as a proportion of all arbitrations are smaller in steel and hospitals than in retail stores and local schools, this finding may help to explain the earlier positive association between the size of the bargaining unit and aggregate arbitration rates. Similar results were discovered for two other independent variables, namely, a union policy to take certain grievances as far as possible through the procedure and the cost of grievance handling, which again aids our understanding of the aggregate regression coefficients reported in Table 5.4.

Third, a management policy of taking certain grievances as far as possible through the procedure was found to be significantly positively associated with category (3)-type arbitrations (work load, work assignment, and so on). Since such arbitrations account for relatively higher proportions of all arbitrations in retail stores and hospitals than in steel manufacturing and local schools, the aggregate regression results reported earlier in Table 5.4 are now more comprehensible.

Fourth, supervisor knowledge of the grievance procedure, which was found to be significantly negatively correlated with arbitration rates outside of steel manufacturing, is shown in the disaggregated analysis to be significantly negatively associated with category (3)-type arbitration issues. These issues occur relatively more often in schools, hospitals, and retail stores than in steel, which helps to explain the pattern of results in the earlier aggregated arbitration-rate analysis.

Level and Speed of Settlement

Do the level and speed of grievance settlement vary by grievance issue? The answer is clearly yes, as indicated by the data in Table 5.10. Grievance issues involving discipline, health and safety, discrimination, management rights, work assignment, working conditions, and work load take the largest time to settle, ranging from 37 to 33 days, on average, across the four industries and sectors. Issues of layoff, recall, leave days, and vacation/holidays take the least time to resolve, at about 25 days, on average, across the industries and sectors. (It is important to keep in mind that these data are for grievances that are committed to writing and, therefore, do not reflect informal grievance settlements.)

The speed of settlement also varies markedly by industry and sector, of course, but the data in Table 5.10 show how much variation exists with respect to specific grievance issues. For example, discipline cases take an average of 30 days to settle in retail department stores and 34 days in steel manufacturing, compared with averages of 43 days in nonprofit hospitals and 41 days in local public schools. Similar differences are evident concerning issues of health and safety, management rights, discrimination, work load, work assignment, and working conditions.

To determine how the independent variables differentially affect the level and speed of grievance settlement by grievance issue, separate regressions were run for three grievance-issue categories: (1) discipline; (2) health and safety, discrimination, work load, work assignment, working conditions, and management rights; and (3) all others. The results of this analysis (the full details of which are not presented here) indicated that, in most cases, the variables previously shown to be significantly associated with the level and speed of grievance settlement (see Tables 5.3 and 5.4) remain significant across these three categories of grievances. As examples, adversarial labor relations, supervisor knowledge of the grievance procedure, and a management policy to take certain grievances as far as possible through the procedure, which were among the most consistently significant of the independent variables in the aggregate analysis of level and speed of grievance settlement, are uniformly significant across the three categories of grievance issues.

A different result emerges, however, concerning provisions for expedited grievance processing. This characteristic of the grievance procedure significantly reduces the time to grievance settlement only for nondisciplinary-type grievances (categories (2) and (3) above). In contrast, expedited grievance procedures significantly *increase* the level of settlement of nondisciplinary-type grievances. Moreover, these

Table 5.10
Level and Speed of Grievance Settlement, by Grievance Issue and Industry/Sector

Grievance Issue	Steel Manufacturing		Retail Department Stores		Industry/Sector — Nonprofit Hospitals		Local Public Schools		All Industries/Sectors	
	Level of Settlement	Days to Settlement	Level of Settlement	Days to Settlement	Level of Settlement	Days to Settlement	Level of Settlement	Days to Settlement	Level of Settlement	Days to Settlement
Pay	2.6	29	1.6	19	1.4	38	2.2	35	1.9	29
Job Grading/Work Standards	2.9	30	1.7	20	1.3	35	2.2	36	2.0	30
Technological Change	2.3	26	1.5	17	1.3	33	1.6	30	1.7	27
Work Assignment	2.2	24	2.2	27	2.1	40	2.4	42	2.2	34
Overtime	2.5	28	2.0	23	1.7	36	NA	NA	2.1	29
Working Conditions	3.0	31	2.2	26	1.9	40	2.3	39	2.4	34
Discipline	3.2	34	2.7	30	2.2	43	2.3	41	2.6	37
Performance Evaluation	2.1	23	1.9	22	1.8	39	2.0	37	2.0	30
Layoff	2.0	24	1.7	18	1.4	33	1.4	24	1.5	25
Recall	2.3	26	1.8	19	NA	NA	NA	NA	2.0	23
Leave Time	1.9	23	1.7	18	1.2	31	1.6	27	1.6	25
Health and Safety	3.1	33	2.7	30	2.4	42	2.5	41	2.7	36

Grievance Issue	Steel Manufacturing		Retail Department Stores		Nonprofit Hospitals		Local Public Schools		All Industries/Sectors	
	Level of Settlement	Days to Settlement	Level of Settlement	Days to Settlement	Level of Settlement	Days to Settlement	Level of Settlement	Days to Settlement	Level of Settlement	Days to Settlement
Transfer	2.5	29	2.0	24	2.1	40	2.4	40	2.3	33
Promotion	2.4	28	2.3	26	1.9	38	2.1	37	2.2	32
Work Hours	2.2	26	2.5	28	1.8	39	2.2	38	2.2	32
Discrimination	3.1	34	2.8	29	2.1	39	2.3	40	2.6	36
Productivity	2.7	27	1.4	16	1.1	32	1.5	27	1.7	26
Fringe Benefits	2.2	25	1.5	17	1.2	33	1.7	29	1.7	26
Union Security	2.8	30	1.8	21	1.2	33	1.9	33	1.9	29
Management Rights	3.1	32	2.3	27	1.9	40	2.3	39	2.4	35
Vacation/Holidays	2.3	24	1.6	15	1.6	37	1.7	29	1.8	26
Seniority	2.5	25	1.7	16	1.5	36	1.8	31	1.9	27
Strikes/Lockouts	3.0	32	NA	NA	1.3	33	2.3	35	2.2	33
Work Load	2.7	27	2.2	28	2.1	41	2.7	41	2.4	34
Subcontracting	3.3	33	NA	NA	NA	NA	NA	NA	3.3	33

effects are strongest in steel manufacturing, followed by nonprofit hospitals. Note that disciplinary-type grievances are relatively more common in steel and hospitals than in retail stores and schools, with the result that the effects of expedited grievance processing on the level and speed of grievance settlement occur in relation to relatively smaller bases of nondisciplinary grievances in steel and hospitals than in retail stores and schools.

To gain additional insight into this matter, consider the data in Table 5.11, which show the presence and use of provisions for expedited grievance processing across the four industries and sectors. Such provisions are most prominent in steel manufacturing, where they appear in more than four-fifths of the contractual grievance procedures, followed by nonprofit hospitals, local public schools, and retail department stores. Note also that, with one exception, steel has the highest proportions of specific provisions for expedited grievance processing (see rows 3-6 of Table 5.11). As an example, more than 90 percent of the steel agreements provide for skipping intermediate steps of the procedure. Across the four industries and sectors, severe discipline and demotion issues are almost always excluded from expedited grievance processing (though about 15 percent of the retail-store agreements permit expedited grievance handling over these issues), as is concerted action (that is, strikes and lockouts). Additionally, however, issues of discrimination, management rights, subcontracting, and work load are excluded from expedited grievance processing in roughly 85 percent of the hospital labor agreements, 80 percent of the local school agreements, and 60 percent of the retail store agreements.

While expedited grievance procedures significantly increase the level of grievance settlement in each of the industries and sectors, their effects are strongest in steel and hospitals (see Table 5.3). This appears to result from the more common presence of provisions for skipping intermediate steps of the grievance procedure in steel and hospitals than in retail stores and schools (see row 3 of Table 5.11), and perhaps also from the more frequent *use* of this specific type of expedited procedure in the former than the latter sectors. A modified regression analysis in which the proportion of agreements that provide for skipping intermediate steps (together with other previously significant independent variables) was regressed on the level of grievance settlement. It yielded significant positive coefficients in steel and hospitals, a marginally significant positive coefficient in schools, and an insignificant coefficient in retail stores. In short, expedited grievance processing leads to higher-level grievance settlements, usually through arbitration, and this is especially true in steel manufacturing and nonprofit hospitals.

A similar analysis (not fully presented here) was performed using the time to settlement (measured in days) as the dependent variable and

Table 5.11
Provisions for Expedited Grievance Processing, by Type of Provision, Excluded Issues, and Industry/Sector[†]
(in percentage of contractual grievance procedures)

Expedited Grievance Procedure	Steel Manufacturing	Industry/Sector Retail Department Stores	Industry/Sector Nonprofit Hospitals	Industry/Sector Local Public Schools
Provision for expedited grievance processing:				
- Yes	81%	32%	53%	45%
- No	19	68	47	55
Type of provision for expedited grievance processing[†]				
- Skipping steps	91	72	84	75
- Shorter time limits	65	60	44	80
- Informal hearings	55	42	54	50
- Dispensing transcripts	45	33	42	35
Grievance issues excluded from expedited processing[†]				
- Discipline	97	84	98	92
· Discharge	98	88	100	94
· Long-term suspension	96	78	97	88
· Demotion	96	80	95	90
- Strikes/lockouts	94	82	94	86
- Discrimination	62	64	88	80
- Management rights	56	62	86	80
- Subcontracting	52	62	86	80
- Work load	32	57	84	74

[†]For agreements with provisions for expedited grievance processing

each of the specific types of expedited grievance-processing provisions as independent variables in four separate regression equations. The findings showed that procedures for skipping intermediate grievance steps were associated with faster grievance settlements in each of the industries and sectors. However, shortened time limits were associated with faster grievance processing in steel, hospitals, and schools, but not in retail stores; informal hearings were associated with faster grievance settlements in steel, hospitals, and schools, but not in retail stores; and dispensing with written transcripts was associated with faster grievance settlements in steel and hospitals, but not in retail stores and schools.

The specific provisions for expedited grievance processing were also regressed on the three categories of grievance issues noted above. The results showed that (a) disciplinary grievances are resolved relatively more quickly by the use of shortened time limits for the parties' responses at each step of the procedure, which are most commonly found in local public schools (see row 4 of Table 5.11); (b) health and safety, discrimination, and other category (2)-type grievances are resolved relatively more quickly by the skipping of intermediate grievance steps, which is most commonly found in steel manufacturing; and (c) other types of grievances (category (3) grievances) are resolved relatively more quickly through informal hearings and dispensing with written transcripts, which are most commonly found in steel manufacturing and nonprofit hospitals. Thus, while expedited grievance procedures as a whole lead to faster grievance settlements across the four industries and sectors, the effects vary by grievance issue and by specific type of expedited grievance-handling provision.

Finally, if expedited grievance procedures reduce the time required to settle grievances across the four industries and sectors, why do hospital grievances take longer to resolve, on average, than grievances in steel, retail stores, and schools? One answer to this question is that other variables may differentially affect the speed of grievance settlement in the four industries and sectors. Recall from Table 5.3 that the hospital sector had the largest number of significant variables that were positively associated with the speed of grievance settlement. Alternatively, it may also be the case that certain expedited procedures, such as faster time limits for the parties' responses to each other, use of informal hearings, and dispensing with written transcripts, are actually used less often in hospitals than elsewhere. This conclusion is partially supported by data showing that, on an annual average basis over the 1980-1982 period, approximately 9 percent of all hospital (nurses') grievances were handled through an expedited procedure, compared to 22 percent in steel, 13 percent in retail stores, and 16 percent in local schools. The conclusion is further supported by analysis of interview data from hospital administrators and union officials, which showed that only one of the seven hospital labor agreements to which these respondents were party contained an expedited grievance procedure. Because the data were not available by specific expedited procedure used, however, this conclusion about the speed of hospital grievance settlement must remain tentative.

Importance of Grievance Issues

Earlier it was shown that the perceived importance of issues raised through the grievance procedure varied by category of respondent (whether union or management and industry/sector (see Table 4.3). It was also found that grievance issue importance scores rose with a management policy of taking certain grievances as far as possible through the procedure, a union policy of committing all grievances to writing, the length of the bargaining relationship, supervisor knowledge of the grievance procedure, and steward knowledge of the grievance procedure (see Table 5.5). Do perceptions of grievance issue importance vary by grievances actually filed? Yes, according to the data presented in Table 5.12, although there are some notable industry/sector differences in this regard.

Observe that the management respondents as a whole rated certain grievance issues as more important than did union respondents. These included grievances about management rights, leave time, strikes/lockouts, and subcontracting. Steel managers rated discipline, working conditions, health and safety, work load, technological change, leave time, and subcontracting as highly important grievance issues.[3] These managers as well as those in retail department stores gave high importance ratings to productivity issues, and store managers also rated work-hour grievances as highly important. Both retail store managers and hospital managers rated work-assignment issues as highly important, and the hospital managers also gave high importance ratings to transfer issues. For school administrators, discipline, performance-evaluation, and transfer issues were rated as highly important. In all four industries and sectors, managers assigned especially high importance ratings to issues of management rights and strikes/lockouts.

Union respondents rated most grievance issues higher in importance than did management respondents, with the differences being largest in the cases of health and safety, discipline, pay, discrimination, overtime, union security, seniority, and recall. Grievances over discipline, working conditions, health and safety, management rights, and discrimination were rated highest in importance by union respondents in steel; grievances over work assignment, transfer, discipline, and work hours were rated highest in importance by union respondents in retail stores; grievances over work load, transfer, discrimination, working conditions, and

Table 5.12

Perceived Importance of Grievance Issues Filed,
by Issue, Respondent, and Industry/Sector
(mean ratings where 1 = low, 5 = high)

| | Industry/Sector | | | | | | | | | | | | | | |
| Grievance Issue | Steel Manufacturing | | | Retail Department Stores | | | Nonprofit Hospitals | | | Local Public Schools | | | All Industries/ Sectors | | |
	M†	U†	C†	M†	U†	C†	M†	U†	C†	M†	U†	C†	M†	U†	C†
Discipline	4.4	4.7	4.6	3.4	4.3	3.9	3.6	4.3	4.0	3.9	4.2	4.0	3.8	4.4	4.1
Working Conditions	4.1	4.6	4.3	3.0	3.9	3.4	3.0	4.3	3.7	3.6	4.0	3.8	3.4	3.7	3.6
Health and Safety	4.2	4.8	4.5	2.2	2.7	2.5	2.6	4.2	3.4	3.0	4.2	3.6	3.0	4.0	3.5
Management Rights	4.8	4.4	4.6	4.2	3.4	3.8	4.5	4.2	4.3	4.2	4.1	4.1	4.4	4.0	4.2
Work Assignment	3.7	4.1	3.9	4.1	4.3	4.2	4.4	4.0	4.2	2.7	4.0	3.3	3.7	4.1	3.9
Pay	3.2	3.9	3.5	2.4	3.3	2.8	2.8	3.8	3.3	2.1	2.7	2.4	2.6	3.4	3.0
Discrimination	3.9	4.5	4.3	2.9	3.7	3.3	3.3	4.3	3.8	3.0	4.1	3.5	3.3	4.2	3.8
Job Grading/Work Standards	4.0	3.9	4.1	3.2	3.3	3.2	3.0	3.6	3.3	3.2	2.9	3.0	3.4	3.5	3.5
Overtime	3.1	4.3	3.7	2.4	2.9	2.7	2.4	3.2	2.8	NA*	NA	NA	2.6	3.5	3.0
Performance Evaluation	3.0	3.6	3.3	3.0	3.4	3.2	3.7	4.2	4.0	3.9	4.1	4.0	3.4	3.8	3.6
Transfer	2.8	3.5	3.2	3.4	4.3	3.8	4.0	4.3	4.1	3.7	3.6	3.6	3.5	3.9	3.6
Promotion	3.2	3.4	3.3	2.5	3.1	2.8	3.2	4.0	3.6	3.6	3.7	3.7	3.1	3.5	3.3
Work Hours	4.3	4.1	4.2	4.1	4.2	4.1	3.4	4.2	3.8	2.0	1.5	1.7	3.4	3.5	3.4

154

Industry/Sector

Grievance Issue	Steel Manufacturing			Retail Department Stores			Nonprofit Hospitals			Local Public Schools			All Industries/ Sectors		
	M†	U†	C†	M†	U†	C†	M†	U†	C†	M†	U†	C†	M†	U†	C†
Work Load	4.6	4.2	4.3	2.1	1.4	1.8	3.6	4.5	4.1	3.4	4.4	3.9	3.4	3.6	3.5
Technological Change	4.4	3.6	4.0	1.6	1.7	1.6	2.2	2.6	2.4	1.5	1.8	1.6	2.4	2.4	2.4
Vacation/Holidays	2.6	4.0	3.3	2.4	2.7	2.6	3.3	3.8	3.6	3.4	2.7	3.0	2.9	3.3	3.1
Layoff	3.8	4.4	4.1	2.2	3.1	2.6	2.1	3.1	2.6	1.7	1.9	1.8	2.4	3.1	2.7
Leave Time	4.2	4.2	4.2	1.7	2.4	2.0	3.2	2.7	2.9	3.6	2.6	3.1	3.2	3.0	3.1
Productivity	4.6	3.7	4.1	4.0	2.6	3.3	2.6	2.2	2.4	2.5	2.0	2.2	3.4	2.6	3.0
Fringe Benefits	2.6	3.3	2.9	3.2	3.3	3.2	1.4	1.9	1.7	1.5	1.9	1.7	2.2	27	2.5
Union Security	2.3	4.4	3.3	2.1	3.8	2.9	1.6	3.7	2.6	1.9	3.6	2.7	2.0	3.9	3.0
Seniority	2.4	3.3	2.8	2.3	2.7	2.5	1.9	3.1	2.5	2.1	2.4	2.2	2.2	2.9	2.6
Strikes/Lockouts	4.7	4.3	4.5	4.2	2.7	3.4	4.1	3.5	3.8	4.3	4.0	4.1	4.3	3.6	3.9
Subcontracting	4.9	4.1	4.5	2.0	1.2	1.6	NA	NA	NA	NA	NA	NA	3.5	2.7	3.2
Recall	2.9	3.8	3.3	NA	NA	NA	NA	NA	NA	NA	NA	NA	2.9	3.8	3.3
TOTALS	3.6	3.9	3.7	2.7	3.2	3.0	3.1	3.7	3.4	3.1	3.4	3.3	3.2	3.6	3.4

†M = management respondent ratings; U = union respondent ratings; C = combined ratings; the data are mean ratings
*NA = not available

155

discipline were rated highest in importance by union respondents in hospitals; and grievances over work load, discipline, health and safety, management rights, discrimination, and performance evaluation were rated highest in importance by union respondents in local schools.

To probe these variances further, separate regression analyses were performed for each industry/sector. In each case, the top, middle, and lower third, respectively, of grievance issue importance ratings were used as the dependent variables. The results (not reproduced here) showed that the independent variables initially found to be significantly related to the perceived importance of grievance issues (see Table 5.5) remained so in steel and schools. However, the labor-management relations variables were positively related to grievance issue importance only for the most important (that is, the top third) grievance issues in retail stores, and for the top two-thirds of grievance issues, rated by importance, in nonprofit hospitals. A union policy of committing all grievances to writing was positively associated with grievance issue importance ratings in all cases in retail stores, hospitals, and schools, but only to the least important issues in steel. A management policy of committing all grievances to writing was statistically significant (and positive) for the middle and lowest tier grievances in retail stores and hospitals. These findings suggest that the fact—the requirement—of writing grievances down elevates their perceived importance, as judged by the responses of both the union and management officials surveyed in this study.

Equity of Grievance Settlement

The data in Table 5.13 show that the perceived equity of grievance settlement varies not only by industry and sector, but by grievance issue and category of respondent. In steel and retail stores, management officials generally have a lower perceived equity of grievance settlement, on average, than union officials. In steel, the differences are largest in the cases of grievances over discipline, working conditions, health and safety, discrimination, performance evaluation, vacation/ holidays, union security, seniority, subcontracting, and recall. In retail stores, the differences are largest in the cases of discipline, health and safety, and union security.

In local schools and especially nonprofit hospitals, management officials generally have a higher perceived equity of grievance settlement than union officials. In schools, the differences are largest over issues of discipline, working conditions, health and safety, transfer, performance evaluation, leave time, and strikes/lock-outs. In hospitals, the differences are largest over issues of discipline, health and safety, management rights, work assignment, overtime, promotion, and union security.

Perceived Equity of Grievance Settlement,
by Issue, Respondent, and Industry/Sector
(mean ratings where 1 = low, 5 = high)

	Industry/Sector														
Grievance Issue	Steel Manufacturing			Retail Department Stores			Nonprofit Hospitals			Local Public Schools			All Industries/ Sectors		
	M†	U†	C†	M†	U†	C†	M†	U†	C†	M†	U†	C†	M†	U†	C†
Discipline	3.4	4.1	3.8	2.4	3.0	2.7	3.7	2.7	3.2	3.7	3.1	3.6	3.3	3.2	3.2
Working Conditions	3.2	4.0	3.6	2.6	2.8	2.7	3.4	2.9	3.1	3.6	3.0	3.3	3.2	3.2	3.2
Health and Safety	3.1	4.2	3.7	2.8	3.3	3.1	3.8	2.5	3.2	3.4	2.9	3.2	3.3	3.2	3.2
Management Rights	3.9	3.8	3.8	3.1	3.2	3.1	3.4	2.4	2.9	3.5	3.0	3.2	3.5	3.1	3.3
Work Assignment	2.7	3.1	2.9	2.4	2.7	2.5	3.1	2.3	2.7	3.1	3.1	3.1	2.8	2.8	2.8
Pay	2.4	2.7	2.6	2.7	2.3	2.5	3.0	2.7	2.9	3.0	3.2	3.1	2.8	2.7	2.7
Discrimination	3.0	2.3	2.7	2.4	2.6	2.5	2.8	2.4	2.6	2.9	3.2	3.1	2.8	2.6	2.7
Job Grading/Work Standards	3.3	3.0	3.1	2.3	2.5	2.4	2.8	2.6	2.7	2.9	2.9	2.9	2.8	2.8	2.8
Overtime	2.7	3.3	3.0	2.9	3.1	3.0	3.4	2.4	2.9	NA*	NA	NA	3.0	2.9	3.0
Performance Evaluation	2.4	3.2	2.6	3.0	3.2	3.1	3.3	2.6	3.0	3.4	2.9	3.2	3.0	3.0	3.0
Transfer	2.1	2.6	2.4	2.6	2.3	2.5	3.2	2.7	2.9	3.6	2.9	3.3	2.9	2.6	2.7
Promotion	2.6	2.9	2.7	2.8	2.4	2.6	3.2	2.2	2.7	3.6	3.2	3.4	3.1	2.8	2.9
Work Hours	3.3	3.1	3.2	2.4	2.6	2.5	2.0	2.3	2.6	3.2	3.0	3.1	3.0	2.8	2.9

Table 5.13 (continued)

Industry/Sector

Grievance Issue	Steel Manufacturing M†	U†	C†	Retail Department Stores M†	U†	C†	Nonprofit Hospitals M†	U†	C†	Local Public Schools M†	U†	C†	All Industries/ Sectors M†	U†	C†
Work Load	3.8	3.3	3.5	2.5	2.7	2.6	2.9	2.1	2.5	3.1	3.2	3.1	3.1	2.8	2.9
Technological Change	3.4	2.9	3.1	3.0	3.2	3.1	2.9	2.6	2.7	2.8	2.9	2.9	3.0	2.9	3.0
Vacation/Holidays	2.2	3.3	2.7	2.7	3.1	2.9	3.0	2.4	2.7	3.9	3.6	3.7	2.9	3.1	3.0
Layoff	3.3	2.9	3.1	2.9	3.2	3.1	2.7	2.9	2.8	3.7	3.4	3.5	3.2	3.1	3.1
Leave Time	3.0	3.2	3.1	2.2	2.6	2.4	3.3	2.4	2.8	4.0	3.4	3.7	3.1	2.9	3.0
Productivity	3.5	3.1	3.3	2.4	2.8	2.6	3.0	2.5	2.7	3.7	3.4	3.5	3.2	2.9	3.1
Fringe Benefits	2.3	2.6	2.4	3.1	3.4	3.2	2.8	2.6	2.7	3.0	2.9	3.0	2.8	2.9	2.8
Union Security	2.1	3.4	2.7	2.1	2.6	2.3	4.0	2.4	3.2	2.9	3.3	3.1	2.8	2.9	2.9
Seniority	2.2	3.7	2.9	2.7	3.1	2.9	3.3	2.3	2.8	3.6	3.3	3.2	2.9	3.1	3.0
Strikes/Lockouts	3.5	3.2	3.3	2.4	2.8	2.6	3.6	2.9	3.3	3.5	2.9	3.2	3.3	3.0	3.1
Subcontracting	3.9	2.4	3.2	3.1	3.4	3.2	NA	NA	NA	NA	NA	NA	3.5	2.9	3.2
Recall	2.4	3.6	3.0	NA	NA	NA	NA	NA	NA	NA	NA	NA	2.4	3.6	3.0
TOTALS	3.0	3.4	3.2	2.6	3.0	2.8	3.2	2.5	2.8	3.4	3.2	3.3	3.0	3.1	3.1

†M = management respondent ratings; U = union respondent ratings; C = combined ratings; the data are mean ratings
*NA = not available

To some extent, union-management differences over the perceived equity of grievance settlement are based on the outcomes of grievance cases. Analysis of the survey data shows that equity ratings are moderately positively correlated with the parties' judgments about "wins" and "losses" in grievance cases. In steel and retail stores, grievances were judged by the respondents to have been decided in favor of employees in about 56 and 58 percent of the cases, respectively, over the 1980-1982 period. In both industries, management respondents assigned about 10 percent lower ratings to the equity of grievance settlement than did union respondents. In local schools, the respondents judged school districts to have "won" slightly over half (52 percent) of the grievance decisions between 1980 and 1982, and management respondents assigned approximately 5 percent higher ratings to the equity of grievance settlement than did union respondents. In nonprofit hospitals, employers were judged by the respondents to have won about 60 percent of the grievance cases decided between 1980 and 1982, and the perceived equity of grievance settlement was almost 30 percent higher among management than among union respondents.

To understand better the union-management differences in perceived equity of grievance settlement, especially in the hospital sector, separate regression analyses were performed for each industry and sector. The dependent variables in this analysis were union-management difference scores with respect to the equity of grievance settlement, and these were separated into the top, middle, and lower third of scores. Only independent variables previously shown to be significantly related to the equity of settlement (see Table 5.6) were included in the analysis.

The regression results (not reproduced here) showed that a management policy of taking certain grievances as far as possible through the procedure was not significantly related to union-management differences in the perceived equity of grievance settlement (though this variable was significantly positively related to management's perceived equity of grievance settlement). However, adversarial labor relations were significantly positively related to the top third of union-management difference scores across the four industries and sectors, to the middle third of difference scores in hospitals and schools, and to the lower third of difference scores in hospitals. These findings are consistent with other data showing that, over the 1980-1982 period, labor-management relations as judged by union and management respondents became less adversarial in steel, were virtually unchanged in retail department stores, became slightly more adversarial in local public schools, and became considerably more adversarial in nonprofit hospitals. Note, too, that provisions for expedited grievance handling were significantly positively related to the perceived equity of grievance settlement for all three dependent variables (that is, union-management difference scores) in steel and schools, but only for the middle category in retail stores and for the middle and lower categories in hospitals. As in the aggregate analysis (Table 5.6), the cost of grievance handling was significantly negatively related to all categories of union-management difference scores in steel and schools. However, in retail stores this variable was negatively related only to the middle and lower categories of difference scores, and in hospitals it remained unrelated to all categories of difference scores.

The "outlier" position of the hospital sector concerning union-management differences in the perceived equity of grievance settlement is further demonstrated by examination of the relationship between perceived importance of grievance issues and the perceived equity of grievance settlement. For all four industries and sectors, the correlation between these two variables was $+.34$, which is statistically significant at $p = < .05$. However, the correlation was $+.63$ in steel, $+.56$ in retail stores, and $+.59$ in local schools, but $-.24$ in nonprofit hospitals. In other words, and as shown in Figure 5.1, the more important the issues raised through the grievance procedure, the higher the perceived equity of grievance settlement, as judged by the union and management parties to grievances in steel, retail stores, and schools. In contrast, in the nonprofit hospital sector the perceived equity of grievance settlement initially rose but then declined as the perceived importance of grievance issues rose. This finding is also consistent with the aforementioned pattern of change in labor-management relations over the 1980-1982 period across the four industries and sectors.

INTERVIEW PERSPECTIVES

The interviews of seventeen management officials and nineteen union officials conducted during this study provided additional support for the quantitative findings about grievance procedure effectiveness that have been reported to this point.[4] This is especially so with respect to the perceived importance of grievance issues and the perceived equity of grievance settlement.

For example, the union interviewees as a whole gave a mean rating (on a 1 = low, 5 = high scale) of 3.9 to the importance of issues raised in the grievance procedure, compared to the overall management inter-viewees' rating of 3.5. Consistent with the survey data, the combined interviewees' ratings of grievance issue importance were highest in steel (3.6) and lowest in retail department stores (2.8).

As to the equity of grievance settlement, this too was rated more highly by the union representatives than by the management officials as a whole, specifically, 3.3 versus 2.9 on a five-point rating scale. However, while the unionists' rating of the equity of grievance settle-ment exceeded the managers' rating in steel and retail stores, the

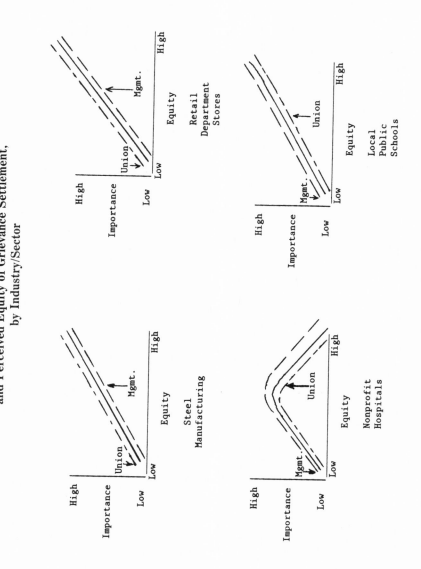

Figure 5.1
Relationships between Perceived Importance of Grievance Issues
and Perceived Equity of Grievance Settlement,
by Industry/Sector

ratings were equal in local schools (at 3.0) and the relationship was reversed in nonprofit hospitals, where managers rated the equity of grievance settlement at 3.3 and union officials rated it at 2.5.

One of the hospital union officials who was interviewed observed the following about the equity of grievance settlement:

> What bothers me most about grievance handling in our hospitals is that the settlements are just not equitable. To the contrary, they are widely perceived to be unfair. What's more, they are most unfair when they involve really important issues, like work load. We had seventeen grievances filed over patient loads by our nurses last year, and not one of them was satisfactorily resolved. And, I'm not talking about winning or loosing the grievances; hell we won eleven of those cases. I'm talking more about the fact that none of the decisions really dealt with the quality of patient care or the job of the nurse, which are key in all of this. That's why I don't think these so-called settlements are very equitable.

A hospital administrator also commented on this issue:

> You ask about the equity of grievance settlements in this hospital. Well, of course, that's a judgment call but from a management point of view I'd say they are reasonably equitable, reasonably fair, on the whole. Where we run into problems is with inconsequential grievances and really big grievances. If a nurse says that her pay was docked for being late to work, she may be right but that ought to be settled informally by talking it through with her supervisor. It's just not an important enough issue to invoke the grievance machinery and its unfair to have to take up lots of people's time dealing with this issue no matter what the result. On a big issue, like a discharge case or a work slowdown, the parties feel so strongly that any settlement is bound to be seen as unfair by someone. Even when we win one of these cases, we rarely get back what we lost or really find that the real causes of the problem have been dealt with in the grievance process.

These comments provide qualitative insights into the negative correlation between grievance issue importance and the equity of grievance settlement which was previously found to exist in the nonprofit-hospital sector. They also contrast with the views of other interviewees. For example, a steelworkers' union official noted the following about grievance settlement:

> We've had a long history of grievance processing in our industry, and all in all I'd say that things work pretty well. By this I mean that we use the procedure to take up important issues—there's not a lot of junk that clogs up the procedure— and the settlements tend to be pretty fair. Sure you may get hundreds of grievances during the course of a year in a big steel plant, but we and management know which of these are really important and we try to settle them by getting at the underlying problems that bring them about. I think our expedited procedure has helped a lot on this score.

A steel-company manager offered the following perspective on this issue:

There was a time when the grievance procedure was abused and settlements just weren't accepted. But what with the competitive problems facing our industry, both the union and the management decided that we'd better get our heads out of the sand and either make the grievance procedure work or find something else. Yes we did go to an expedited grievance procedure several years ago, but there's also been some attitude changes on both sides. Today when grievances are filed, they get acted on promptly and we go by the merits of the case. There's no splitting differences just to split them, even on the important or big cases. I think that's a key reason why we think the settlements are pretty fair, even if we lose some.

These comments are consistent with the significant positive correlation between the importance of grievance issues and the equity of grievance settlement reported earlier for steel manufacturing.

In retail department stores, both management and union interviewees commented on grievance-handling costs and expedited arbitration as they bore upon the equity of grievance settlements. For example, an RWDSU official noted the following:

How equitable are grievance settlements, you ask? I'll tell you. The issues themselves matter less than how they are treated, how much it costs, and how quickly we get them resolved. A few years ago we found that grievance-handling costs were going through the roof, so we went to an expedited procedure. Since then, we've found that important issues get treated more quickly and cost us a hell of a lot less than before. Everyone is aware of this so now most people think the settlements are pretty fair even if your own side loses a case.

A department store manager also commented on this matter:

We have a policy of taking our grievances as far as possible through our procedure so as to get definitive settlements. However, this often proved to be a long, costly procedure. In recent years, our expedited procedure has helped reduce grievance-handling costs greatly, speed up the procedure, and create more favorable opinions about the fairness of the procedure. I think it's also true that we take up more important issues than we used to and that most people see the settlements of these issues as pretty fair. I know I feel this way even if we lose a case.

These two similar sets of comments reinforce the earlier quantitative findings about the determinants of the attitudinal measures of grievance procedure effectiveness in retail department stores, and about the relationship between grievance issue importance and the perceived equity of grievance settlement.

Public school officials and union representatives who were interviewed for this study tended to focus on the nature and length of the labor-management relationship in discussing grievance settlement. A school administrator with several years of grievance-handling experience commented as follows:

> What I've seen here and in two other school districts before this is that, early on in a labor relationship, the parties don't know how to deal with each other and the grievance procedure gets flooded with all sorts of cases—most of which are trivial. Later on as they gain experience they stop beating each other over the head, they adopt a more mature attitude, and the grievance procedure takes up fewer but more important issues. At least that's what I've seen in this district. Today, I think our school administrators and managers think that grievance settlements are pretty fair.

An NEA official who also had several years of grievance-handling experience in the schools offered these observations:

> Well, so-called maturity of the labor relationship can cut both ways, but from what I've seen here and elsewhere it does tend to make the parties act more responsibly. This is reflected in the grievance process where we generally get important, or at least not trivial, issues and where the settlements are seen as reasonably equitable. Both we and the school district administration have policies to pursue grievances through the procedure, but we try to do so judiciously so that we don't spend our whole lives in the process. All in all, it's a pretty cooperative relationship—but that's not the way it was at the beginning.

These comments are consistent with the strong positive relationship between grievance issue importance and the perceived equity of grievance settlement earlier found to exist in local public schools. They are also consistent with the quantitative evidence about the determinants of the attitudinal measures of grievance procedure effectiveness in the schools.

SUMMARY AND CONCLUSIONS

This chapter has investigated differences by industry and sector in six measures of grievance procedure effectiveness as well as in the determinants of effectiveness. Certain independent variables, especially characteristics of the labor-management relationship, are generally if not uniformly significantly related to the dependent variables across the four industries and sectors; other variables are occasionally significant in this regard; and still other variables are rarely, if ever, significant.

In steel, expedited grievance processing, the size of the bargaining unit, and adversarial labor relations were consistently significant across the behavioral measures of grievance procedure effectiveness, and the first and last of these variables were also significantly related to perceived equity of grievance settlement. Voluntary employee turnover was significantly negatively associated with grievance and arbitration rates in the steel industry, thereby supporting the notion that exit is an alternative to voice in the employment relationship (Hirschman, 1970; Freeman and Medoff, 1984). Adversarial labor relations, supervisor knowledge of the grievance procedure, and expedited grievance processing significantly affected the behavioral measures of grievance procedure effectiveness in retail department stores, while a management policy to take certain grievances as far as possible through the procedure was significantly positively related to the two attitudinal measures of grievance procedure effectiveness in retail stores.

In nonprofit hospitals, union and management policies to take certain grievances as far as possible through the procedure, the size of the bargaining unit, adversarial labor relations, supervisor knowledge of the grievance procedure, and expedited grievance handling were consistently significantly related to the behavioral measures of grievance procedure effectiveness, but only the management policy variable was significantly (positively) related to the two attitudinal measures of grievance procedure effectiveness. In local public schools, only adversarial labor relations were consistently significantly related to the grievance rate, level of settlement, speed of settlement, and arbitration rate, with the relationship being positive in all cases. Management and union policies to take certain grievances as far as possible through the procedure and the length of the bargaining relationship were significantly related to both the perceived importance of grievance issues and the perceived equity of grievance settlement in the schools.

The empirical analyses also showed that the four industries and sectors differed notably in the type and incidence of grievances filed over the 1980-1982 period, with work-load issues being especially prominent in schools and hospitals, work hours, vacation/holidays, and pay issues being especially prominent in retail stores, and job grading, subcontracting, discrimination, and overtime being particularly notable in steel. Health and safety issues were a key subject of grievances in steel, schools and, to a lesser extent, hospitals, and work-assignment grievances were frequently filed in retail stores, hospitals, and schools. Three issues, discipline, working conditions, and management rights, were major subjects of grievances in all four industries and sectors.

Finally, clear differences in the perceived importance of grievance issues and the perceived equity of grievance settlement were observed among the industries and sectors. While union respondents, on average, rated grievance issues as more important than did management respondents in each of the four industries and sectors, union respondents had a higher perceived equity of grievance settlement than did management respondents in steel and retail stores, but a lower perceived equity of grievance settlement than did management respondents in schools and especially hospitals. Moreover, in steel, retail stores and schools, the perceived equity of grievance settlement was consistently significantly positively correlated with the perceived importance of grievance issues, whereas in nonprofit hospitals the relationship was positive to the midpoint of grievance issue importance scores but turned negative thereafter.

NOTES

1. Recall that the speed of grievance settlement is measured in the number of days to settlement. Thus, a positive coefficient in Table 5.3 means that a particular independent variable is associated with slower grievance settlements, a negative coefficient with faster settlements.

2. Note that the total grievance rates presented in this table differ from those shown in Table 4.2 because only subsamples of respondents provided sufficiently complete survey responses to permit the construction of Table 5.8.

3. Because mean ratings of grievance issue importance varied by industry and sector, different cut-off scores on the five-point rating scales were used to identify the most important issues in each case. These were 4.1 in steel manufacturing, 4.0 in retail department stores, 4.0 in nonprofit hospitals, and 3.7 in local public schools.

4. The interviewee respondents were distributed as follows:

Industry/Sector	Management Respondents	Union Respondents
Steel Manufacturing	4	5
Retail Department Stores	4	4
Nonprofit Hospitals	3	4
Local Public Schools	6	6
Total	17	19

6

Post-Grievance
Settlement Behavior
and Outcomes

A unique opportunity was provided in this study to examine the post-grievance settlement behavior of workers and supervisors/managers. As was observed in Chapter 3, the grievance literature has been almost exclusively concerned with grievance activity and settlement. But just how do grievance settlements and variation in settlements affect employee performance, work attendance, promotions, turnover, and other aspects of the employment relationship? These as well as related questions and issues are addressed in this chapter.

DATA SOURCES

As was also noted in Chapter 3, one employer organization and one corresponding union in each of the four industries and sectors cooperated in and furnished data for this portion of the study. Grievance filing data were obtained for the 1980-1983 period for certain locations and facilities in each of the four employer organizations.[1] Selected personnel data for the employees and supervisors/managers who were direct parties to these grievances were then obtained and merged with the grievance data to create a file of grievance system users. Then, samples of non-grievance users and their supervisors/managers were drawn from the same locations and time period, and relevant personnel data were also obtained for them. This data base allowed us to conduct ex post facto control group type research for the purpose of identifying the effects of grievance filing and grievance settlement on the post-settlement behavior of employees and supervisors/managers.[2]

GRIEVANCE PROCEDURE CHARACTERISTICS
AND USAGE

Each of the four organizations included in this portion of the study maintains a multistep grievance procedure that at the first or second step requires grievances to be put in writing if they are to be further considered and if they are eligible to progress through the procedure. The structure of these grievance procedures is summarized in Table 6.1.

In organizations A and C, informal discussion of a grievance between the employee and the immediate supervisor constitutes the first step of the grievance-handling process. While this appears not to be the case in organizations B and D, document analysis and interview data clearly indicated that such informal discussion is, de facto, the initial grievance-processing step. In each of the four organizations, then, four written steps are provided for the filing and appeal of grievances.

In all four of these organizations, the employee's immediate supervisor is the lowest-level management representative in the grievance process. Other, higher-level management representatives are involved in the later stages of grievance processing. However, only the nonprofit hospital uses the personnel director as a management representative in the grievance process, and only the hospital and organized nurses fail to use a grievance committee. In all four organizations, arbitration is the final step of the grievance procedure.

Table 6.2 shows rates of grievance filing, by step, over the 1980-1983 period in each of the four organizations. Consistent with the aggregate industry/sector data presented earlier, grievance rates were consistently higher in the steel company than in the other three organizations; the nonprofit hospital, the local school district, and the retail department store followed next in order. Interestingly and somewhat unexpectedly, the rates of grievance-appeal filing to higher steps of the procedure are quite similar across the four organizations so that, at the arbitration step, between two and four cases per 1,000 employees were processed annually, on average, between 1980 and 1983. Note further from Table 6.2 that, on a longitudinal basis, these organization-level grievance data partially parallel the experience with the aggregate industry/sector-level data presented previously; that is, annual grievance rates fell between 1980 and 1982 and rose in 1983 (but not to 1980 levels).

Grievance Procedure Users and Nonusers

Who uses these grievance procedures and who doesn't? To answer this question, data on the individual characteristics of grievance filers and the total membership of the relevant bargaining units in each of the four organizations were obtained from union membership files and employer

Table 6.1

Grievance Procedures in Four Organizations

Grievance Procedure Structure	Organization A (Steel Mfg.)	Organization B (Retail Department Store)	Organization C (Nonprofit Hospital)	Organization D (Local School District)
First Step	Informal discussion required between grievant and immediate supervisor	Written grievance filed and written response required from immediate supervisor	Informal discussion required between grievant and immediate supervisor	Written grievance filed and written response required from immediate supervisor
Second Step	Written grievance filed and written response required from general foreman	Written appeal filed and written response required from area or store manager	Written grievance filed and written response required from immediate supervisor	Written appeal filed and written response required from school principal
Third Step	Written appeal filed and written response required from plant manager	Written appeal filed and written response required from grievance committee	Written appeal filed and written response required from area or head supervisor	Written appeal filed and written response required from grievance committee
Fourth Step	Written appeal filed and written response required from grievance committee	Third party arbitration	Written appeal filed and written response required from personnel director	Third party arbitration
Fifth Step	Third party arbitration	--	Third party arbitration	--

Table 6.2

Grievance Rates by Grievance Step in Four Organizations, 1980-1983*

Grievance Step	Organization A					Organization B					Organization C					Organization D				
	'80	'81	'82	'83	'80-83**	'80	'81	'82	'83	'80-83**	'80	'81	'82	'83	'80-83**	'80	'81	'82	'83	'80-83**
Step 1	13.8	11.3	10.2	12.1	12.0	8.4	7.9	6.1	7.6	7.4	10.4	9.7	9.0	10.3	9.8	8.6	7.8	7.2	8.3	7.9
Step 2	6.4	5.1	4.4	5.2	5.2	3.7	3.2	2.9.	3.8	3.6	5.1	4.3	3.9	4.7	4.5	4.2	3.0	2.8	3.7	4.4
Step 3	2.3	1.9	1.4	2.0	1.9	1.4	1.1	0.9	1.3	1.2	2.1	1.8	1.1	2.0	1.8	2.1	1.6	1.3	1.8	1.7
Step 4	0.5	0.4	0.2	0.4	0.4	0.4	0.2	0.2	0.4	0.3	0.4	0.2	0.1	0.3	0.2	0.5	0.3	0.2	0.4	0.3

* Grievances per 100 employees
** Annual average per 100 employees

personnel records. The "grievance user" data were then separated (subtracted) from the bargaining-unit membership and employment data to create a "grievance nonuser" category. The relevant data for both categories of employees are shown in Table 6.3.

These data suggest that, across the four organizations, grievance procedure users share certain personal characteristics. In particular, grievance procedure users are younger on average than nonusers, men are more likely than women to be grievance users, blacks are more likely than any other racial minorities to use the grievance procedure, and the probability of using the grievance procedure increases with education (schooling) level. Employees with little or a large amount of work experience are less likely to be grievance procedure users than employees with intermediate amounts of work experience.

To identify more fully the relationships among employee characteristics and grievance procedure usage, correlation and regression analyses were performed for each organization separately and in total. The regression results are shown in Tables 6.4 and 6.5. In each organization, age is significantly negatively associated with grievance procedure usage, while men, blacks, and relatively more educated employees were significantly more likely than women, nonblacks, and relatively less educated employees to use the grievance procedure (Table 6.4). Work experience is not significantly associated with grievance filing in any of the equations; however, a subsequent decomposition analysis found that, in three of the four organizations, employees with from five to twelve years of experience were significantly more likely to use the grievance procedure than employees with less than five or more than twelve years of experience. All of these findings are basically replicated when data from the four organizations are aggregated (see Table 6.5); this is especially noteworthy in view of the otherwise major differences among these organizations in the type of work performed and the characteristics of employees. In addition, the regression results from Table 6.5 show that grievance procedure usage was significantly greater in the steel manufacturing firm than in the three other organizations included in this portion of the study.

Explaining Nonuse of the Procedure

While the quantitative analysis helps to distinguish the characteristics of grievance procedure users from nonusers, it does not illuminate the motivational dimensions of grievance procedure usage. Why do some employees, but not others, make use of these procedures? To deal with this question, we initially consider the exclusion of informal grievance handling from the data presented so far.

Recall that interviews and document analysis indicated that informal

Table 6.3
Selected Characteristics of Grievance Procedure
Users and Nonusers in Four Organizations, 1980-1983

Employee Characteristic	Organization A		Organization B		Organization C		Organization D	
	Grievance Procedure		Grievance Procedure		Grievance Procedure		Grievance Procedure	
	Users	Nonusers	Users	Nonusers	Users	Nonusers	Users	Nonusers
Age (mean, in years)	34.7	37.6	32.4	34.7	32.1	37.6	32.8	35.3
Sex:								
• Male	98.0	95.0	45.9	37.5	7.7	6.4	39.7	31.4
• Female	2.0	5.0	54.1	62.5	92.3	93.6	60.3	68.6
Race:								
• Caucasian	44.6	48.4	73.3	74.3	45.5	47.6	63.8	66.6
• Black	39.4	30.7	17.4	14.4	18.9	16.4	15.6	12.0
• Hispanic	8.2	10.3	3.4	3.6	18.9	17.3	9.1	8.3
• Asian	3.3	6.5	4.3	6.4	9.7	11.1	8.2	10.4
• Other minority	4.5	4.1	1.6	1.3	7.0	7.6	3.3	2.7
Education (schooling):								
• < 9 years	15.2	17.4	5.1	6.4	0.3	0.6	0.0	0.0
• 9-11 years	32.4	37.7	10.0	12.6	3.1	4.4	1.0	2.0
• High school graduate	43.9	37.2	51.2	48.2	9.7	15.6	1.4	3.3
• 1-3 years college	6.7	6.3	25.4	21.4	21.3	18.9	8.0	9.4
• College graduate	1.8	1.4	10.3	8.1	32.8	32.2	41.8	40.6
• Some graduate school				3.0	17.3	15.4	28.4	26.6
• Master's degree				0.3	11.4	9.3	12.3	11.4
• Some doctoral work			–	–	4.1	3.6	5.0	4.6
• Ph.D. degree			–	–	–	–	2.1	2.1

Employee Characteristic	Organization A		Organization B		Organization C		Organization D	
	Grievance Procedure		Grievance Procedure		Grievance Procedure		Grievance Procedure	
	Users	Nonusers	Users	Nonusers	Users	Nonusers	Users	Nonusers
Work experience (with the employer, in years):								
· < 1 year	2.1	4.0	3.6	7.3	4.7	6.6	4.2	7.3
· 1-2 years	9.4	7.2	16.3	15.7	15.4	17.1	7.6	9.2
· 3-5 years	11.3	8.3	31.7	28.3	24.6	21.7	17.3	16.4
· 6-8 years	20.6	16.7	19.7	18.9	22.4	18.7	21.7	18.5
· 9-12 years	29.1	26.6	16.2	14.6	16.4	14.6	21.5	18.3
· 13-15 years	17.9	23.2	7.8	9.5	9.6	10.5	15.9	14.4
· 16-19 years	5.4	7.3	2.9	3.4	4.6	6.3	6.7	7.6
· 20-24 years	2.7	4.2	1.3	1.5	2.0	3.3	2.7	4.2
· 25-29 years	1.3	2.1	0.4	0.6	0.3	1.2	1.8	2.7
· 30+ years	0.2	0.4	0.1	0.2	0.0	0.0	0.6	1.4
N	452	414	364	344	326	318	382	368

Table 6.4
Regression Coefficients on Grievance
Procedure Usage, by Organization,
1980-1983

(t-values in parentheses)

Independent Variable	Organization A	Organization B	Organization C	Organization D
Age (in years)	-3.26* (-2.15)	-2.84* (-2.02)	-4.31** (-2.63)	-3.10* (-2.12)
Sex (male = 1 female = 0)	+0.17 (+1.62)	+0.36** (+2.94)	+0.19* (+1.92)	+0.28** (+2.64)
Race (black = 1, others = 0)	+0.27** (+2.73)	+0.22* (+2.39)	+0.29** (+2.83)	+0.24* (+2.51)
Education (in years of schooling)	+2.95* (+2.14)	+3.22* (+2.36)	+3.47** (+2.68)	+3.53** (+2.81)
Work Experience (in years)	+1.43 (+1.21)	+1.61 (+1.35)	+1.54 (+1.29)	+1.52 (+1.61)
R^2	.42	.39	.45	.51
N	866	708	644	750

 * Significant at $p =< .05$
** Significant at $p =< .01$

grievance processing occurs in all four organizations. Additionally and because organizations A and C require informal discussion of grievances at the first step of their respective procedures, some data are available on the extent of informal grievance handling. For the 1980-1983 period, these data indicated that on an annual basis approximately 42 percent of all steelworkers (in Organization A) and 34 percent of all hospital employees (in Organization C) "filed" grievances in that they discussed a workplace or employment issue with their immediate supervisors. Further, schoolteachers employed by organization D were surveyed (by the school district and the teachers' union jointly) in 1982 to determine the extent of informal grievance settlement. This survey found that approximately 23 percent of all teachers had initiated grievance discussions with (the equivalent of) their immediate supervisors. Still further, interviews with three management officials and four union officials conducted during this study indicated that between 16 and 21 percent of all department store employees in Organization B annually initiated informal grievance discussions with their immediate supervisors. In other words and confirming a point that has been made in other studies, a substantial (if not precisely known) amount of informal grievance handling apparently does occur in U.S. industrial relations.

Table 6.5
Regression Coefficients on Grievance Procedure Usage, All Employees in Four Organizations, 1980-1983

(t-values in parentheses)

Independent Variable	All Employees in Four Organizations
Age (in years)	-3.62**
	(-2.73)
Sex (male = 1, female = 0)	+0.36**
	(+2.83)
Race (black = 1, others = 0)	+0.26*
	(+2.57)
Education (in years of schooling)	+3.24*
	(+2.49)
Experience (in years)	+1.31
	(+1.15)
Industry (steel = 1, others = 0)	+0.42*
	(+2.45)
R^2	.45
N	2968

* Significant at p =< .05
** Significant at p =< .01

Next, consider the true nonusers of grievance procedures in the organizations studied here. Do these employees simply not encounter workplace issues or problems that would lead them either informally to discuss or formally to file grievances, or do other factors determine their nonuse of the procedure? The aforementioned survey conducted by organization D sheds light on this question. Among 625 teachers surveyed (of whom roughly 65 percent had not initiated informal or formal grievance usage between 1980 and 1983), 16 percent indicated that they had no employment-related issue that warranted initiation of a grievance; 12 percent said that they had asked their immediate supervisor for clarification of a personnel or employment policy; 10 percent said that a grievance wasn't worth filing because "management wouldn't change its mind" or "the chances of winning were small"; 6 percent said that either school policy or the collective bargaining agreement excluded employment-related issues of special concern to them; and 18 percent indicated that they feared "management reprisal" if a written grievance was filed.

This last point was further supported by the responses of some union officials and even certain management representatives in these four organizations to questions posed during interviews conducted for the present study. Six union officials and five management officials who were interviewed mentioned the "fear of" or the "potential for" managerial reprisal as a reason why employees did not initiate grievance discussions or processing. This point will be further discussed and, in a limited sense, tested later in this chapter. For now, the significance of the discussion is to support the importance of "unobservable events" in analyzing and assessing grievance procedures. Put differently, it is a relatively straightforward matter to identify grievances actually filed and to distinguish the characteristics of grievance procedure users from those of nonusers. It is far more difficult, however, to understand why nonusers refrain from using a procedure that has been negotiated on their behalf by their bargaining representatives.

GRIEVANCE ISSUES AND EMPLOYEE CHARACTERISTICS

What kinds of issues are taken up in the grievance procedures studied here? The relevant data for the 1980-1983 period are presented in Table 6.6 for eight major categories of grievances in the four organizations. In Organization A, the steel company, issues concerning pay and work, working conditions, and discipline accounted for fully three-fifths of all grievances filed between 1980 and 1983. Issues of pay and work and working conditions were also leading subjects of grievance issues in Organization C, the nonprofit hospital, as were performance and mobility issues; together, these three categories accounted for 55 percent of all grievances filed in Organization C. In Organization B, the retail department store, issues of performance and mobility, pay and work, benefits, and discipline represented two-thirds of all grievances filed between 1980 and 1983. In Organization D, the school district, performance and mobility issues were most often the subject of grievances during the 1980-1983 period, followed by working conditions and supervisory relations issues.

Detailed Grievance Issues

As to more detailed grievance issues, safety and health-related issues predominated in the steel company. Examination of grievance files and interviews with union and management officials indicated that exposure to dangerous substances, inadequate ventilation, inadequate machinery safeguards, and inadequate treatment of minor on-the-job injuries were the most common allegations made by steelworkers who filed griev-

Table 6.6
Distribution of Grievance Issues, by
Organization, 1980-1983
(in percent)

Grievance Issue	Organization A	Organization B	Organization C	Organization D
Pay and Work	21%	17%	18%	12%
· Pay rate, grade and level	7	3	3	3
· Overtime assignment	6	2	3	1
· Job classification	3	3	3	4
· Job assignment	5	9	9	4
Benefits	14%	16%	11%	13%
· Vacation	4	6	4	3
· Holidays	2	1	1	1
· Personal leave	5	6	3	4
· Seniority	2	1	2	3
· Medical, life insurance and pension benefits or coverage	1	2	1	2
Working Conditions	17%	13%	19%	15%
· Safety and health	12	3	4	7
· Work hours	3	6	4	1
· Work lead	2	4	11	7
Performance and Mobility	9%	17%	18%	21%
· Performance appraisal	2	8	4	3
· Promotion	1	3	8	3
· Transfer	2	1	3	10
· Training	1	2	3	2
· Layoff	2	2	0	2
· Recall	1	1	0	1
Discipline	22%	15%	9%	10%
· Supervisor	9	5	4	5
· Demotion	8	6	3	3
· Discharge	5	4	2	2
Discrimination	3%	6%	7%	6%
· Sex	1	3	2	2
· Race	2	2	3	2
· Age	0	1	2	2
Management Rights	6%	4%	7%	9%
· Subcontracting	3	1	2	3
· Technological change	2	2	3	4
· Other	1	1	2	2
Supervisory Relations	8%	12%	11%	14%
TOTAL	100%	100%	100%	100%

ances. Challenges to supervisors and demotions for alleged violations of company policies and practices were also heavily represented in specific steelworker grievances.

In the retail department store, job assignment, performance appraisal, and vacation and personal leave scheduling were the most common of the detailed grievance issues. Department store employees relatively frequently filed grievances over changes of work location and departments within stores, management denial of personal leave, and management scheduling of vacations with little or no employee consultation. Also a frequent subject of grievances in the retail department store were performance evaluations, which were alleged by some employees to be unfair and not communicated to them in direct or timely fashion. Interview data indicated that management was most strongly concerned about the performance evaluation grievances, given that store policy called for employees to be directly informed of their appraisals by supervisors and, indeed, for employees to "sign-off" on their appraisals.

In the nonprofit hospital, work load, job assignment, and promotion were the most common detailed subjects of grievances. Examination of grievance records and interviews with management and union officials indicated that nurses were most prone to file grievances over patient loads that were alleged to be too large, too unevenly distributed among nurses, and subject to change without adequate employee consultation or advance communication. Interestingly, three of the five management officials interviewed tended to support nurses' claims in this regard, although they pointed to the inability to control local community demand for hospital services as a major contributing factor to this problem. Nurses also frequently claimed that certain promotions were unfairly denied them and that favoritism characterized the granting of some promotions.

In the school district, transfers, safety and health, and work load were the most common detailed subjects of grievances. Examination of grievance files and interviews with union and management officials indicated that, in this school district, teachers consistently alleged that transfers were made without adequate consultation and with a retribution motive, personal safety was not adequately addressed by management, and class size was both too large and too varied. All of the management officials interviewed disagreed strongly with teacher claims about transfers, as did three of the five union officials interviewed, but there was some agreement among management officials and strong agreement among union officials with teacher allegations about matters of personal safety and class size.

To gain better understanding of the determinants of issues raised in the grievance procedures, two sets of regression analyses were performed. The first of these treated major category of grievance as the dependent variable and characteristics of grievance filers as independent variables. For this purpose, the data were pooled across the four years and the four organizations studied. The results of this analysis (which are not reproduced here) showed that younger workers filed significantly more disciplinary grievances than middle-aged or older workers; female employees filed significantly more performance and mobility grievances than male employees; members of minority groups filed significantly more discrimination and supervisory relations grievances than white employees; more-experienced employees filed significantly more benefits grievances than less-experienced employees; and blue-collar employees filed significantly more pay and work grievances than white-collar employees.

The second regression analysis used detailed grievance issue as the dependent variable, which was then regressed on grievance filer characteristics. These results (which, again, are not reproduced here) showed that more-educated employees were significantly more likely than less-educated employees to file grievances over promotion and transfer issues; women were significantly more likely than men to file grievances over work load, job assignment, and promotion issues; men were significantly more likely than women to file grievances over pay rate and overtime assignment issues; blue-collar workers were significantly more likely than white-collar workers to file grievances over issues of safety and health; and younger employees were significantly more likely than older employees to file grievances over suspension and demotion (but not discharge) issues.

Because the unit of analysis in this portion of the study is the individual grievance filer, it was deemed inappropriate to enter an industry/sector control variable into the analysis. Yet, because employee characteristics differ considerably among the four organizations, separate regressions were run for each of these organizations, with major grievance categories and detailed grievance issues again serving as dependent variables and employee characteristics again serving as independent variables. These results generally supported the findings from the pooled regressions. Of particular interest are the regression results for grievance filers in Organization B, the retail department store, where the work force composition was approximately two-thirds women and one-third men during the 1980-1983 period. In this organization and controlling for the size of the two groups, women were significantly more likely than men to file grievances over job assignment, personal leave, performance appraisal, and discrimination issues, whereas men were significantly more likely than women to file grievances over suspension, demotion, pay rate, and layoff issues. Content analysis of grievance files in Organization B also showed that supervisory relations grievances were significantly more likely to be filed when the supervisor and the subordinate were of opposite sexes than when they were of the same sex. While the data underlying this individual grievance filer analysis have certain limitations, and while the organization from which they were drawn cannot be claimed to be representative of the other organizations included in this chapter (or in this study more broadly), these findings nevertheless suggest that the types of grievances filed by unionized workers vary systematically by individual employee characteristics. This, in turn, supports the inclusion of employee characteristics variables (apart from organizational characteristics variables) in models of grievance procedure dynamics and effectiveness.

GRIEVANCE ISSUES AND LEVELS OF SETTLEMENT

How does the level of grievance settlement vary, if at all, by grievance issue? Recall that each of the organizational grievance procedures included in this study contains four steps for the processing of written grievances. Table 6.7 presents data on the level of grievance settlement by category of grievances over the 1980-1983 period in each of the four organizations studied.

Consistent with the data in Table 6.2, the data in Table 6.7 show that about 55 percent of all grievances filed by employees of these four organizations were settled at the first written step of the grievance procedure. However, the level of grievance settlement clearly varies by category of grievance issue in each of these organizations. For example, a majority of grievances over working conditions issues were settled beyond the first grievance step in Organizations A, C, and D, while a majority of grievances over issues involving management rights were settled at the first step of the grievance procedure in all four organizations.

Organization A

In Organization A, the steel company, fully 40 percent of all grievances over working conditions issues were settled at the last two steps of the grievance procedure. Indeed, 10 percent of these grievances went to arbitration during the 1980-1983 period. Discipline-related grievances were also relatively frequently appealed to the last steps of the grievance procedure in Organization A. In contrast, more than three-fifths of all grievances over pay and work, benefits, and discrimination issues in Organization A were settled at the first step of the grievance procedure, and less than 1 percent of these grievances were taken to arbitration.

Table 6.7
Level of Grievance Settlement, by Step in Four
Organizations, 1980-1983
(in percent)

Grievance Issue	Organization A Step #				Organization B Step #				Organization C Step #				Organization D Step #			
	1	2	3	4	1	2	3	4	1	2	3	4	1	2	3	4
Pay and Work	61%	25%	13%	1%	49%	21%	22%	8%	47%	25%	23%	5%	54%	23%	20%	3%
Benefits	64%	24%	11%	1%	50%	20%	22%	8%	62%	22%	16%	0%	62%	18%	19%	2%
Working Conditions	39%	21%	30%	10%	54%	28%	16%	2%	49%	27%	19%	5%	44%	20%	28%	8%
Performance and Mobility	58%	27%	13%	2%	50%	22%	21%	7%	48%	27%	21%	4%	52%	16%	26%	6%
Discipline	44%	22%	26%	8%	54%	27%	17%	2%	58%	26%	15%	1%	59%	18%	18%	5%
Discrimination	64%	22%	14%	0%	58%	26%	15%	1%	64%	19%	16%	1%	56%	20%	22%	2%
Management Rights	52%	29%	14%	5%	60%	29%	9%	2%	60%	24%	14%	2%	58%	21%	20%	1%
Supervisory Relations	58%	27%	13%	2%	62%	25%	12%	1%	57%	25%	17%	1%	60%	15%	22%	3%
TOTAL	54%	25%	17%	4%	56%	24%	16%	4%	54%	26%	18%	2%	56%	18%	22%	4%

Organization B

In Organization B, the retail department store, about 4 percent of all grievances filed between 1980 and 1983 went to arbitration, the same percentage as in Organization A. However, 8 percent of all grievances over pay and work and benefits issues were taken to arbitration, and another 22 percent of these grievances were settled at the third step of the grievance procedure. About the same pattern of grievance-settlement level occurred for performance and mobility related grievances. Conversely, grievances over working conditions and discipline issues, which often reached the last steps of the grievance procedure in Organization A, were most commonly settled at the first step of the grievance procedure in Organization B, and less than 2 percent of these grievances were decided in arbitration. In fact, the same can be said about grievances over discrimination, management rights, and supervisory relations issues in Organization B; between 80 and 90 percent of these grievances were settled at the first two steps of the grievance procedure.

Organization C

Organization C, the nonprofit hospital, had the lowest grievance arbitration rate over the 1980-1983 period among the four organizations, namely, 2 percent. However, 44 percent of all grievances filed by employees of this organization were settled at the second and third steps of the grievance procedure—a higher percentage than in the three other organizations. Grievances over pay and work, working conditions, and performance and mobility were especially prone to be carried beyond the first step of the grievance procedure in Organization C, and about 5 percent of all grievances involving these categories of issues were settled in arbitration. In contrast, about three-fifths of all grievances over benefits, discipline, discrimination, management rights, and supervisory relations were settled at the first step of the grievance procedure in this organization.

Organization D

In Organization D, the school district, the grievance arbitration rate, 4 percent, equalled that in Organizations A and B, but this was the only organization studied in which the percentage of grievances settled was larger at the third than at the second step of the grievance procedure. Fully 22 percent of all grievances were settled at the third step of Organization D's grievance procedure, and approximately one-third of all grievances over working conditions and mobility issues were taken to the last two steps of the grievance procedure. Conversely, between 75 and 85 percent of all grievances over pay and work, benefits, discipline, discrimination, management rights, and supervisory relations were settled at the first and second steps of Organization D's grievance procedure.

Regression analysis, using level of grievance settlement as the dependent variable and category of grievance issue as independent variables, largely confirmed the main conclusion drawn from the frequency data presented in Table 6.7 (the full regression results are not presented here). Namely, certain categories of grievances are more likely than others to be settled at higher steps of the grievance procedure in these four organizations. However, the addition of employee characteristics variables to the regressions showed that women and white-collar employees were significantly more likely than men and blue-collar employees to pursue grievances over performance mobility, pay and work, and discrimination to the final steps of the grievance procedure. Further, the regressions also showed that men and blue-collar employees were far more likely than women and white-collar workers to take grievances over discipline issues to the third and fourth steps of the grievance procedure. However, there were no significant differences between men and women or between blue-collar and white-collar employees with respect to the appeal of grievances over working conditions issues to higher steps of the grievance procedure. Finally, older employees were significantly more liklely than younger employees to appeal grievance rulings over benefits issues to higher steps of the grievance procedure. In contrast, younger employees were significantly more likely than older employees to take grievances over pay and work and discipline issues to the third and fourth steps of the grievance procedure.

BEYOND GRIEVANCE SETTLEMENT: BEHAVIOR AND CONSEQUENCES

The grievance procedure literature offers a dominant perspective on the value of the procedure, namely, that grievances provide important information to management about workplace problems—information that can be used for corrective purposes so as to improve employee and organizational performance (Gandz, 1979; Kuhn, 1961; Slichter, Healy, and Livernash, 1960). From this perspective, grievance handling and settlement is a positive process that perhaps can be analogized to other organizational systems and processes that are intended to improve and sustain the organization's achievement of goals and objectives. In this light, employees who bring workplace problems to the fore via the grievance procedure should, at best, be commended or otherwise rewarded for doing so. At worst, grievance filers should be treated no differently than employees who do not file grievances.

An alternative perspective on the grievance procedure, nested in organizational punishment and industrial discipline research (Arvey and Jones, 1985; O'Reilly and Weitz, 1980; Selznick, 1969), suggests that employees who file grievances (or otherwise call attention to organizational problems) run the risk of being judged negatively by employers, that is, of being labeled complainers, troublemakers, even misfits. From this perspective, the grievance procedure and grievance users do not provide useful information so much as they impose costs on the organization that reduce the organization's overall effectiveness. Both the professional and popular management literature that deal with employee loyalty can also be interpreted to support this view of the consequences of grievance filing (Hirschman, 1970; Ewing, 1977, 1983).

From an empirical perspective, the important question becomes "What happens to employees who use the grievance procedure?" Apparently, no study has addressed this question, yet responses to the question are essential if collective bargaining specifically and employee relations more broadly are to be connected to organizational outcomes and not treated solely as organizational processes.

In an attempt to answer this question in the present study, grievance and personnel records for selected grievance filers in each of the four organizations were extracted and analyzed. All grievances filed in 1982 by these employees were treated as "baseline" data, and these were joined to performance evaluation, work attendance, promotion, and turnover data for the 1981-1983 period. Next, comparable data for the same years were extracted for samples of comparable employees (that is, members of the respective bargaining units) in each of the four organizations who did not file grievances during 1982. Using these data and analyzing them for the three-year period in question, we sought to determine whether or not employers treated grievance procedure users differently from nonusers after grievances were settled. In research design terminology, 1981 is the pre-experimental year, 1982 is the experimental year, and 1983 is the post-experimental year in this portion of the study. What do these data tell us?[3]

Consider first the data presented in Table 6.8. They show that, in 1981, grievance procedure users (in 1982) had slightly higher performance ratings, proportionately fewer work absences, lower involuntary turnover rates, and a higher incidence of promotions than nonusers of the grievance procedures.[4] Chi-square tests indicated that these differences were uniformly significant in the cases of turnover and promotions, insignificant in the case of performance rating, and significant in the case of work attendance in Organizations A and C only. The overall picture that emerges in 1981, that is, immediately prior to grievance usage, shows that subsequent users of the grievance procedures were somewhat more stable employees and more upwardly mobile employees than nonusers of the grievance procedures.

Table 6.8
Personnel Data and Activity for Grievance Procedure Users and Nonusers in Four Organizations, 1980-1983

Year and Personnel Activity	Organization A		Organization B		Organization C		Organization D	
	Grievance Users	Grievance Nonusers	Grievance Users	Grievance Nonusers	Grievance Users	Grievance Nonusers	Grievance Users	Grievance Nonusers
1981								
Performance Rating (mean rating, 1 = low and 5 = high)	3.3	3.2	3.4	3.3	3.8	3.5	3.6	3.7
Work Attendance (in percent of days absent or late)	7.6	8.2	6.2	6.7	4.7	5.3	6.8	7.2
Turnover (in percent)	7.3	8.1	8.2	8.7	9.2	9.6	7.3	7.7
Voluntary	5.2	5.0	5.7	6.3	7.2	6.4	6.4	6.0
Involuntary (excluding retirements)	2.1	3.1	2.5	2.4	2.0	3.2	.9	1.7
Promotion (in percent, promoted to higher step, grade or position from prior year)	4.6	3.5	6.3	5.8	5.1	4.8	10.3	9.4
1982								
Performance Rating	3.4	3.5	3.5	3.3	3.6	3.4	3.5	3.5
Work Attendance	6.9	7.3	5.9	6.4	4.6	5.0	6.5	7.0
Turnover	6.1	6.6	7.0	7.6	8.1	8.5	6.4	6.9
Voluntary	3.3	3.2	4.2	4.3	5.8	6.0	3.9	4.0
Involuntary	2.8	3.4	2.8	3.3	2.3	2.5	2.5	2.9
Promotion	3.1	2.7	4.9	4.7	4.3	4.5	7.3	7.9
1983								
Performance Rating	3.2	3.6	3.3	3.7	3.4	3.6	3.3	3.6
Work Attendance	7.3	7.1	6.0	6.2	4.9	5.1	7.1	6.8
Turnover	6.7	6.4	7.9	7.3	8.6	8.4	6.8	6.3
Voluntary	5.2	3.5	5.8	4.3	6.9	5.7	4.8	3.8
Involuntary	1.5	2.9	2.1	3.0	1.7	2.7	2.0	2.5
Promotion	1.6	2.8	4.2	5.6	3.8	4.6	5.6	8.2
N	212	195	186	174	164	157	183	172

This picture was not substantially different in 1982, though promotion rates were no longer significantly different between grievance procedure users and nonusers, except in Organization D where they slightly favored nonusers. By 1983, however, the picture had changed. Relative to nonusers of the grievance procedures, the users had significantly lower performance ratings in two of the organizations, significantly lower promotion rates in all four organizations, and significantly higher voluntary turnover rates in three of the four organizations studied. Moreover, the earlier record of better, if nor uniformly significantly different work attendance among grievance procedure users changed markedly in all four organizations. In two of these organizations, the work attendance differentials declined and in two other cases they were reversed. Recognizing that the "stock" of employees in each of these organizations changed somewhat from year to year, these data nevertheless provide some support for the second of the two dominant perspectives discussed above, namely, that the use of the grievance procedure brings about some employer retribution or employee disillusionment, or both.

To test this proposition further, the data in Table 6.8 were reassembled and reanalyzed to take account of both the levels of grievance settlement and the outcomes of grievance cases filed in the four organizations during 1982. Table 6.9 presents these data for the post-settlement period, that is, 1983. In all cases, performance ratings were higher for employees whose grievances were settled at the first step than at higher steps of the grievance procedure. Using chi-square tests, these differences were found to be statistically significant in Organizations B and D. Even more marked were the differences in performance ratings by the outcome of grievance cases; those ratings were consistently and statistically significantly higher for employees whose grievances were decided in favor of the employer than for employees whose grievances were decided in their own favor.

Work attendance data indicate that the incidence of absences and lateness was higher for grievants whose cases were settled at the first step than for grievants whose cases were settled at later steps of the grievance procedure, and the differences were statistically significant in Organizations B and C. In three of the four organizations studied, grievants whose cases were decided in favor of the employer had significantly higher work-absence (and lateness) rates than grievants who won their cases.

Voluntary employee turnover was insignificantly lower among grievants whose cases were settled at the first step than at higher steps of the grievance procedure. However, voluntary turnover was significantly higher among grievants who lost their cases than among grievants who won their cases. Further, the data show that, in Organizations A and B, the incidence of promotions was significantly higher among grievants

Table 6.9
Personnel Data and Activity in 1983 for
Grievance Procedure Users in 1982

Personnel Activity	Organization A				Organization B				Organization C				Organization D			
	Grievance Settled at Step Steps		Decision in favor of		Grievance Settled at Step Steps		Decision in favor of		Grievance Settled at Step Steps		Decision in favor of		Grievance Settled at Step Steps		Decision in favor of	
	1	2,3,4	G*	E*	1	2,3,4	G*	E*	1	2,3,4	G*	E*	1	2,3,4	G*	E*
Performance Rating (mean rating, 1 = low and 5 = high)	3.4	3.1	3.0	3.5	3.5	3.1	2.9	3.6	3.6	3.3	3.1	3.7	3.5	3.1	3.0	3.6
Work Attendance (in percent of days absent and late)	7.6	7.0	6.8	7.8	6.3	5.6	5.5	6.4	5.3	4.6	4.4	5.5	7.3	6.9	6.8	7.4
Turnover (in percent)	6.5	6.9	5.5	7.8	7.6	8.2	7.5	8.4	8.3	8.7	7.9	9.4	6.5	7.1	6.3	7.4
Voluntary	4.9	5.5	3.6	6.0	5.7	6.0	5.4	6.7	6.7	7.1	6.4	7.7	4.6	5.0	4.4	5.2
Involuntary	1.6	1.4	1.9	1.8	1.9	2.2	2.1	1.7	1.6	1.6	1.5	1.7	1.9	2.1	1.9	2.2
Promotion (in percent promoted to higher step, grade or position from prior year)	2.0	1.1	.7	1.2	4.5	3.8	3.3	4.9	3.9	3.6	3.2	4.3	5.8	5.4	4.7	6.5
N	126	86	100	112	104	82	90	96	86	78	77	87	101	82	86	97

*G = grievant, E = employer

whose cases were settled at the first step of the grievance procedure than among grievants whose cases were settled at higher steps. Moreover, in all four organizations, the promotion rate was significantly higher for grievants whose cases were decided in favor of the employer than for grievants who won their cases. These findings appear to strengthen the notion that grievance procedure users run considerable personal and organizational risks when they appeal grievances to higher levels, especially when they prevail in grievance settlement.

Still more evidence on this matter may be adduced by examining the post-grievance settlement behavior of supervisors and managers against whom grievances were filed in these four organizations. In this respect, data extraction and partitioning procedures comparable to those used to study grievance filers were adopted. Specifically, personnel records for 1983 were obtained from each of the four organizations for samples of supervisors and managers who were and were not direct parties to employee grievances filed in 1982. These data are shown in Table 6.10.

Supervisors and managers who did not have grievances filed against them in 1982 had higher performance ratings one year later than supervisors and managers against whom grievances were filed in 1982. The differences ranged between .4 and .6 on a five-point scale and were statistically significant in three of the four organizations. Also in three of the four organizations, work attendance data showed that supervisors and managers against whom grievances were filed in 1982 had a lower incidence of absent and late days in 1983 than supervisors and managers against whom grievances were not filed in 1982. However, this difference was statistically significant only in Organization D, the school district.

Turnover of supervisors and managers in 1983 was uniformly higher among those against whom grievances were filed in 1982 than among those against whom no grievances were filed. In terms of voluntary turnover, the difference between the two groups of supervisors and managers was significant only in Organization A, the steel company. However, the differences in involuntary turnover—a category that consists largely of discharges—between the two groups of supervisors and managers were statistically significant in three of the four organizations (the school district being the exception). Taken together, these data suggest that supervisors and managers against whom grievances are filed subsequently leave their employers *and* are separated by their employers more often than supervisors and managers against whom grievances are not filed. Relatedly, supervisors and managers who are not directly involved in grievance actions are subsequently promoted more often than supervisors and managers who are direct parties to grievance actions. The promotion differences were statistically significant in three of the four organizations studied (the steel company being the exception).

Table 6.10
Personnel Data and Activity in 1983 for Supervisors and Managers, by Grievance Involvement in 1982

	Organization A Supervisors-Managers		Organization B Supervisors-Managers		Organization C Supervisors-Managers		Organization D Supervisors-Managers	
	DPG*	NDPG*	DPG*	NDPG*	DPG*	NDPG*	DPG*	NDPG*
Performance Rating (mean rating, 1 = low, 5 = high)	3.6	4.1	3.3	3.9	3.5	4.0	3.4	3.8
Work Attendance (in percent of days absent or late)	4.4	4.7	5.2	5.5	6.1	5.9	5.6	6.2
Turnover (in percent)	3.3	2.0	4.1	3.0	5.2	3.9	3.4	2.7
Voluntary	1.4	.7	1.8	1.3	1.6	1.3	1.6	1.2
Involuntary (excluding retirements)	1.9	1.3	2.3	1.8	3.6	2.6	1.8	1.5
Promotion (in percent promoted to higher step grade or position from prior year)	1.7	2.0	2.2	2.9	3.1	3.6	2.4	2.9
N =	82	80	64	60	52	50	66	62

*DPG = direct party to grievances, NDPG = non-direct party to grievances

These data add to the picture that emerged earlier of the individual consequences of grievance activity in work organizations. It appears that both employees who file grievances and the supervisors and managers against whom grievances are filed behave differently and are treated differently by their employers in the post-grievance settlement period than employees and supervisors/managers who are not involved in grievance activity. In particular, the work attendance record of grievance procedure users worsened in the post-settlement period, both absolutely and relative to nonusers; the grievance users' promotion rates and performance ratings declined, both absolutely and relative to nonusers; and the grievance users' turnover rates increased relative to those of nonusers. These effects of grievance procedure usage are larger still for grievants who appeal their cases to higher steps of the grievance procedure and for grievants who win their cases. Similarly, supervisors and managers involved in grievance cases subsequently received proportionately fewer promotions and lower performance ratings than supervisors and managers who were not involved in grievance cases; the former also experienced greater voluntary and involuntary turnover than the latter in the post-grievance settlement period.

As a final test of the consequences of grievance procedure usage and involvement, 1983 data for samples of grievance procedure users and nonusers and for supervisors/managers who were and were not directly involved in grievance activity in 1982 across the four organizations were extracted from the larger data set and pooled for the purpose of conducting regression analyses. Separate regressions were run using performance ratings, promotion rates, work attendance, and turnover rates as dependent variables.[5] The independent variables included various personal characteristics as well as a grievance procedure usage dummy variable. The results of this analysis are shown in Table 6.11.

Note first that none of the independent variables was significant in the work attendance equation, and that variations in promotion rates and turnover rates were better explained by the independent variables than were variations in performance ratings and work attendance. Second, age was significantly positively related to promotion rates and negatively related to turnover rates. Third, and related, men were more likely to be promoted and less prone to turnover than women. Fourth, education and work experience were significant explanatory variables in only one of the four equations. Fifth, and most important, grievance procedure users and supervisors/managers who were direct parties to grievances received lower performance ratings, had lower promotion rates, and were significantly more prone to turnover than their counterparts who were not directly involved in grievance activity. Additionally (and not shown in Table 6.11), grievance procedure users and their supervisors/managers were significantly more likely to have been separated from their employers—that is, to have experienced involun-

Table 6.11
Regression Coefficients on Performance Ratings, Promotion Rates, Work Attendance, and Turnover among Employees and Supervisors/Managers in 1983, by Grievance Involvement in 1982

(t-values in parentheses)

Independent Variable	Performance Rating	Dependent Variable Promotion Rates	Work Attendance	Turnover Rates
Age (in years)	+1.74 (+0.68)	+2.79* (+1.99)	-1.63 (-0.84)	-3.42** (-2.73)
Sex (male = 1, female = 0)	+1.43 (+0.61)	+2.69* (+2.02)	+1.23 (+0.43)	-2.95* (-2.31)
Race (black = 1, others = 0)	-0.09 (-0.17)	-1.03 (-0.47)	-0.82 (-0.29)	-1.73 (-0.79)
Education (in years of schooling)	+2.45 (+1.76)	_2.83* (+2.11)	+0.79 (+0.32)	+1.76 (+0.50)
Work Experience (in years)	+1.69 (+0.61)	+2.04 (+1.39)	+1.40 (+0.42)	-3.41* (-2.30)
Grievance Procedure (usage/involvement = 1, nonusage/noninvolvement = 0, for 1982)	-3.23* (-2.28)	-4.12* (-2.74)	-1.47 (-0.57)	+3.41** (+2.17)
R^2	.32	44	.26	.40
N	1642	1626	1634	1564

* Significant at $p =< .05$
** Significant at $p =< .01$

tary turnover—than grievance procedure nonusers and supervisors/ managers who were not directly involved in grievance activity. These findings provide additional confirmation of the fact that considerable risk is involved for users of (direct participants in) the grievance process in the sense that their post-grievance settlement behavior and treatment by employers is different from and less favorable than that experienced by grievance procedure nonusers (non-direct nonparticipants).

GRIEVANCE SPILLOVERS TO THE BARGAINING PROCESS

In all four organizations studied, interview data and organizational records indicated that certain notably contentious grievance issues were later interjected into the collective bargaining process. For example, in Organization A, the steel company, a wildcat strike over employer-initiated changes in workplace technology and job design occurred in 1982, and the strike itself was preceded by a surge of grievances over the same issues. Both steel company and steel union officials interviewed indicated that the enlarged grievance activity and the work stoppage were instrumental to the parties' subsequent (that is, 1983) negotiations over technological change and job design issues. Examination of the collective bargaining agreements negotiated by the parties in 1977, 1980, and 1983 showed that only in the last of these agreements were specific provisions included that dealt with technological change and job redesign.

In Organization B, the retail department store, a surge of job assignment and promotion-related grievances in 1980 and 1981 apparently led to the negotiation in 1982 of specific contractual provisions that addressed both of these issues. Four management representatives who were interviewed specifically observed that the company's management had long opposed negotiations over job assignments and promotions, but then altered this position in 1982 in response to the enlarged volume of grievances in the two preceding years. Again, examination of the 1982 contract and three predecessor labor agreements revealed that only the latest of these agreements included specific provisions dealing with job assignments and promotions.

In Organization C, the nonprofit hospital, the 1983 labor agreement between nurses and hospital management included specific provisions dealing with patient loads, job assignments, and promotions. In 1982, this hospital experienced both a substantial increase in grievances over these issues as well as a two-day "sick out" of nurses that was aimed at inducing the hospital to reduce patient loads and adopt new promotional criteria. Both the hospital managers and union officials interviewed in the course of this study judged the increased volume of grievances in the prebargaining period to have strongly contributed to the adoption of new contract language to deal with patient loads, job assignments, and promotions. A comparison of three predecessor agreements with the 1983 labor agreement showed that only the last of these dealt explicitly with patient loads and promotion criteria.

In Organization D, the school district, grievances over safety conditions and transfer policy predominated in the early 1980s (see Table 6.6), and apparently led to the negotiation in 1983 of new provisions to deal with these issues. Interviews with school district administrators and teachers' union officials indicated that the combination of numerous grievances over safety and transfer issues and the resignation of several highly rated teachers in 1981 and 1982 were instrumental to the negotiation in 1983 of new contractual provisions to deal with these issues. In fact, both school district administrators and union officials explicitly stated that grievances were carefully examined in preparing for the 1983 negotiations. A comparison of the 1974, 1977, 1980, and 1983 teacher labor agreements in this school district showed that only the last of these contracts dealt specifically with both safety and transfer issues.

AN OVERALL ASSESSMENT

These experiences of four organizations in four different industries and sectors suggest several lessons about the role and function of the modern grievance procedure. First, at a macro-organizational level, the grievance procedure does indeed appear to provide useful information for the reappraisal and sometimes redesign of employee relations policies and practices. Each of the four organizations included in this study had one or more experiences with grievance filing and settlement in the early 1980s that led to the restructuring of policies dealing with technological change, job design, promotions, performance evaluations, job assignments, work load, workplace safety, and employee transfers. Furthermore, management officials in three of the four organizations indicated in interviews that they had mounted new supervisor and management training and development programs in direct response to issues raised in the grievance procedure.

Second, the use of grievance procedures to influence collective bargaining confirms that the grievance procedure can properly be conceptualized as part of the negotiating process. While the work of Kuhn (1961), among others, attests to the fractional bargaining aspects of grievance procedures in certain manufacturing industries, the findings of the present study suggest that such fractional bargaining is both a more widespread and more enduring phenomenon. Put differently, collective bargaining in each of these organizations is not a periodic once-every-three-years event but, instead, is a continuing, if not fully continuous, process.

Third, the positive organizational consequences of grievance activity in the four organizations studied here must in some respects be offset against the apparent negative individual consequences of grievance procedure usage and settlement. The data presented in this chapter clearly indicate that some organizational retribution is meted out to employee grievants—especially grievants who pursue their cases to higher steps of the grievance procedure and grievants who win their cases. Compared to nonusers of the grievance procedure, grievance users experienced higher post-settlement voluntary turnover rates, lower performance ratings and promotion rates, and larger amounts of work absenteeism and lateness.

Fourth, negative individual consequences of grievance procedure involvement are also apparent for supervisors and managers against

whom grievances are filed. Compared to supervisors and managers who
were not directly involved in grievance cases, the involved supervisors
and managers had lower post-settlement performance ratings, lower
promotion rates, and higher turnover rates, especially involuntary turnover rates. It appears, therefore, that both employees and their direct
supervisors/managers run considerable individual risks when they
become directly involved in grievance activity and resolution.

This last point may be especially helpful in understanding why scholars
and practitioners universally contend that most grievances are settled
either informally without entering the grievance process or at the first
step of the grievance procedure. Recall that the first grievance step
usually involves oral discussion between the employee and the immediate supervisor. No doubt some employees are not able to reduce their
grievances to writing, some decide that the written (as opposed to the
oral) facts do not justify pursuing a grievance, some decide that the time
involved in pursuing a formal grievance is excessive, and some accept
supervisors' explanations of particular personnel actions and decide not
to pursue their grievances beyond the oral-discussion stage. But the
results of this study suggest that the fear of organizational reprisal after
using the grievance procedure, particularly after winning a grievance, is
a primary factor in the decision of most employees to settle grievances
at the informal-discussion stage of the process. Moreover, the preference for informal grievance settlement is a joint preference in that it is
shared by supervisors/managers, who also recognize the risks they run
in becoming formally involved in grievance activity.

INTERVIEW PERSPECTIVES

It is useful to recall that, in all four of the organizations studied here,
management and union officials observed that most grievances were
settled informally via oral discussions between employees and supervisors. Those interviewed gave various reasons for this judgment, including some that were noted earlier, but several of the union and management officials also commented (though not always directly) on the
risk factor in grievance involvement. According to a hospital manager,
for example:

Grievances are tricky things. On the one hand, we've got a structured procedure for resolving disputes with our nurses, and the procedure is helpful to us in
spotting certain problems and in correcting certain abuses. On the other hand,
the grievance procedure is often used for frivolous purposes and unwarranted
claims, and we don't think that nurses who continually file grievances are the
type of people we want to put in charge of things. As a matter of fact and despite

the fact that, like most hospitals, we sometimes have nursing shortages, an unhappy nurse is probably better off leaving here, and we've occasionaly taken steps to see that that happens.

A manager of a department store offered this observation about the grievance procedure:

A supervisor who is the subject of grievances creates red flags for us. We expect supervisors to be able to handle most employee relations issues, and if they can't then we question whether or not they have a future with us. I know that grievances are sometimes filed with no justification whatsoever, but on the whole a supervisor who avoids formal grievances looks a lot better to management than a supervisor who's tying up his and our time in grievance hearings.

A teachers' union official commented as follows:

I've been involved in grievance handling for a long time. After a while, you learn that certain teachers come to understand how to get things done informally, while others go by the book. Now, the same is true of school administrators, but I represent teachers and I would admit privately that a teacher who constantly raises grievances is, in effect, telling me that he doesn't understand how things operate. You're better off settling these things informally, and if you can't maybe you ought to look into another line of work. I certainly wouldn't promote such a teacher if I were running a school.

A steelworkers' union official had this to say about the grievance process:

It's true that management brings a lot of grievances on itself, but this isn't one-sided by any means. Some workers insist on filing grievances even when they are without merit, and some workers can't understand why a case is decided against them. I know that I wouldn't want these people working for me if I were running the business, especially when you have other employees who are able to settle their grievances without making a big thing of it. When you think about it, the grievances that are really important to us are the ones that we can use in collective bargaining. In those cases, the grievance process is very valuable to us.

While clearly anecdotal, these comments nevertheless support the view that individual employees as well as individual supervisors and managers who become involved in formal grievance activity run certain risks in terms of their future standing and careers with their employers. Recognizing this, most employees and most supervisors/managers display risk-averse behavior by settling most grievances informally. Ironically, when certain grievance issues are widely shared by employees and when these grievances are vigorously pursued, it becomes possible to influence the collective bargaining agenda and bargaining outcomes. This, in turn, offers a certain collective or organization level protection to employees and also to supervisors/managers who, according to the data presented here, are likely to suffer negative consequences after grievances are resolved. Such is the apparent real-life duality of grievance procedures in the modern private and public sectors.

NOTES

1. The opportunity to conduct this analysis arose during the later stages of survey and interview data collection, when it become known that certain organizations were willing to provide the relevant grievance data and access to personnel files. Consequently, data were obtained for the 1980-1983 period, or one year beyond the data base assembled for the grievance effectiveness portion of this study. As a condition of obtaining the post-grievance settlement data, neither the individual employers nor the characteristics of the employing organizations are identified. Selected characteristics of these organizations are available from the authors, on written request.

2. The details of these data collection procedures were more fully described in Chapter 3.

3. These data were made available for selected plants, facilities, and office locations in each of the four organizations. The selection of non-grievance user samples was based on an every nth name randomization process applied to alphabetized lists of employees, excluding grievance users; the total sample sizes are shown in Table 6.8. Certain analyses to be reported later in this chapter will use subsets of these samples. Keep in mind that, from a strict research design perspective, these are all "purposive" rather than random samples.

4. In this analysis, involuntary turnover includes retirements, discharges for cause, layoffs, deaths, and certain other separations, but not transfers and promotions; voluntary turnover refers to employee quits.

5. The samples differ by the particular dependent variable shown in Table 6.11 due to missing or incomplete grievance and personnel file data.

7
Conclusions
and Implications

Having completed our analysis of the data bases assembled for this study, we now ask, "What have we learned about the modern grievance procedure in the United States?" We will attempt to answer this question in the present chapter. We begin by reconsidering the significance of our study for the larger body of literature on the unionized grievance procedure. Then we summarize and briefly discuss the major findings and conclusions reached during the study. Last, we identify and elaborate on the implications of our work for future grievance procedure research and practice.

SIGNIFICANCE OF THE STUDY

The central purpose of this study was to analyze the dynamics of grievance procedures in four unionized industries and sectors during the early 1980s (that is, 1980-1983). The four research settings were chosen because they provided a rich mix of industries and sectors, occupational groups, labor organizations, and employer organizations.

The steel industry is the most traditional of these industries and sectors, with its heavily male blue-collar production work force long having been represented by an industrial union. In contrast, retail department stores employ primarily white-collar workers, of whom a large proportion are female, but these employees are also organized on an industrial union model. The unionization of nurses is a relatively recent phenomenon, and this study provided a rare opportunity to examine grievance procedure dynamics involving a predominantly female quasi-professional work force and not-for-profit hospital employers.

Professionally oriented and relatively highly educated public school teachers are heavily unionized, and their grievance interactions with school administrators and managers were also examined in this research.

To our knowledge, this is the first study of grievance procedures to cover portions of the private, public, and not-for-profit sectors, whether in the United States or abroad. Beyond this, however, we believe that the study is important for three additional reasons. First, it contrasts with the largely descriptive literature on the grievance procedure. Second, it responds to a number of shortcomings that have characterized grievance procedure research. Third, the research design employed in this study is distinctive compared to those used in other grievance studies. Each of these points is more fully discussed in the remainder of this section.

Contribution to the Grievance Literature

In this study, we sought to provide several contributions to the literature on unionized grievance procedures. Foremost, perhaps, the study provides something of an update of the early classic studies of grievance procedures conducted by Slichter, Healy, and Livernash (1960) and Kuhn (1961). The data used in those studies are now 30 to 40 years old, so there has been a long-standing need to take a fresh look at the grievance procedure—and not just in one industry or sector. This we have attempted to do, not by replicating older studies but by studying some newer as well as some traditonal labor-management relationships and by using newer types of analysis. We believe that our study and the associated data give the reader a reasonably clear picture of how modern grievance procedures operate.

In terms of its breadth, the present study is probably less reflective of the typical U.S. grievance study than of the works of Thomson and Murray (1976) and Hyman (1972), which were done in Britain. Comparison of our data with theirs should enable the reader to identify similarities and differences between the U.S. and British grievance systems.

Another contribution of this study lies in its emphasis on quantification rather than description. Our extensive review and assessment of the grievance procedure literature showed that much of it has concentrated on describing how the grievance procedure works or should work. Invariably when something was quantified in those studies it was the grievance rate, with an occasional foray into measuring certain personal characteristics of grievants. We have sought to go beyond this to wrestle with the knotty issues involved in quantitatively measuring the behavioral actions and interactions of the parties that are germane to grievance handling and resolution.

This is not to say that quantification is to be valued for its own sake or that it can't be overdone. The excellent quantitative study by Kuhn (1961), for example, shows how it is possible to advance our understanding of the grievance process by perceptively interpreting field data and observations. In fact, we have built on Kuhn's work and that of other industrial relations researchers by conducting a multistage field study. Nevertheless, we have more strongly emphasized quantification than previous researchers because we believe that, within limits, it too can advance our knowledge of the dynamics and consequences of grievance activity.

Much of the quantification in this research has been directed toward the measurement of grievance procedure effectiveness. For the most part, the descriptive literature has simply not recognized the variety of ways and measures by which one may judge the effectiveness of the grievance procedure. Typically, a single measure, such as the grievance rate or the arbitration rate, has been used to draw conclusions about grievance procedure effectiveness. More recently, a few researchers (Briggs, 1984; Anderson, 1979) have experimented with multiple measures of effectiveness, and we have also built upon their work in the present study. But to the best of our knowledge, this is the only research that quantifies and combines behavioral with attitudinal measures of grievance procedure effectiveness.

All of this quantification, however, has not (we hope) blinded us to the fact that for many, especially those who are directly involved in grievance activity, effectiveness is in the eye of the beholder. Union officials, for example, are likely to view the grievance procedure as a means of exercising leadership as well as showing the union's membership that the union can deliver an important service to them. Management, in contrast, is most likely to view the grievance procedure as a means of assuring continuity of production (of goods or services) during the life of the labor agreement. Management may also value highly the information received through the grievance procedure because it is helpful for monitoring supervisory behavior.

In still sharper contrast, the individual employee is most likely to be concerned about due process considerations in the operation of the grievance procedure—and also, of course, with the outcomes of grievance cases. Put differently, grievance procedure effectiveness is most likely to be assessed by an employee according to whether or not he feels that he has had his "day in court." The public at large is most likely to assess grievance procedure effectiveness in terms of the checks and balances (that is, the industrial jurisprudence) associated with a particular procedure, and with whether or not the procedure prevents strikes and lockouts. Thus, we recognize that any attempt to construct and quantify multiple measures of grievance procedure effectiveness is bound to simplify the reality of day-to-day labor-management relations. But this should not serve as an excuse for failing to develop more robust measures of grievance procedure effectiveness. Indeed, we have shown how it is possible for employers and unionists to monitor the effectiveness of their own grievance procedures on a systematic basis by using some of the measures of effectiveness developed in this study.

Note, further, that by highlighting the measurement of grievance procedure effectiveness, we also call attention to what is not known about the effectiveness of the tens of thousands of grievance procedures (other than those we looked at) that exist in U.S. labor-management relations. Recall our estimate that perhaps as many as 1.2 million written grievances were filed in the unionized sector in 1986—and that the total might approach 11 million if grievances not put into writing were accurately accounted for! These are staggering figures even if one thinks only of the time and effort of management and union officials required to resolve grievances. It would indeed be helpful if the measures of grievance procedure effectiveness developed here could be applied to a larger portion of the voluminous grievance activity that occurs in the United States.

Shortcomings of Prior Research

The computerized literature search that was conducted at the outset of this study revealed that about 60 empirical articles and books have been published on the unionized grievance procedure in the United States during the post-World War II period. This translates into about one and one-half studies per year, or far less than the average dozen or more books, articles, and monographs on collective bargaining that have been produced annually over the same time period. The irony and the unfortunate aspect of this is that contract administration is a continuous event that takes considerably more of the time and attention of union and management officials than does periodically recurring collective bargaining.

The grievance procedure literature has several shortcomings in addition to those noted above, and we attempted to address some of these in the present research effort. First, and probably foremost, grievance studies have been largely atheoretical. This was true some ten years ago, as pointed out by Thomson and Murray (1976), and it is by and large still true today, although studies by Katz, Kochan, and Gobeille (1983), Freeman and Medoff (1984), Norswsorthy and Zabala (1985), and especially Ichniowski (1986) and Ichniowski and Lewin (1987) have some theoretical content. However, none of these studies sought to measure grievance procedure effectiveness or to test for the effects of grievance resolution on post-settlement outcomes at the individual employee level. We have suggested, but have not provided full tests of, theoretical frameworks for the analysis of grievance procedure effectiveness and post-grievance settlement outcomes. For example, we began with a systems model of the grievance procedure, subsequently revised it, and then used the revised model as a foundation to direct the questions asked in the field study. We believe that this and related theoretical frameworks merit further testing in other contexts and with richer data sets; we hope that other researchers will join us in building on this work and further developing theoretical insights into the grievance procedure.

Second, few grievance studies have tested more general models of collective bargaining and industrial relations. In this study, we provided partial tests of the exit-voice model of unionism (Hirschman, 1970; Freeman and Medoff, 1984) at the individual employee level. As will be more fully discussed later, some of the evidence produced in this study did not support the exit-voice model.

Third, relatively few grievance procedure studies have specified or tested a priori hypotheses. In the few cases where hypotheses were tested, the data base and the number of variables incorporated into the analysis were quite small. Our analytical framework, large number of variables, and sizable data base allowed us to specify and test several key hypotheses about grievance procedure effectiveness.

Fourth, the vast majority of prior grievance studies were typically limited to reporting grievance activity among factory employees in one or two plants or companies, or public employees in one or another federal agency, municipal government, or school district.[1] This study, in contrast, ranged across numerous employers, plants, facilities, locations, occupations, and labor organizations. In particular, it covered portions of three major economic sectors (private, public, and nonprofit) and incorporated grievance data involving blue-collar, white-collar, professional, and supervisory-managerial employees.

Fifth, most prior studies have employed fairly modest research designs that specify a small number of independent variables and one or, at most, two dependent variables. A few studies (such as Fleischman and Harris, 1962) have gathered substantial data on the characteristics of grievants and non-grievants, but these are the exceptions. The present study featured a comprehensive research design that will be further discussed below.

Sixth, most previous grievance studies made limited use of questionnaires, interviews, or company or union records. No study of which we are aware has combined these three types of data. In contrast, we sought from the outset of this study to use a variety of data collection methods and to assemble several data bases in order to gain a better understanding of the dynamics of the grievance procedure.

Seventh, we found that most grievance studies used limited descriptive statistics and simple tests of statistical significance. In many cases this was understandable, given the limited data available for analysis. In this study, we purposely used a variety of statistical methods, including chi-square, factor analysis, correlation analysis, and multiple regression analysis. We did so because we wanted to identify those variables that had the strongest influences on grievance procedure effectiveness and post-grievance settlement outcomes. In other words, these statistical methods helped us to conduct actual behavioral research on the grievance procedure.

Distinctiveness of the Research Design

A few of the distinctive features of the research design used in this study have already been mentioned. Here we elaborate on some additional features of the design that underscore its distinctiveness within the larger body of grievance procedure research.

First, our research involved a multistage field study with three major components. Initially we conducted a large-scale mail survey of union and management officials in each of four industries and sectors. This was followed by 36 semistructured interviews with union and management officials who had primary responsibility for grievance handling within their organizations. Then, content analysis of grievance files and personnel records in one employer organization in each of the four industries/sectors was undertaken. This procedure in particular enabled us to collect data unobtained in previous studies. Moreover, all of these data were gathered directly from the parties rather than relying on secondary sources. We are not aware of any other grievance study that is as comprehensive as this one—although a few other researchers (for example, Peach and Livernash, 1974) have used two of the afore-mentioned approaches to data collection.

A second distinctive feature of the research design involved the use of multiple measures of grievance procedure effectiveness, including both behavioral and attitudinal measures. The behavioral measures were the grievance rate, level of settlement, speed of settlement, and the arbitration rate; the attitudinal measures were the perceived importance of grievance issues and the perceived equity of grievance settlement. We know of no other study that has used this combination or variety of effectiveness measures.

Third, drawing on the empirical research that was assessed in our literature review, we identified and tested some sixteen independent and intervening variables that were expected to influence grievance procedure effectiveness. Each independent variable was assigned to one of five major groupings: characteristics of the bargaining unit, grievance policies of the parties, characteristics of the labor-management relationship, grievance procedure characteristics, and environmental influences. Hypothesis testing was carried out only in those cases in which the research literature supported the a priori specification of a relationship between particular variables.

Fourth, the fact that data were collected from organizations and respondents in four industries and sectors permitted us to generalize the findings beyond a single organization, sector, or occupational group. This, too, sets the present study apart from virtually all others.

Fifth, this study is also distinctive because of our having used random rather than convenience samples for most phases of the research.[2] The literature review clearly indicated that most researchers have been limited to reporting data for one or two organizations that were typically located close to the researcher or that were willing to provide access to the researcher. Additionally, many researchers have obtained grievance data from management officials or union representatives, but not both. Our study was designed to obtain survey and interview data from large samples of management and union officials.

Sixth, we used model testing and model refinement as means of better understanding the questionnaire data. Few other grievance studies have featured the reanalyses of initial data to refine an analytical model, provide a cross-check on the data, or gain additional insights into grievance handling dynamics. This procedure enhanced our confidence in the empirical findings of the study.

Seventh, the survey questionnaire was carefully pretested among experienced academics and union and management officials. This procedure led to the development and use of eight separate versions of the basic questionnaire (one for union and for management respondents in each industry/sector), which helped us address the variation among organizations, industries/sectors, and union and management respondents.

Eighth, although the interview method of data collection has been used by other grievance procedure researchers, rarely have in-depth interviews or interview comments been reported. In this study, we developed a semistructured interview schedule that elicited certain systematic responses across the 36 union and management officials who had major responsibility for their grievance handling systems. The interviews, which lasted two hours on average, provided an important means of interpreting and supplementing the survey questionnaire data.

Ninth, the most distinctive feature of this study and its accompanying research design concerned the consequences of grievance procedure usage. By obtaining personnel file information for samples of grievance procedure users and nonusers in four separate organizations, we were able to identify and measure the post-settlement behavior of employees and supervisors/managers in terms of job performance, promotions, work attendance, and turnover. To our knowledge, this is the first study to have systematically addressed the question, "What happens to grievance procedure users following grievance settlement?"

In the next section, we turn to a summary of the major findings and conclusions drawn from this multistage field study of grievance procedures in steel, retail stores, hospitals, and local schools.

MAJOR FINDINGS AND CONCLUSIONS

Based on the data and analyses presented in Chapters 4 through 6, we believe that we have learned a great deal about the unionized grievance procedure. However, some caveats are in order. To begin with, even though we covered portions of four industries and sectors, we did not go beyond them so that, like other studies, our findings are not fully generalizable to other U.S. settings or to grievance procedures abroad. Next, most of our data were obtained for the 1980-1982 period, during which a major economic recession occurred. We were able (partially) to test only one hypothesis about the effects of recession on grievance activity, so our findings may not be representative of grievance filing and settlement during periods of economic expansion or stability. Additionally, we were not able to determine how representative the survey respondents were of the total samples to whom questionnaires were sent. This may not, at first glance, appear to be a major problem because the percentages of usable questionnaire responses ranged between 53 and 64 percent for the eight groups of management and union respondents surveyed (see Table 4.1). Indeed, for the samples as a whole, about 58 percent of the management officials and 57 percent of the union representatives completed the questionnaires. These are impressive response rates for social science research, especially in light of the length and complexity of the questionnaires (Kerlinger, 1973). Nevertheless, concepts of grievance procedure effectiveness are at an early stage of development, and the findings reported here about such effectiveness might not apply (or apply as fully) to the nonrespondent individuals and organizations.

Key Findings

Turning to the major findings of the study, the following stand out:

1. With respect to the four behavioral measures of procedure effectiveness, the steel industry had the highest grievance rate, level of settlement, and arbitration rate; retail department stores had the lowest grievance and arbitration rates and the fastest speed of settlement; and nonprofit hospitals had both the lowest average step of grievance settlement and the slowest speed of settlement.

2. Grievance activity declined over the 1980-1982 period in the organizations that supplied survey data, with the nonprofit hospitals constituting a slight exception in this regard. We judged this to have resulted in

part from economic recession, although other factors were undoubtedly at work. This is a provocative finding because it is well known that voluntary employee turnover, or exit, declines during recessions so that employee exercise of voice might be thought to rise during such periods (Freeman, 1980). However, our findings do not support this proposition.

3. Combining union and management responses for the perceptual/attitudinal measures of grievance procedure effectiveness, we found that steel industry respondents gave the highest ratings to grievance issue importance while department store respondents had the lowest importance ratings. Union and management respondents in the public schools had the highest equity of grievance settlement ratings, while respondents from department stores and hospitals had the lowest equity ratings.

4. Correlation analysis showed that some of the measures of grievance procedure effectiveness were significantly intercorrelated. Specifically, seven of the fifteen correlations attained statistical significance (see Table 4.4). Unsurprisingly, the highest correlation coefficients were those for (a) the level of settlement and the speed of settlement, and (b) the importance of grievance issues and the arbitration rate. Still, the coefficients were not so large as to cause us to discard one or more of the effectiveness measures.

5. Factor analysis indicated that the sixteen original independent variables could be grouped into four categories, which were identified in the revised model of grievance procedure effectiveness presented in Chapter 1. These were management characteristics, union characteristics, labor-management characteristics, and characteristics of the grievance procedure. In this regard, empirical support varied by the particular measure of grievance procedure effectiveness employed. In general, the strongest support was found in correlations with the grievance rate, level of settlement, and speed of settlement, where between one-half and two-thirds of the coefficients attained statistical significance.

6. Several independent variables stood out when regression analysis was used to test the full systems model of the grievance procedure (see Figure 1.2). In particular, the following variables consistently yielded the most significant regression coefficients: management and union policies to take certain grievances as far as possible through the procedure, a union policy of committing grievances to writing, adversarial labor relations, the supervisor's knowledge of the grievance procedure, and the use of expedited arbitration. In general and except for the supervisor's knowledge of the grievance procedure, these variables were likely to result in higher grievance and arbitration rates, higher-step settlements, slower settlements, greater perceived importance of grievance issues, and higher perceived equity of grievance settlement. The supervisory knowledge variable was negatively related to the behavioral

measures of grievance procedure effectiveness and positively related to the attitudinal measures. (These and other findings for this portion of the study are summarized in Table 7.1.)

Two modified models of grievance procedure effectiveness were also tested in this study. The first of these excluded those independent variables that were seldom if ever significantly associated with the six measures of grievance procedure effectiveness. The second model involved the decomposition of the six dependent variables into three combinations of two variables each. We concluded that the full model captured the largest amount of variance in grievance procedure effectiveness. Note that the R^2s in these empirical tests ranged between 34 percent for the equity of grievance settlement and 53 percent for the grievance rate.

7. Our field and interview data confirmed a notion expressed in the grievance literature (Kuhn, 1961), namely, that grievance activity is greatest during the period immediately preceding the negotiation (or renegotiation) of a labor agreement. Across the four industries and sectors, unionized workers signal their discontent with one or another condition of employment or the contract itself by filing more written grievances than normal. Such activity also appears to reflect a more general building of militancy among the rank and file, especially where a strike is contemplated or undertaken.

8. When the model of grievance procedure effectiveness was tested separately for the individual industries and sectors included in the study, some notable similarities and differences were found. Significant regression coefficients were obtained for between one-third and one-half of the independent variables for at least one grievance procedure effectiveness measure in each of the four industries and sectors. As to other independent variables, few if any significant regression coefficients were obtained on any effectiveness measure in any of the four industries and sectors.

While the variables that were most consistently significantly related to grievance procedure effectiveness in the aggregate analysis (see number 6) were also generally significant in the individual industry/sector regression tests, certain other variables had differential effects by industry/sector. As examples, union steward knowledge of the grievance procedure was associated with lower grievance rates, a lower average settlement step, and faster grievance settlements in nonprofit hospitals; the cost of grievance handling was negatively associated with four measures of grievance procedure effectiveness in steel manufacturing; and occupational diversity of the bargaining unit was associated with slower grievance settlements and a lower perceived equity of settlement only in retail department stores (see Table 5.7).

The strongest support for the full model of grievance procedure effectiveness was obtained in nonprofit hospitals and steel manufacturing, where about 50 percent of the regression coefficients were significant.

Across specific measures of grievance procedure effectiveness, we were able to explain between 30 and 60 percent of the variance in the four industries and sectors. While all of this attests to the difficulty of generalizing about grievance procedures, we believe that we have accurately identified some of the key variables that affect grievance procedure effectiveness irrespective of industry and sector.

9. It is probably not surprising that grievance issues vary in frequency and rate of grievance filing across the industries and sectors. Discipline, health and safety, working conditions, and management rights issues were the most common subjects of grievances in steel manufacturing during the 1980-1982 period. Union security, working conditions, and work assignment issues predominated in retail department store grievances. In nonprofit hospitals, the most frequently grieved issues included discipline, working conditions, and workload. The predominant grievance issues in local public schools were working conditions, health and safety, and work assignments.

10. Contractual provisions for expedited arbitration were most prominent in steel manufacturing, least prominent in retail department stores. Skipping certain steps of the grievance procedure and shortening the time limits for grievance processing were the most common features of these expedited procedures. Grievances over discipline, strikes/lockouts, discrimination, management rights, subcontracting, and work load were the most likely to be excluded from expedited arbitration provisions.

11. The perceived importance of grievance issues and the perceived equity of grievance settlement were positively and linearly related in steel manufacturing, retail department stores, and local public schools. However, in nonprofit hospitals the relationship between these two variables was positive but curvilinear. In other words, those grievance issues that were judged to be of intermediate importance by management and union officials in the hospital sector were also viewed as resulting in the most equitable grievance settlements.

12. Grievance file and personnel data obtained from four organizations, one per each industry and sector, showed that grievance procedure users were more likely than nonusers to be young, male, black, and relatively better educated, and to be low- to mid-career service employees. It was also clear that the issues over which grievances were filed varied significantly by the age, race, sex, education, and work experience of employees. Further, internal organizational surveys (not conducted by the authors) indicated that some nonusers of the grievance procedures did indeed have a variety of "felt" grievances, but they also had several reasons for not filing grievances, of which the single most prominent was fear of management reprisal.

13. There was substantial evidence of negative outcomes for grievance

.procedure users in the immediate post-grievance settlement period. Using 1982 as the baseline or "experimental" year of grievance filing, we found that, compared to control groups of nonusers, grievance procedure users had significantly lower job performance ratings, lower promotion rates, poorer work attendance, and higher turnover in the year following grievance settlement (that is, 1983). These effects were even more pronounced for employees who pursued their grievances to higher steps of the procedures and those who won their grievances.

14. A comparable post-grievance settlement analysis was performed for samples of supervisors/managers who were and were not direct parties to grievance activity in the four organizations in 1982. This analysis clearly showed that supervisors/managers against whom grievances were filed had lower job performance ratings, lower promotion rates, poorer work attendance, and higher turnover, especially involuntary turnover, in the year after grievance settlement than supervisors/managers who were not directly involved in grievance activity. In both the supervisor/manager and employee analyses, little or no significant pre-baseline-year differences between the experimental and control groups were found with respect to performance ratings, promotion rates, work attendance, and turnover rates.

15. Interview data obtained from management and union officials in each of the four organizations showed that the grievance process is closely linked to the collective bargaining process. In each organization and labor relationship, certain specific issues raised in the grievance process during the early 1980s subsequently became subjects of bargaining and were often translated into contractual provisions. These issues and provisions dealt with such matters as technological change, job design, job assignments, promotions, work load, health and safety, and employee transfers.

Key Conclusions

What conclusions can be drawn from the empirical findings just summarized? The following conclusions seem especially notable. First, the concept of grievance procedure effectiveness can be operationalized and measured using survey instruments. While any one of the effectiveness measures employed in this study has inherent limitations and is open to criticism, it is nevertheless critical to have multiple measures of effectiveness. Much of the research on grievance procedures has relied on a single measure of grievance activity or effectiveness—typically the grievance rate—but even the authors of that research acknowledge the shortcomings of single measure studies (Dalton and Todor, 1981; Fleishman and Harris, 1962). This problem has been overcome in the present study.

Second, it has been shown that behavioral-type measures can be combined with perceptual/attitudinal-type measures of grievance procedure effectiveness. In other words, "real" data can be combined with "non-observable" data to study this topic—and presumably other industrial relations topics as well.[3] This is especially important when one is dealing with a constructed dependent variable, such as effectiveness, as distinct from a directly observable dependent variable, such as the grievance rate.

Third, we have shown that grievance settlement can be treated and measured as an intervening variable, which is associated with certain "final" outcomes. Specifically, the grievance user-nonuser analyses clearly indicated that certain "negative" consequences accrue to those who are directly involved in grievance activity, and this includes both employees and their supervisors/managers. These findings also validate the systems model of the grievance procedure employed here, which links determinants of grievance activity and settlement to post-grievance settlement outcomes.

Fourth, despite differences along a variety of dimensions, grievance procedures and grievance data from several industries and sectors can be combined and subjected to theoretical and empirical analysis. Most grievance studies have been confined to a single industry, firm (or government agency), or plant (facility) location, which severely limits the generalizability of the research. By drawing on data from 77 separate employers, six major unions, hundreds of survey and interview respondents, and thousands of grievance and personnel files, this study has yielded the most generalizable findings so far produced about the grievance procedure in the United States.

Fifth, expedited grievance procedures appear to be associated with higher levels of grievance procedure effectiveness. Specifically, such procedures contribute to faster grievance settlement and to heightened perceptions of the importance of grievance issues and the equity of grievance settlement. While certain limited evidence of the benefits of expedited grievance procedures has been assembled by other researchers (Sandver, Blain, and Woyar, 1981; Stessin, 1977; Zalusky, 1976), this is the first study to substantiate such benefits via quantitative analyses of a large data base drawn from several industries and sectors.

Sixth, there is little or no evidence from this study to suggest that employers (or unionists) wish to abandon or substantially modify existing grievance procedures. This is perhaps surprising in view of the expressed and documented desire of employers to avoid unions and disinvest in unionized facilities (Kochan, McKersie, and Cappelli, 1984). However, the post-grievance settlement analysis presented here can be interpreted to show that employers exercise some retribution against grievance filers, especially those who pursue their cases to higher levels of the grievance procedure and those who win their cases. In other words and framed sharply, employers apparently seek to rid themselves of (or punish) grievance activists irrespective of whether or not these same employers seek to rid themselves of unions. At the theoretical level, this evidence runs directly counter to the exit-voice explanation of union and firm behavior that has been offered by other researchers (Freeman and Medoff, 1984).

IMPLICATIONS FOR RESEARCH AND PRACTICE

What are the major implications of this study for grievance procedure research and practice? In part, this is a question best answered by the reader, but there are several such implications that we believe are worth noting here. The research implications will be taken up first, followed by the implications for practice.

Research Implications

In our judgment, the leading implication for research that stems from the present study concerns the treatment of grievance activity and settlement as an intervening variable. Put differently, most researchers have treated grievance filing, processing, and settlement as dependent variables and have sought to identify and explain the determinants of one or another of these dependent variables. In contrast, this research has shown how grievance activity can be linked to subsequent individual- and organizational-level outcomes, such as turnover, internal mobility, and job performance. We believe, therefore, that models of the griev- ance procedure should be revised to incorporate outcome variables asso- ciated with grievance activity. Katz, Kochan, and Gobeille (1983) and Ickniowski (1986), among others, have done this at the plant or establish- ment level, but no other researchers have done this at the individual level in unionized workplaces. If industrial relations research is to be able to contribute to outcome-type questions—if the research is to be able to address the "what difference does it make"-type question—then it is essential for grievance procedure researchers to strike a better balance between process- and outcome-oriented research. We have pro- vided one example of how this can be done.

Another research implication of this study concerns the level or unit of analysis. Most grievance research has focused on individual grievants and their immediate worksites. This study also used individual-level data, both in the survey and grievance-personnel file phases of the research, but the dominant orientation of the study was toward the organizational level. That is, we began by selecting samples of employers and union organizations and then selected samples of individual respondents. More or less the same procedure was followed in the post-grievance settlement portion of the research. Although we did not incorporate organization-level measures, per se, into this study, the individual-level data that were employed in terms of both grievance effectiveness and post-settlement outcomes have much more substantial organization-level implications than have heretofore been produced by grievance procedure research. In the future, grievance procedure research should include individual- and organizational-level variables so as to provide potentially more robust measures of grievance procedure determinants, effectiveness, and outcomes.

At the theoretical level, this study additionally suggests that several dominant perspectives on the grievance procedure merit further testing, especially simultaneously. For example, classic industrial relations treatments of the grievance procedure emphasize the procedure's conflict resolution and due process functions (Chamberlain and Kuhn, 1986). The labor-economics literature emphasizes the positive consequences of voice exercised through the grievance procedure—consequences such as reduced turnover and improved job performance (Freeman and Medoff, 1984). The organizational punishment–industrial discipline research calls attention to the sanctions meted out to organizational dissidents (Arvey and Jones, 1985; Scott, 1965). We have accumulated evidence that is partially consistent with the first and third of these perspectives and partially inconsistent with the second. However, we did attempt formally to test hypotheses derived from each of these perspectives. Such future hypothesis testing on multi-industry/sector data bases holds the potential for substantially advancing theoretical formulations about the grievance procedure.[4]

A substantial research opportunity for grievance procedure researchers appears to exist in the nonunion sector, where apparently a majority of large firms (and perhaps also government and nonprofit employers) have adopted grievance-like complaint and appeal systems for their employees (Berenbeim, 1980; Freedman, 1985). Lewin (1987a) has recently shown how the uses and consequences of these procedures can be subjected to the same type of analyses carried out in the present study. However, his data were limited to three large firms and, consequently, much more remains to be learned about the dynamics and outcomes of grievance-like procedures in the growing nonunion sector of the U.S. economy.

Finally, the validity and reliability of grievance procedure research, whether conducted in unionized or nonunion settings, could be significantly enhanced by the collection and analysis of longitudinal data. The present study has made some progress in this respect, especially in the post-grievance settlement portion of the research, but survey instruments basically yield only cross-sectional data (even when respondents are asked to recall grievance activity or events from prior periods). Thus, if grievance initiation, resolution, and outcomes are dynamic processes, as surely they must be, and if we are interested in measuring changes in independent, intervening, and dependent variables, as surely we are, then longitudinal studies of the grievance procedure are vital. The challenge here is for scholars to formulate and implement research designs, including most especially field studies, that emphasize data collection from multiple sources at multiple points in time. We fully recognize that this is not an easy task and is unlikely to be accomplished by individual scholars working alone. Nevertheless, it is precisely this kind of large-scale, field-based, longitudinal research that is required if we are to significantly advance both theoretical and empirical knowledge of the grievance procedure.

Implications for Practice

The initial implication of this study for grievance procedure practice flows directly from the last of the research implications noted. Specifically, employers and unionists who are involved in grievance activity would do well to forge closer links with researchers whose work holds the potential for improving the uses, functioning, and effectiveness of the grievance procedure. Certainly there are understandable requirements for the confidentiality of grievance (and personnel) files to be maintained, but researchers are generally uninterested in identifying individual grievants and their supervisors/managers, individual firms and unions, individual respondents to surveys, or individual interview subjects. Rather, the researcher's objective is to gain a better understanding of the uses and consequences of grievance procedures, and this should also benefit employers, union officials, and employees. But this can only occur if those who are engaged in grievance handling and who control the relevant records make the requisite data available to interested researchers. In other words, a closer link between the academic and practitioner communities must be formed if the type of grievance procedure research that has been advocated here is to be carried out. And, from a data availability standpoint, practitioners must be willing to do their share of the work required to forge this link.

In the same vein, employers (and probably also union officials) can potentially benefit by using existing internal data to assess the grievance procedure. Recall that, in the present study, virtually all of the grievance effectiveness and post-grievance settlement data were provided by respondent management and union officials. In other words, much of these data came from existing grievance and personnel files. There is no apparent reason why managers or managers and unionists together cannot use these data for their own purposes. The interviews we conducted clearly indicated that neither management nor union officials were aware of the negative consequences for users of the grievance procedure, yet it was their own grievance data that, when properly analyzed, attested to these consequences. We believe that management and union officials should treat grievance data as part of an employee relations information system, much in the same way that performance appraisal and turnover data are typically used in this regard. Thus, a clear implication of this study is that practitioners have at their disposal information that can be used to improve the functioning and effectiveness of the grievance procedure.

Also of importance to labor and management officials is the evidence showing that grievance activity increases as contract negotiations draw near. This evidence can be interpreted to support the adoption of multistage or even continuous bargaining so as to better integrate the issues raised in the grievance process with those treated in collective bargaining. Once more, if grievance activity is viewed from an informational perspective, the parties to a bargaining relationship can potentially benefit by more closely integrating the grievance and bargaining processes.

Related to this point is the evidence from this study showing that adversarial labor relations are consistently negatively related to both behavioral and attitudinal measures of grievance procedure effectiveness. We recognize that modifying adversarial labor relations, especially to achieve cooperative labor relations, is a formidable task, but other industrial relations research shows that this can be done—particularly when the parties are pressed to do so by external factors (Katz, Kochan, and Weber, 1985; Katz, Kochan, and Gobeille, 1983). Among the industries and sectors included in the present study, steel manufacturing probably offers the leading example of a recent movement from adversarial to more cooperative labor relations. The more general point or implication for practitioners is that grievance initiation, processing, settlement, and effectiveness are adversely affected by adversarial labor relations. Herein lies an incentive for the parties to attempt to develop alternative approaches to interorganizational relationships.

Indeed, one such alternative in the context of the grievance procedure is expedited arbitration. Recall that this form of grievance processing was significantly associated with more effective procedures, but also recall that several key types of grievance issues—for example, discharges—were excluded from expedited grievance processing. We believe that the parties to labor relations could substantilaly expand the scope of issues that are subject to expedited grievance processing without fundamentally sacrificing due process, record keeping, or other relevant considerations in the grievance procedure. Within the context of the present study, this recommendation is most germane to the parties in retail department stores and local public schools, who have a relatively low incidence and narrow scope of expedited grievance procedures. However, the recommendation is meant to apply to union and management officials in general.

The final implication of this study for practitioners stems from the findings about post-grievance settlement consequences. If grievance procedure users and their direct supervisors/managers do indeed suffer retribution from their employers, then middle- and senior-level management officials must consider whether or not corrective action is warranted. One reason for this is that a grievance procedure promises fair and ultimately neutral third-party resolution of workplace conflict, which contrasts strikingly with the evidence of post-grievance settlement consequences produced here. Another reason is that middle-and lower-level management may be exercising retribution against organizational dissidents, whereas senior management expects that this will not occur. Hence, an important question arises out of our findings concerning the ability of the management organization to coordinate employee relations policies and practices and to induce all levels of management to adhere to those policies and practices.

An alternative explanation of our post-grievance settlement findings is that grievance users and their direct supervisors/managers are, on average, less competent performers than their nonuser and nondirectly involved counterparts. This explanation is not supported by the data from this study, which showed no significant job performance rating differences between grievance procedure users and nonusers prior to grievance filing. Nevertheless, if such performance differences are claimed or thought to exist, then a clear implication of the present study is that performance appraisal systems and policies are not properly used until after grievances are filed. In other words, grievance activity "shocks" management into more parsimonious uses of performance appraisals. In any case, the post-grievance settlement findings of this study should, above all, alert practitioners to the unanticipated consequences of grievance filing and resolution.[5]

NOTES

1. See Table 2.1 for a summary of the relevant studies.

2. Recall that a randomization procedure was used in the survey portion of the research, as descibed in Chapter 3. However, purposive or convenience samples were used in the post-grievance settlement portion of the research, as described in Chapters 3 and 6.

3. See, for example, Lewin and Feuille (1983).

4. In this section, we have identified only a few of the possible theoretical

formulations about the grievance procedure. For other perspectives, see Ichniowski and Lewin (1987).

5. One additional unanticipated consequence in this regard is that employees (and supervisors/managers) will, over time, "learn" not to use the grievance procedure. For some evidence on this matter in nonunion settings, see Lewin (1987a, 1987b; Knight, 1986).

Appendix 1: Mail Questionnaires

MANAGEMENT QUESTIONNAIRE
STEEL COMPANIES

708 Uris Hall
Columbia University
New York, New York 10027

Attached is a questionnaire that we would like you to fill out and
return to us in the enclosed self-addressed envelope. The questionnaire
is part of a study, sponsored by the National Science Foundation (NSF),
of the modern grievance procedure in the United States. We are attempting to learn more about grievance handling in four sectors: steel,
retail trade, nonprofit hospitals and local public schools.

Your company has been chosen at random from a list of steel companies to receive and complete the questionnaire. The American Iron
and Steel Institute assisted us in preparing the list and is cooperating
in the study. We recognize that we are imposing on your time, but
believe that purposes for doing so are sound, and we will provide you
with a copy of our detailed report, which is scheduled for completion in
1985. We assure you in the strongest possible terms that the answers
you provide us will remain completely confidential. Further, no one
steel company among those being surveyed will be singled out for analysis; to the contrary, the analysis will be done only on aggregated data.

Your completion and return of this questionnaire is of great
importance to us. Note that your responses should pertain only to your
collective bargaining agreement with and grievance procedure for steelworkers. Also, please enclose a copy of the current collective bargaining agreement with the steelworkers. If one of your peers or someone on
your staff is more properly the person to complete the questionnaire,
please transmit it to him or her. If you have any further questions
about this questionnaire or the larger study of which it is a part,
please do not hesitate to write to me at the address shown above or call
me at the telephone number listed below. Thank you in advance for your
cooperation in this matter.

Sincerely,

David Lewin
Professor of
Business

Tel: (212) 280-4418

Enc.

Note: Please answer all questions as they pertain to steelworkers only!

I. Collective Bargaining Characteristics

1.   Who are the parties to this collective bargaining agreement?

Employer_____

Union   _____

2.   What is your position with the company?

Title   _____

3.   What is the composition of the bargaining unit? (check one)

Steelworkers only   _____

Steelworkers and other employees   _____
(e.g., maintenance personnel)

Other   _____
(please describe
  briefly)
          _____

          _____

          _____

4.   Does the collective bargaining agreement cover your company
     only? (check one)

          Yes_____

          No _____

     4A. If no, please briefly describe the employer coverage of
          the agreement. That is, indicate if the agreement has
          been negotiated by a multiemployer association.

          Specify_____

                  _____

5.   What are the beginning and ending dates of the collective
     bargaining agreement?

     Beginning date_____   Ending date_____

6. Please list the main job titles of steelworkers (and others) who are in the bargaining unit.

    _____

    _____

    _____

    _____

    _____

    _____

    _____

    _____

    _____

7. How large is the bargaining unit? That is, how many steelworkers are in the bargaining unit? (If other personnel are in the unit, list their total(s) separately.)

    Steelworkers   _____

    Others   _____

    Total   _____

8. Does the collective bargaining agreement contain a grievance procedure? (check one)

    Yes_____

    No _____

9. How many steps are there in the grievance procedure (including arbitration)? (check one)

    One   _____   Five _____

    Two   _____   Six _____

    Three_____   Seven or more _____

    Four _____

10. Is arbitration the final step of the grievance procedure?

        Yes_____

        No _____

10A. If no, please identify the last step

        Right to strike   _____

        Advisory arbitration   _____

        Binding arbitration   _____

        Joint committee vote   _____

        Other (briefly describe) _____

11. Is the first step of the grievance procedure a formal one in the
sense that a grievance form is filled out?

        Yes_____

        No _____

11A. If no, please explain briefly_____

_____

_____

_____

12. Does the collective bargaining agreement permit expedited grievance
processing?

        Yes_____

        No_____

12A. If yes, please indicate what type of expedited procedures exist.
(check those that apply)

        Skipping intermediate steps   _____

        Speeding up time limits   _____

        Use of informal hearings   _____

        Dispensing with transcripts   _____

        Other (please describe briefly) _____

_____

12B. If you answered yes to question 12, please list the types
of grievances for which expedited arbitration is permitted
(specify or describe briefly)

_____

_____

_____

_____

_____

12C. If you answered yes to question 12, please list the types of
grievances for which expedited arbitration is not permitted
(specify or describe briefly)

_____

_____

_____

_____

_____

13. If the collective bargaining agreement provides for grievance
arbitration, does it require

An ad hoc arbitrator   _____

A permanent arbitrator,
umpire or referee   _____

An arbitration panel   _____

Other (please describe briefly) _____

_____

14. What is the method of paying the arbitrator?

Parties pay equal shares   _____

"Losing" party pays all costs   _____

"Losing" party pays a majority
of the cost (e.g., 2/3 or 3/4 ─────────────────────────────

Other (please describe briefly) _____

_____

15. How common is the use of lawyers to represent your company in arbitration? (check one)

| Very | | | | Very |
Uncommon				Common
1	2	3	4	5

16. Are grievance meetings scheduled on a regular basis?

    Yes_____

    No _____

16A. If yes, how often? (please specify)

    _____

    _____

III.   Grievance Procedure Usage

17. Based upon your written records, how many grievances were filed in the last three years under this contractual grievance procedure? (give number)

    1982_____

    1981_____

    1980_____

18. Approximately what percent of the grievances in each of the last three years were settled in each of the time periods listed below? (give percentages)

Year	10 days or less	11-30 days	31-60 days	61-90 days	More than 90 days	Total
1982	_____	_____	_____	_____	_____	100%
1981	_____	_____	_____	_____	_____	100%
1980	_____	_____	_____	_____	_____	100%

19. Approximately what percent of the grievances in each of the last three years were settled at each of the steps listed below? (Give percentages)

Year	Step 1	Step 2	Step 3	Step 4	Step 5	Step 6	Step 7 or above	Total
1982								100%
1981								100%
1980								100%

20. Approximately what percent of the grievances in each of the last three years were handled by an expedited procedure? (Give percent)

    1982_____

    1981_____

    1980_____

21. Approximately what percent of the grievances in each of the last three years were settled in arbitration? (Give percent)

    1982_____

    1981_____

    1980_____

22. Please indicate the frequency with which each of the following issues was the subject of grievances during the most recent year for which data are available? (check one per issue, where relevant)

Specify year: 19____

		Very Rarely 1	2	3	4	Very Often 5
a.	Pay (wages or salaries)	___	___	___	___	___
b.	Job grading/work standards	___	___	___	___	___
c.	Technological change	___	___	___	___	___
d.	Work assignment	___	___	___	___	___
e.	Overtime	___	___	___	___	___
f.	Working conditions	___	___	___	___	___
g.	Discipline	___	___	___	___	___
h.	Performance evaluation	___	___	___	___	___

22.   (Continued)

		Very Rarely				Very Often
		1	2	3	4	5
i.	Layoff	___	___	___	___	___
j.	Recall	___	___	___	___	___
k.	Leave Time	___	___	___	___	___
l.	Health and safety	___	___	___	___	___
m.	Transfer	___	___	___	___	___
n.	Promotion	___	___	___	___	___
o.	Work hours	___	___	___	___	___
p.	Discrimination (race, sex, age, religion)	___	___	___	___	___
q.	Productivity	___	___	___	___	___
r.	Fringe benefits	___	___	___	___	___
s.	Union security	___	___	___	___	___
t.	Management rights	___	___	___	___	___
u.	Vacations/holidays	___	___	___	___	___
v.	Seniority	___	___	___	___	___
w.	Strikes/lockouts	___	___	___	___	___
x.	Other (please specify below)					

_____   ___ ___ ___ ___ ___

_____   ___ ___ ___ ___ ___

_____   ___ ___ ___ ___ ___

_____   ___ ___ ___ ___ ___

23. If the data are available, please provide a numerical breakdown of formal grievances filed over the last three years. Use either your own categories or those listed in question 22, items a through x.

Category	1982	Number filed in 1981	1980
_____	_____	_____	_____
_____	_____	_____	_____
_____	_____	_____	_____
_____	_____	_____	_____
_____	_____	_____	_____
_____	_____	_____	_____
_____	_____	_____	_____
_____	_____	_____	_____
_____	_____	_____	_____
_____	_____	_____	_____
_____	_____	_____	_____
_____	_____	_____	_____
_____	_____	_____	_____
_____	_____	_____	_____
_____	_____	_____	_____
_____	_____	_____	_____
_____	_____	_____	_____
_____	_____	_____	_____
_____	_____	_____	_____
_____	_____	_____	_____
_____	_____	_____	_____
_____	_____	_____	_____
_____	_____	_____	_____

24. Were there particular events, such as those listed below, that contributed to either a very high or very low rate/number of grievances
filed in each of the last three years? (check event and year or years).

Event	1982	1981	1980
Work force reductions	——	——	——
Wildcat strikes	——	——	——
Depressed economic conditions	——	——	——
Technological change	——	——	——
Job/work redesign and/or reallocation	——	——	——
Contract negotiation or rejection	——	——	——
Other (please describe below)			
_____	——	——	——
_____	——	——	——
_____	——	——	——
_____	——	——	——

25. Approximately what percentage of grievance arbitrations were
decided in favor of the company (management) in each of the last
three years? (give percent)

    1982_____%

    1981_____%

    1980_____%

26. How often do top management officials become involved in the
settlement of grievances? (check one)

    Never____   Seldom____   Occasionally____   Frequently____   Always____

27. Approximately what percentage of grievances in each of the last
three years were initiated by management? (give percent)

    1982_____%

    1981_____%

    1980_____%

28. For nonunion employees (hourly, salaried, management, etc.) of your company, are any of the following available? (check those that apply)

Open door policy _____

Appeal system with
steps to middle
management _____

Appeal system with
steps to top
management _____

Appeals or
grievance system
with arbitration
as the final step _____

Other (please
describe briefly) _____

_____

IV. Perceptions of the Grievance Procedure

29. In general, how important are the issues that are raised in the grievance procedure? (please circle one)

Very Unimportant				Very Important
1	2	3	4	5

30. In general, how has the importance of the issues raised in the grievance procedure changed over the 1980-82 period? (please circle one)

Issues have become much less important				Issues have become much more important
1	2	3	4	5

31. Without regard to the merits of the grievances filed or their settlements, how would you assess the grievance procedure in terms of the process it provides for grievance discussions? (please circle one)

Very Unfair				Very Fair
1	2	3	4	5

32. In your judgment, how equitable were grievance settlements in the most recent year for which data are available? (please circle one)

    Specify year: 19____

Very Inequitable				Very Equitable
1	2	3	4	5

33. If the data are available, how would you describe the changes in grievance settlements over the 1980-82 period? (please circle one)

Settlements have become much less equitable				Settlements have become much more equitable
1	2	3	4	5

34. In general, how would you describe the results of grievance discussions with the union at step one of the procedure? (please circle one)

Very Unfair				Very Fair
1	2	3	4	5

35. In general, how would you describe the results of grievance discussions with the union at intermediate steps of the procedure, that is at other than the first or last steps? (please circle one)

Very Unfair				Very Fair
1	2	3	4	5

36. In general, how would you describe the settlements resulting from the final step of the grievance procedure? (please circle one)

Very Unfair				Very Fair
1	2	3	4	5

37. Do you think that one or more steps of the grievance procedure should be eliminated?

     Yes_____

     No _____

37A. If yes, which step(s)?_____

_____

Why?_____

_____

_____

_____

38. How would you characterize the scope of issues covered by the grievance procedure? (please circle one)

Too Narrow				Too Broad
1	2	3	4	5

39. How would you characterize the time limits prescribed by the grievance procedure? (please circle one)

Too Short				Too Long
1	2	3	4	5

V. Grievance Procedure Functions, Management and Audit

40. In your opinion, what are the principal functions of the grievance procedure? (check those that apply)

A safety valve for employees to let off steam   _____

A mechanism to resolve labor-management disputes   _____

A vehicle for exercising power   _____

A method of providing justice   _____

A mechanism to maintain production   _____

40. (Continued)

Provides information for management   _____
  decision-making

Other (please describe briefly)_____

_____

_____

_____

_____

_____

41. Please briefly describe how the structure of the grievance procedure
     has changed, if at all, during the last three years.

_____

_____

_____

_____

_____

_____

42. Do you conduct annual or periodic audits of grievance procedure
     usage and outcomes?

          Yes_____

          No _____

42A. If yes, for which of the following purposes is the information
     generated by such audits used? (check those that apply)

     To prepare for arbitration cases   _____

     To formulate collective bargaining strategy   _____

     To identify trouble spots in employee relations   _____

     To appraise supervisory performance   _____

     To counsel/train supervisors   _____

     To redesign jobs and work   _____

42A. Continued

To redesign compensation systems _____

To change production methods _____

To change discipline policies _____

To change other employee relations policies
(please describe briefly) _____

_____

_____

_____

Other (please describe briefly) _____

_____

_____

_____

43. Do you maintain data on post-grievance settlement behavior of
employees and supervisors who were parties to grievances?

Yes_____

No _____

43A. If yes, please indicate which of the following post-grievance
settlement data are maintained? (check those that apply)

Employee productivity and/or performance _____

Employee absenteeism_____, tardiness_____, and turnover_____

Employee morale _____

Supervisor's enforcement of the labor agreement _____

Supervisory's enforcement of work standards _____

Other (Please describe briefly)

_____

_____

_____

44. In general, how knowledgeable are supervisors about the structure
    content and uses of the grievance procedure? (please circle one)

    Not at all   Completely
    knowledgeable   knowledgeable

        1   2   3   4   5

45. In general, how knowledgeable is management about the structure
    content and uses of the grievance procedure? (please circle one)

    Not at all   Completely
    knowledgeable   knowledgeable

        1   2   3   4   5

46. In general, how knowledgeable are employees about the structure
    content and uses of the grievance procedure? (please circle one)

    Not at all   Completely
    knowledgeable   knowledgeable

        1   2   3   4   5

47. If data are available, please provide the average cost to the
    company of grievance handling per employee.

        Average cost per employee_____   Year_____

48. If data are available, please provide the average cost to the
    company of grievance arbitration cases.

        Average cost per arbitration case_____   Year_____

49. In your opinion, what are the major benefits of the grievance
    procedure in your company? (please describe briefly)

    _____

    _____

    _____

    _____

    _____

    _____

    _____

    _____

50. In your opinion, what are the major costs and/or abuses of the grievance procedure in your company? (please describe briefly)

_____

_____

_____

_____

_____

_____

_____

_____

_____

VI. Employer Characteristics

51. How many people are employed by your company?

      Number_____   Year_____

52. What is the production capacity, as measured by tons of steel, of your company?

      Total capacity_____   Year_____

53. If the data are available, what has been the actual production in terms of steel in your company in each of the last three years?

                              <u>Total Steel Production (in tons)</u>

      1982   _____

      1981   _____

      1980   _____

54. What is the job title of the individual who negotiates the company's collective bargaining agreement with this bargaining unit?

      Job Title_____

VII. Demographic Characteristics

55. What is your age (in years)?   _____

56. How long have been employed by
     the company (in years)?   _____

57. How many years of labor relations
     experience have you had?   _____

58. How many years of grievance handling
     experience have you had?   _____

59. What is your sex?   Male_____   Female_____

60. What is your race? (check one)

               Caucasian   _____

               Black   _____

               Hispanic   _____

               Oriental   _____

               Other   _____
               (please specify)

61. What level of schooling have you completed? (check one)

               Eighth grade or less   _____

               Some high school   _____

               High school   _____

               Some college   _____

               College graduate   _____ Specify field_____

               Some graduate work   _____

               Graduate degree   _____

                  Specify degree(s) _____ Specify field_____

                          _____   _____

62. What is your marital status? (check one)

      Single, never married   _____

      Married   _____

      Widowed   _____

      Divorced   _____

      Other (please specify)   _____

UNION QUESTIONNAIRE
NONPROFIT HOSPITALS
(NURSES)

708 Uris Hall
Columbia University
New York, New York   10027

Attached is a questionnaire that we would like you to fill out and return to us in the enclosed self-addressed envelope. The questionnaire is part of a study, sponsored by the National Science Foundation (NSF), of the modern grievance procedure in the United States. We are attempting to learn more about grievance handling in four sectors: steel, retail trade, nonprofit hospitals and local public schools.

You have been chosen from a list of union officials to receive and complete the questionnaire. The American Nurses Association assisted us in preparing the list and is cooperating in the study. We recognize that we are imposing on your time, but believe that the purposes for doing so are sound, and we will provide you with a copy of our detailed report, which is scheduled for completion in 1985. We assure you in the strongest possible terms that the answers you provide us will remain completely confidential. Further, no one single ANA local organization or official will be identified in the report. To the contrary, the analysis will be done only on aggregated data.

Your completion and return of this questionnaire is of great importance to us. Note that your responses should pertain only to your collective bargaining agreement with and grievance procedure for the hospital in which you are employed. Also, please enclose a copy of the current collective bargaining agreement with your employer. If one of your peers is more properly the person to complete the questionnaire, please transmit it to him or her. If you have any further questions about this questionnaire or the larger study of which it is a part, please do not hesitate to write to me at the address shown above or call me at the telephone number listed below. Thank you in advance for your cooperation in this matter.

Sincerely,

David Lewin
Professor of
Business

Tel: (212) 280-4418

Enc.

Note: Please answer all questions as they pertain to nurses only!

I. Collective Bargaining Characteristics

1. Who are the parties to this collective bargaining agreement?

    Association_____

    Employer   _____

2. What is your position with the association?

    Title   _____

3. What is the composition of the bargaining unit? (check one)

    Nurses only   _____

    Nurses and other hospital personnel
    (e.g., attendants, technicians)   _____

    Other
    (please describe   _____
      briefly)

    _____

    _____

    _____

4. Does the collective bargaining agreement cover your association
    only? (check one)

          Yes_____

          No _____

    4A. If no, please briefly describe the coverage of the agreement.
         That is, indicate if the agreement has been negotiated by a
         union coalition.

         Specify_____

         _____

5. What are the beginning and ending dates of the collective
    bargaining agreement with this hospital?

    Beginning date_____   Ending date_____

6. Please list the main job titles of nurses (and others) who are in
    the bargaining unit.

    _____

    _____

    _____

    _____

    _____

    _____

    _____

    _____

7. How large is the bargaining unit? That is, how many nurses are in
    the bargaining unit? (If other personnel are in the unit, list
    their total(s) separately.)

        Nurses   _____

        Others   _____

        Total   _____

II. Grievance Procedure Characteristics

8. Does the collective bargaining agreement contain a grievance
    procedure? (check one)

        Yes_____

        No _____

9. How many steps are there in the grievance procedure (including
    arbitration)? (check one)

        One   _____   Five _____

        Two   _____   Six _____

        Three_____   Seven or more _____

        Four _____

10. Is arbitration the final step of the grievance procedure?

      Yes_____

      No _____

    10A. If no, please identify the last step

      Right to strike   _____

      Advisory arbitration   _____

      Binding arbitration   _____

      Joint committee vote   _____

      Other (briefly describe) _____

11. Is the first step of the grievance procedure a formal one in the sense that a grievance form is filled out?

      Yes_____

      No _____

    11A. If no, please explain briefly_____

      _____

      _____

      _____

12. Does the collective bargaining agreement permit expedited grievance processing?

      Yes_____

      No_____

    12A. If yes, please indicate what type of expedited procedures exist. (check those that apply)

      Skipping intermediate steps   _____

      Speeding up time limits   _____

      Use of informal hearings   _____

      Dispensing with transcripts   _____

      Other (please describe briefly) _____

      _____

12B. If you answered yes to question 12, please list the types
of grievances for which expedited arbitration is permitted
(specify or describe briefly)

_____

_____

_____

_____

_____

12C. If you answered yes to question 12, please list the types of
grievances for which expedited arbitration is <u>not</u> permitted
(specify or describe briefly)

_____

_____

_____

_____

_____

13. If the collective bargaining agreement provides for grievance
arbitration, does it require

An ad hoc arbitrator   _____

A permanent arbitrator,
umpire or referee   _____

An arbitration panel   _____

Other (please describe briefly) _____

_____

14. What is the method of paying the arbitrator?

Parties pay equal shares   _____

"Losing" party pays all costs   _____

"Losing" party pays a majority
of the cost (e.g., 2/3 or 3/4 _____

Other (please describe briefly) _____

_____

15. How common is the use of lawyers to represent your company in
     arbitration? (check one)

            Very   Very
          Uncommon   Common

         _____   _____   _____   _____   _____
           1   2   3   4   5

15A. How common is the use of state ANA officials in grievance
     handling? (check one)

            Very   Very
          Uncommon   Common

         _____   _____   _____   _____   _____
           1   2   3   4   5

15B. How common is the use of national ANA officials in grievance
     handling? (check one)

            Very   Very
          Uncommon   Common

         _____   _____   _____   _____   _____
           1   2   3   4   5

16. Are grievance meetings scheduled on a regular basis?

          Yes_____

          No _____

16A. If yes, how often? (please specify)

     _____

     _____

III.   Grievance Procedure Usage

17. Based upon your written records, how many grievances were filed in
     the last three years under this contractual grievance procedure?
     (give number)

          1982_____

          1981_____

          1980_____

18. Approximately what percent of the grievances in each of the last three years were settled in each of the time periods listed below? (give percentages)

Year	10 days or less	11-30 days	31-60 days	61-90 days	More than 90 days	Total
1982	_____	_____	_____	_____	_____	100%
1981	_____	_____	_____	_____	_____	100%
1980	_____	_____	_____	_____	_____	100%

19. Approximately what percent of the grievances in each of the last three years were settled at each of the steps listed below? (Give percentages)

Year	Step 1	Step 2	Step 3	Step 4	Step 5	Step 6	Step 7 or above	Total
1982								100%
1981								100%
1980								100%

20. Approximately what percent of the grievances in each of the last three years were handled by an expedited procedure? (give percent)

1982_____

1981_____

1980_____

21. Approximately what percent of the grievances in each of the last three years were settled in arbitration? (give percent)

1982_____

1981_____

1980_____

22. Please indicate the frequency with which each of the following issues was the subject of grievances during the most recent year for which data are available? (check one per issue, where relevant)

Specify year: 19____

		Very Rarely 1	2	3	4	Very Often 5
a.	Pay (wages or salaries)					
b.	Job grading/work standards					
c.	Technological change					
d.	Work assignment					
e.	Overtime					
f.	Working conditions					
g.	Discipline					
h.	Performance evaluation					
i.	Layoff					
j.	Recall					
k.	Leave Time					
l.	Health and safety					
m.	Transfer					
n.	Promotion					
o.	Work hours					
p.	Discrimination (race, sex, age, religion)					
q.	Productivity					
r.	Fringe benefits					
s.	Union security					
t.	Management rights					
u.	Vacations/holidays					
v.	Seniority					
w.	Strikes/lockouts					

22. (Continued)

		Very Rarely				Very Often
		1	2	3	4	5
x.	Patient load	____	____	____	____	____
y.	Subcontracting	____	____	____	____	____
z.	Other (please specify below)					
	_____	____	____	____	____	____
	_____	____	____	____	____	____
	_____	____	____	____	____	____
	_____	____	____	____	____	____

23. If the data are available, please provide a numerical breakdown of formal grievances filed over the last three years. Use either your own categories or those listed in question 22, items a through z.

Category	Number filed in		
	1982	1981	1980
_____	_____	_____	_____
_____	_____	_____	_____
_____	_____	_____	_____
_____	_____	_____	_____
_____	_____	_____	_____
_____	_____	_____	_____
_____	_____	_____	_____
_____	_____	_____	_____
_____	_____	_____	_____
_____	_____	_____	_____
_____	_____	_____	_____
_____	_____	_____	_____
_____	_____	_____	_____
_____	_____	_____	_____

23. (Continued)

Category	1982	Number filed in 1981	1980
_____	_____	_____	_____
_____	_____	_____	_____
_____	_____	_____	_____
_____	_____	_____	_____
_____	_____	_____	_____
_____	_____	_____	_____
_____	_____	_____	_____
_____	_____	_____	_____
_____	_____	_____	_____
_____	_____	_____	_____
_____	_____	_____	_____
_____	_____	_____	_____

24. Were there particular events, such as those listed below, that con-
    tributed to either a very high or very low rate/number of grievances
    filed in each of the last three years? (check event and year or years).

Event	1982	1981	1980
Work force reductions	_____	_____	_____
Wildcat strikes	_____	_____	_____
Depressed economic conditions	_____	_____	_____
Technological change	_____	_____	_____
Job/work redesign and/or reallocation	_____	_____	_____
Contract negotiation or renegotiation	_____	_____	_____

24. (Continued)

    Other (please describe below)

    _____   _____   _____   _____

    _____   _____   _____   _____

    _____   _____   _____   _____

    _____   _____   _____   _____

25. Approximately what percentage of grievance arbitrations were
    decided in favor of the association (employee) in each of the last
    three years? (give percent)

    1982_____%

    1981_____%

    1980_____%

26. How often do top association officials become involved in the
    settlement of grievances? (please check one)

    Never_____   Seldom_____   Occasionally_____   Frequently_____   Always_____

27. Approximately what percentage of grievances in each of the last
    three years were initiated by management? (give percent)

    1982_____%

    1981_____%

    1980_____%

28. For nonunion employees (hourly, salaried, management, etc.) of your
    hospital, are any of the following available? (check those that apply)

            Open door policy   _____

            Appeal system with
            steps to middle   _____
            management

            Appeal system with
            steps to top   _____
            management

            Appeals or
            grievance system   _____
            with arbitration
            as the final step

28. (Continued)

Other (please
describe briefly)

_____

_____

IV. Perceptions of the Grievance Procedure

29. In general, how important are the issues raised in the grievance
procedure? (please circle one)

Very Unimportant				Very Important
1	2	3	4	5

30. In general, how has the importance of the issues raised in the grievance procedure changed over the 1980-82 period? (please circle one).

Issues have become much less important				Issues have become much more important
1	2	3	4	5

31. Without regard to the merits of the grievances filed or their settlements, how would you assess the grievance procedure in terms of the
process it provides for grievance discussions? (please circle one).

Very Unfair				Very Fair
1	2	3	4	5

32. In your judgment, how equitable were grievance settlements in the
most recent year for which data are available? (please circle one)

Specify year: 19____

Very Inequitable				Very Equitable
1	2	3	4	5

33. If the data are available, how would you describe the changes in grievance settlements over the 1980-82 period? (please circle one)

Settlements have become much less equitable				Settlements have become much more equitable
1	2	3	4	5

34. In general, how would you describe the results of grievance discussions with management at step one of the procedure? (please circle one).

Very Unfair				Very Fair
1	2	3	4	5

35. In general, how would you describe the results of grievance discussions with management at intermediate steps of the procedure, that is at other than the first or last steps? (please circle one)

Very Unfair				Very Fair
1	2	3	4	5

36. In general, how would you describe the settlements resulting from the final step of the grievance procedure? (please circle one)

Very Unfair				Very Fair
1	2	3	4	5

37. Do you think that one or more steps of the grievance procedure should be eliminated?

    Yes_____

    No _____

37A. If yes, which step(s)_____

    _____

    Why?_____

    _____

    _____

    _____

38. How would you characterize the scope of issues covered by the grievance procedure? (please circle one)

Too
Narrow

Too
Broad

1   2   3   4   5

39. How would you characterize the time limits prescribed by the grievance procedure? (please circle one)

Too
Short

Too
Long

1   2   3   4   5

V.   Grievance Procedure Functions,
Management and Audit

40. In your opinion, what are the principal functions of the grievance procedure? (check those that apply)

A safety valve (for employees to let off steam)   _____

A mechanism to resolve labor-management disputes   _____

A vehicle for exercising power   _____

A method of providing justice   _____

A mechanism to maintain production   _____

Provides information for management
decision-making   _____

Other (please describe briefly)_____

_____

_____

_____

_____

41. Please briefly describe how the structure of the grievance procedure
    has changed, if at all, during the last three years.

    _____

    _____

    _____

    _____

    _____

    _____

42. Do you conduct annual or periodic audits or evaluations of grievance
    procedure usage and outcomes?

              Yes_____

              No _____

   42A. If yes, for which of the following purposes is the information
        generated by such audits used? (check those that apply)

        To prepare for arbitration cases   _____

        To formulate collective bargaining strategy   _____

        To identify trouble spots in employee relations _____

        To appraise grievance handling   _____

        To counsel/train grievance handlers   _____

        Other (please specify)   _____

        _____

        _____

        _____

43. Do you maintain data on post-grievance settlement behavior of
    employees and supervisors who were parties to grievances?

              Yes_____

              No _____

43A. If yes, please indicate which of the following post-grievance settlement data are maintained? (check those that apply).

Employee productivity and/or performance _____

Employee absenteeism_____, tardiness_____, and turnover____

Employee morale _____

Grievance handler's enforcement of the labor agreement _____

Other (please describe briefly)

_____

_____

_____

44. In general, how knowledgeable are stewards/grievance handlers about the structure content and uses of the grievance procedure? (please circle one).

Not at all   Completely
knowledgeable   knowledgeable

       1   2   3   4   5

45. In general, how knowledgeable are supervisors/managers about the structure content and uses of the grievance procedure? (please circle one).

Not at all   Completely
knowledgeable   knowledgeable

       1   2   3   4   5

46. In general, how knowledgeable are employees about the structure content and uses of the grievance procedure? (please circle one).

Not at all   Completely
knowledgeable   knowledgeable

       1   2   3   4   5

47. If data are available, please provide the average cost to the association of grievance handling per employee.

Average cost per employee_____ Year_____

48. If data are available, please provide the average cost to the association of grievance arbitration cases.

Average cost per arbitration case_____ Year_____

49. In your opinion, what are the major benefits of the grievance pro-
    cedure to the association and to employees? (please describe briefly)

    _____

    _____

    _____

    _____

    _____

    _____

    _____

    _____

    _____

50. In your opinion, what are the major costs and/or abuses of the
    grievance procedure in your association and hospital?
    (please describe briefly)

    _____

    _____

    _____

    _____

    _____

    _____

    _____

    _____

                        VI.   Association Characteristics

51. How many people belong to your association?

            Number_____   Year_____

52. How many elected officials of your association are there?
    (Local ANA)

            Number_____   Year_____

53. How many association officials/members handle grievances in this hospital?

      Number_____   Year_____

54. What is the patient capacity, as measured by the number of beds, of your hospital?

      Total beds_____   Year_____

55. If the data are available, what has been the average bed occupancy rate in each of the last three years?

	Bed Occupancy Rate %
1982	_____
1981	_____
1980	_____

56. What is the title of the individual who negotiates the collective bargaining agreement with this hospital?

      Job Title_____

VII. Demographic Characteristics

57. What is your age (in years)?   _____

58. How long have been employed by the hospital (in years)?   _____

59. How long have you been a union official   _____

60. How many years of grievance handling experience have you had?   _____

61. What is your sex?   Male_____   Female_____

62. What is your race? (check one)

      Caucasian _____

      Black   _____

      Hispanic   _____

      Oriental   _____

      Other   _____
      (please specify)

Appendix 2:
Interview Schedules

I. Collective Bargaining Characteristics

1. Who are the parties to this collective bargaining agreement?

Employer_____

Union   _____

2. What are the beginning and ending dates of the collective bargaining agreement with this bargaining unit?

Beginning date_____   Ending date_____

3. How large is the bargaining unit? That is, how many employees are in the unit?

Size of bargaining unit_____   Year_____

4. What are the main job titles of employees in this unit?

_____

_____

_____

_____

_____

_____

_____

II. Grievance Procedure Characteristics

5. How many steps are there in the grievance procedure (including arbitration)?

No. of steps_____

6. Is the first step of the grievance procedure a formal one in the sense that a grievance form is filled out?

Yes_____   No_____

Other_____

6A. If no, please describe how the employer keeps track of first step grievance resolution.

_____

_____

_____

_____

_____

_____

7. When does the labor relations/industrial relations staff first become involved in the processing of a grievance?

_____

_____

_____

_____

8. Does the grievance procedure provide for the expedited processing of grievances?

    Yes_____   No_____

8A. If yes, please briefly describe the expedited procedure.

_____

_____

_____

_____

8B. If yes, for what types of grievances may expedited procedures be invoked?

_____

_____

_____

_____

9. If you have a step that provides for joint committee processing of grievances, please give your judgment about the effectiveness of this step.

                Very   Very
             Ineffective   Effective

        ――――   ――――   ――――   ――――   ――――
          1   2   3   4   5

    9A. If yes, what is the basis of your judgment?

        _____

        _____

        _____

        _____

10. If lawyers are used by one or both parties in grievance processing (including arbitration), please give your judgment about their effectiveness.

                Very   Very
             Ineffective   Effective

        ――――   ――――   ――――   ――――   ――――
          1   2   3   4   5

    10A. If yes, what is the basis of your judgment?

        _____

        _____

        _____

        _____

11. Please comment on the "political" uses of the grievance procedure.

        _____

        _____

        _____

        _____

        _____

        _____

12. If the collective bargaining agreement provides for grievance
    arbitration, please describe the specific procedure used.

    _____

    _____

    _____

    _____

III.   Grievance Procedure Usage

13. Based upon written records, how many grievances were filed in the
    last three years under this contractual grievance procedure?

    1982_____

    1981_____

    1980_____

14. Approximately what percent of the grievances in each of the last
    three years went to arbitration?

    1982_____

    1981_____

    1980_____

15. In the most recent year for which data are available, what were the
    most common grievance issues?

    Year_____

    Issues_____

    _____

    _____

    _____

    _____

16. In your judgment, what factors account for the variation in grievance activity over the last three years?

_____

_____

_____

_____

IV. Perceptions of the Grievance Procedure

17. In general, how important are the issues that are raised in the grievance procedure?

     Very   Very
Unimportant   Important

   1   2   3   4   5

18. In general, how equitable were grievance settlements in the most recent year for which data are available?

Year_____

     Very   Very
Inequitable   Equitable

   1   2   3   4   5

V. Grievance Procedure Audit

19. Does management conduct annual or periodic audits of grievance procedure usage and outcomes?

Yes_____   No_____

19A. If yes, please briefly describe the purposes and uses of the audits.

_____

_____

_____

_____

20. In your judgement, what are the major benefits of the grievance
    procedure to the employer?

    _____

    _____

    _____

    _____

    _____

    _____

21. In your judgment, what are the major costs of the grievance
    procedure to the employer?

    _____

    _____

    _____

    _____

    _____

    _____

22. What specific "management rights" issues have been taken up in
    the grievance procedure in the last three years?

    _____

    _____

    _____

    _____

    _____

    _____

23. If you personally could make changes to improve the grievance procedure, what would they be?

_____

_____

_____

_____

_____

_____

24. Does your firm track or analyze the post-grievance settlement behavior of employees and supervisors (that is, track performance, attendance, internal job changes and/or turnover)?

      Yes_____   No_____

24A. If yes, please give examples.

_____

_____

_____

_____

_____

_____

25. Please comment on any other aspects of the grievance procedure that you think are important and that haven't been covered in this interview.

_____

_____

_____

_____

_____

_____

_____

_____

UNION INTERVIEW
LOCAL PUBLIC SCHOOLS

I. Collective Bargaining Characteristics

1. Who are the parties to this collective bargaining agreement?

    Union _____

    Employer_____

2. What are the beginning and ending dates of the collective
    bargaining agreement with this bargaining unit?

    Beginning date_____   Ending date_____

3. How large is the bargaining unit? That is, how many employees are
    in the unit?

    Size of bargaining unit_____   Year_____

4. What are the main job titles of employees in this unit?

    _____

    _____

    _____

    _____

    _____

    _____

    _____

II. Grievance Procedure Characteristics

5. How many steps are there in the grievance procedure (including
    arbitration)?

    No. of steps_____

6. Is the first step of the grievance procedure a formal one in the
    sense that a grievance form is filled out?

    Yes_____   No_____

    Other_____

6A. If no, please describe how the employer keeps track of first step grievance resolution.

_____

_____

_____

_____

_____

_____

7. When does the union's staff first become involved in the processing of a grievance?

_____

_____

_____

_____

8. Does the grievance procedure provide for the expedited processing of grievances?

   Yes_____   No_____

8A. If yes, please briefly describe the expedited procedure.

_____

_____

_____

_____

8B. If yes, for what types of grievances may expedited procedures be invoked?

_____

_____

_____

_____

9.   If you have a step that provides for joint committee processing of
     grievances, please give your judgment about the effectiveness of
     this step.

                 Very   Very
              Ineffective   Effective

          ___   ___   ___   ___   ___
           1   2   3   4   5

     9A. If yes, what is the basis of your judgment?

     _____

     _____

     _____

     _____

10. If lawyers are used by one or both parties in grievance processing
     (including arbitration), please give your judgment about their
     effectiveness.

                 Very   Very
              Ineffective   Effective

          ___   ___   ___   ___   ___
           1   2   3   4   5

     10A. If yes, what is the basis of your judgment?

     _____

     _____

     _____

     _____

11. Please comment on the "political" uses of the grievance procedure.

     _____

     _____

     _____

     _____

     _____

     _____

12. If the collective bargaining agreement provides for grievance
arbitration, please describe the specific procedure used.

_____

_____

_____

_____

III. Grievance Procedure Usage

13. Based upon written records, how many grievances were filed in the
last three years under this contractual grievance procedure?

     1982_____

     1981_____

     1980_____

14. Approximately what percent of the grievances in each of the last
three years went to arbitration?

     1982_____

     1981_____

     1980_____

15. In the most recent year for which data are available, what were the
most common grievance issues?

     Year_____

     Issues_____

_____

_____

_____

_____

16. In your judgment, what factors account for the variation in grievance activity over the last three years?

_____

_____

_____

_____

IV. Perceptions of the Grievance Procedure

17. In general, how important are the issues that are raised in the grievance procedure?

```
        Very                                    Very
     Unimportant                             Important


      ___      ___      ___      ___      ___
       1        2        3        4        5
```

18. In general, how equitable were grievance settlements in the most recent year for which data are available?

                        Year_____

```
        Very                                    Very
     Inequitable                             Equitable


      ___      ___      ___      ___      ___
       1        2        3        4        5
```

V. Grievance Procedure Audit

19. Does your union conduct annual or periodic audits of grievance procedure usage and outcomes?

      Yes_____   No_____

19A. If yes, please briefly describe the purposes and uses of the audits.

_____

_____

_____

_____

20. In your judgement, what are the major benefits of the grievance
procedure to employees?

_____

_____

_____

_____

_____

_____

21. In your judgment, what are the major costs of the grievance
procedure to the employees?

_____

_____

_____

_____

_____

_____

22. What specific management policies or "rights" issues have been
taken up in the grievance procedure in the last three years?

_____

_____

_____

_____

_____

_____

23. If you personally could make changes to improve the grievance
    procedure, what would they be?

    _____

    _____

    _____

    _____

    _____

    _____

24. Does your union track or analyze the post-grievance settlement
    behavior of employees and supervisors/administrators (that is, track
    performance, attendance, internal job changes and/or turnover)?

        Yes_____   No_____

    24A. If yes, please give examples.

    _____

    _____

    _____

    _____

    _____

    _____

25. Please comment on any other aspects of the grievance procedure that
    you think are important and that haven't been covered in this
    interview.

    _____

    _____

    _____

    _____

    _____

    _____

    _____

    _____

Bibliography

Adams, J. Stacy. "Inequity in Social Exchange." In L. Berkowitz (ed.), *Advances in Experimental Social Psychology*, vol. 2. New York: Academic Press, 1965, pp. 272-283.

Anderson, John C. "The Grievance Process in Canadian Municipal Labor Relations." Paper presented at the 39th Annual Meeting of the Academy of Management, Atlanta, Georgia, August 1979.

Appleby, Gavin S. "A Union's Right to Company Information: Encumbrances in the Grievance-Arbitration Process." *Employee Relations Law Journal* 10, no. 4 (Spring 1985): 736-744.

Aram, John D., and Paul F. Salipante, Jr. "An Evaluation of Organizational Due Process in the Resolution of Employee/Employer Conflict." *Academy of Management Review* 6, no. 2 (April 1981): 197-204.

Arvey, Richard D., and Allen P. Jones. "The Use of Discipline in Organizational Settings: A Framework for Future Research." In B. M. Staw and L. L. Cummings (eds.), *Research in Organizational Behavior*, vol. 7. Greenwich, Conn.: JAI Press, 1985, pp. 367-408.

Ash, Philip. "The Parties to the Grievance." *Personnel Psychology* 23, no. 1 Spring 1970): 13-37.

Ashenfelter, Orley, and John Pencavel. "American Trade Union Growth, 1900-1960." *Quarterly Journal of Economics* 83, no. 3 (August 1969): 434-448.

Begin, James P. "Grievance Mechanisms and Faculty Collegiality: The Rutgers Case." *Industrial and Labor Relations Review* 31, no. 3 (April 1978): 295-309.

Berenbeim, Ronald. *Non-Union Complaint Systems: A Corporate Appraisal.* Report No. 770. New York: The Conference Board, 1980.

Bloom, David E. "Is Arbitration Really Compatible with Bargaining?" *Industrial Relations* 20, no. 3 (Fall 1981): 233-244.

Bloom, Gordon F., and Herbert R. Northrup. *Economics of Labor Relations.* 9th ed. Homewood, Ill.: Irwin, 1981.

Bloom, Gordon F., Charles R. Perry, and Marion Fletcher. *Negro Employment in*

Retail Trade: A Study of Racial Policies in the Department Store, Drug-store, and Supermarket Industries. Major Industrial Research Unit Studies No. 51. Philadelphia, Pa.: The Wharton School, University of Pennsylvania, 1972.

Bowers, Mollie H. "Grievance Mediation: Another Route to Resolution." *Personnel Journal* 59, no. 1 (February 1980): 132-136.

Bowers, Mollie H., Ronald L. Seeber, and Lamont E. Stallworth. "Grievance Mediation: A Route to Resolution for the Cost-Conscious 1980s" *Labor Law Journal* 33, no. 8 (August 1982): 459-466.

Brett, Jeanne M., and Stephen B. Goldberg. "Wildcat Strikes in Bituminous Coal Mining." *Industrial and Labor Relations Review* 32, no. 4 (July 1979): 465-483.

――――. "Grievance Mediation in the Coal Industry." *Industrial and Labor Relations Review* 37, no. 1 (October 1983): 49-69.

Brett, Jeanne M., Stephen B. Goldberg, and William Ury. "Mediation and Organizational Development: Models for Conflict Management." *Proceedings of the Thirty-Third Annual Meeting, Industrial Relations Research Association.* Madison, Wis.: IRRA, 1981, pp. 195-202.

Briggs, Steven. "The Grievance Procedure: Focal Tool of Organizational Health." Working paper, University of California, Los Angeles, 1981.

――――. "The Steward, the Supervisor, and the Grievance Process." *Proceedings of the Thirty-Fourth Annual Meeting, Industrial Relations Research Association.* Madison, Wis.: IRRA, 1982a, pp. 313-319.

――――. "Beyond the Grievance Procedure: Fact Finding in Employee Complaint Resolution." *Labor Law Journal* 33, no. 8 (August 1982b): 454-459.

――――. *The Municipal Grievance Process.* Los Angeles: Institute of Industrial Relations, University of California, 1984.

Brinker, Paul A. "Labor Union Coercion: The Misuse of the Grievance Procedure." *Journal of Labor Research* 5, no. 1 (Winter 1984): 93-102.

Brown, Charles, and James L. Medoff. "Trade Unions in the Production Process." *Journal of Political Economy* 86, no. 3 (June 1978): 355-378.

Cahn, Sidney L. "Justice and Dignity." *Arbitration Journal* 38, no. 4 (December 1983): 52-54.

Campbell, Donald T., and Julian C. Stanley. *Experimental and Quasi-Experimental Designs for Research.* Chicago, Ill.: Rand McNally, 1963.

Cassidy, George W. "Entropy and Negentropy in Grievance Subsystems." *Journal of Collective Negotiations in the Public Sector* 6, no. 3 (1977: 259-274.

Chamberlain, Neil W. *The Labor Sector.* New York: McGraw-Hill, 1965.

Chamberlain, Neil W., and James W. Kuhn. *Collective Bargaining.* 3d ed. New York: McGraw-Hill, 1986.

Clark, Kim B. "The Impact of Unionization on Productivity: A Case Study." *Industrial and Labor Relations Review* 34, no. 4 (July 1980): 451-468.

Crane, B. R., and R. M. Hoffman. *Successful Handling of Labor Grievances.* New York: Central Book Company, 1956.

Cushman, Bernard. "Current Experiments in Collective Bargaining." *Proceedings of the Twenty-Sixth Annual Meeting, Industrial Relations Research Association.* Madison, Wis.: IRRA, 1974, pp. 129-136.

Dalton, Dan R., and William D. Todor. "Manifest Needs of Stewards: Propensity to File a Grievance." *Journal of Applied Psychology* 64, no. 6 (December 1979): 654-659.

_____. "Win, Lose, Draw: The Grievance Process in Practice." *Personnel Administrator* 26, no. 3 (May-June 1981): 25-29.

_____. "Union Steward Locus of Control, Job, Union Involvement, and Grievance Behavior." *Journal of Business Research* 10, no. 1 (February 1982a): 85-101.

_____. "Antecedents of Grievance Filing Behavior: Attitude/Behavioral Consistency and the Union Steward." *Academy of Management Journal* 25, no. 1 (March 1982b): 158-169.

Dalton, Melville. *Men Who Manage*. New York: Wiley, 1959.

Davey, Harold W., Mario F. Bognanno, and David L. Estenson. *Contemporary Collective Bargaining*. 4th ed. Englewood Cliffs, N.J.: Prentice-Hall, 1982.

Delaney, John Thomas, Donna Sockell, and Joel Brockner. "The Mandatory-Permissive Distinction and the Collective Bargaining Process." *Industrial Relations* 27, no. 1 (Winter 1988): 21-36.

Doherty, Robert E. "Public Education." In G. G. Somers (ed.), *Collective Bargaining: Contemporary American Experience*. Madison, Wis.: Industrial Relations Research Association, 1980, pp. 487-552.

Dolnick, David. "The Settlement of Grievances and the 'Job-Conscious' Theory." *Labor Law Journal* 21, no. 4 (April 1970): 240-247.

Donaldson, Lex, and Malcolm Warner. "Bureaucratic and Electoral Control in Occupational Interest Associations." *Sociology* 8, no. 1 (January 1974): 45-57.

Eckerman, Arthur C. "An Analysis of Grievances and Aggrieved Employees in a Machine Shop and Foundry." *Journal of Applied Psychology* 32, no. 3 (June 1948): 255-269.

Ewing, D. *Freedom Inside the Organization*. New York: Dutton, 1977.

Ewing, David W. *Do It My Way or You're Fired*. New York: Wiley, 1983.

Flanagan, Robert J., Robert S. Smith, and Ronald G. Ehrenberg. *Labor Economics and Labor Relations*. Glenview, Ill.: Scott, Foresman, 1984.

Fleishman, Edwin A., and Edwin F. Harris. "Patterns of Leadership Behavior Related to Employee Grievances and Turnover." *Personnel Psychology* 15, no. 1 (Winter 1962): 43-56.

Fleming, Robin W. *The Labor Arbitration Process*. Urbana, Ill.: University of Illinois Press, 1965.

Freedman, Audrey. *The New Look in Wage Policy and Employee Relations*. Report No. 865. New York: The Conference Board, 1985.

Freeman, Richard. "The Exit-Voice Tradeoff in the Labor Market: Unionism, Job Tenure, Quits, and Separations." *Quarterly Journal of Economics* 94, no. 3 (September 1980): 643-673.

Freeman, Richard B., and James L. Medoff. *What Do Unions Do?* New York: Basic Books, 1984.

Gandz, Jeffrey. "Resolving Conflict: A Guide for the Industrial Relations Manager." *Personnel* 56, no. 6 (June 1979): 22-31.

Gandz, Jeffrey, and J. David Whitehead. "The Relationship Between Industrial Relations Climate and Grievance Initiation and Resolution." *Proceedings of the Thirty-Fourth Annual Meeting, Industrial Relations Research Association.* Madison, Wis.: IRRA, 1982, pp. 320-328.

Getman, Julius G. "Labor Arbitration and Dispute Resolution." *Yale Law Journal* 88, no. 2 (1979): 916-949.

Gideon, Thomas F., and Richard B. Peterson. "A Comparison of Alternate Grievance Procedures." *Employee Relations Law Journal* 5, no. 3 (September 1979): 222-223.

Glassman, Alan M., and James A. Belasco. "The Chapter Chairman and School Grievances." *Industrial Relations* 14, no. 2 (Spring 1975): 233-241.

Goldberg, Stephen B. "The Mediation of Grievances Under a Collective Bargaining Contract: An Alternative to Arbitration." *Northwestern University Law Review* 77, no. 3 (October 1982): 270-315.

Goldberg, Stephen B., and Jeanne M. Brett. "Grievance Mediation: An Alternative to Arbitration." *Proceedings of the Thirty-Fifth Annual Meeting, Industrial Relations Research Association*, Madison, Wis.: IRRA, 1983a, pp. 256-259.

_____. "An Experiment in the Mediation of Grievances." *Monthly Labor Review* 106, no. 3 (March 1983b): 23-30.

Gordan, Michael E., and Sandra J. Miller. "Grievances: A Review of Research and Practice." *Personnel Psychology* 37, no. 2 (Spring 1984): 117-146.

Graham, Harry E., and Brian P. Heshizer. "The Effect of Contract Language on Low-Level Settlement of Grievances." *Labor Law Journal* 30, no. 7 (July 1979): 427-432.

Graham, Harry E., Brian P. Heshizer, and David B. Johnson. "Grievance Arbitration: Labor Officials' Attitudes." *Arbitration Journal* 33, no. 2 (June 1978): 21-24.

Gregory, Gordon A., and Robert E. Rooney, Jr. "Grievance Mediation: A Trend in the Cost-Conscious Eighties." *Labor Law Journal* 31, no. 8 (August 1980): 502-508.

Gross, Ernest. "Grievance Activity and Union Membership: A Conceptual View." *Journal of Collective Negotiations in the Public Sector* 9, no. 1 (1980): 59-80.

Hall, Richard J. "Effectiveness Theory and Organizational Effectiveness." *Journal of Applied Behavioral Science* 16, no. 2 (June 1980): 536-545.

Harbison, Frederick H., and John R. Coleman. "Procedures and Methods." In C. S. Golden and V. D. Parker (eds.), *Causes of Industrial Peace under Collective Bargaining.* New York: Harper and Brothers, 1955, pp. 331-349.

Hayford, Stephen L., and Richard Pegnetter. "Grievance Adjudication for Public Employees." *Arbitration Journal* 35, no. 3 (September 1980): 22-29.

Heneman, Herbert G., III, and Marcus H. Sandver. "Predicting the Outcome of Union Certification Elections." *Industrial and Labor Relations Review* 36, no. 4 (July 1983): 537-559.

Hirschman, Albert O. *Exit, Voice and Loyalty.* Cambridge: Harvard University Press, 1970.

Hoellering, M. F. "Expedited Labor Arbitration Tribunal: A New AAA Forum for Companies and Union," *Labor Law Journal* 23, no. 9 (September 1972): 679-700.

Holley, William H., and Kenneth M. Jennings. *The Labor Relations Process.* New York: Dryden Press, 1980.

Hyman, Richard. *Disputes Procedure in Action: A Study of the Engineering Industry Disputes Procedure in Coventry.* London: Heinemann, 1972.

Ichniowski, Casey. "The Effects of Grievance Activity on Productivity." *Industrial and Labor Relations Review* 40, no. 1 (October 1986): 75-89.

Ichniowski, Casey, and David Lewin. "Grievance Procedures and Firm Performance." In Morris Kleiner et al. (eds.), *Human Resources and the Performance of the Firm.* Industrial Relations Research Association Research Series. Madison, Wis.: IRRA, 1987, pp. 159-194.

Jacoby, Sanford M. "Progressive Discipline in American Industry: Origins, Development, and Consequences." In D. Lipsky and D. Lewin (eds.), *Advances in Industrial and Labor Relations*, vol. 3. Greenwich, Conn.: JAI Press, 1986, pp. 213-260.

Jennings, Ken. "Foremen's Views of Their Involvement with Other Management Officials in the Grievance Process." *Labor Law Journal* 25, no. 5 (May 1974a): 305-316.

―――. "Foremen's Views of Their Involvement with the Union Steward in the Grievance Process." *Labor Law Journal* 25, no. 9 (September 1974b): 541-549.

Katz, Harry C., Thomas A. Kochan, and Kenneth R. Gobeille. "Industrial Relations Performance, Economic Performance and QWL Programs: An Interplant Analysis." *Industrial and Labor Relations Review* 37, no. 1 (October 1983): 3-17.

Katz, Harry C., Thomas A. Kochan, and Mark Weber. "Assessing the Effects of Industrial Relations Systems and Efforts to Improve the Quality of Working Life on Organizational Effectiveness." *Academy of Management Journal* 28, no. 3 (September 1985): 509-526.

Kaufman, Bruce E. "The Determinants of Strikes in the United States, 1900-1977." *Industrial and Labor Relations Review* 35, no. 4 (July 1982): 473-490.

Kerlinger, Fred N. *Foundations of Behavioral Research.* New York: Holt, Reinhart, Winston, 1973.

Kerr, Clark. "The Collective Bargaining Environment." In C. S. Golden and V. D. Parker (eds.), *Causes of Industrial Peace under Collective Bargaining.* New York: Harper and Brothers, 1955, pp. 10-22.

Kissler, Gary D. "Grievance Activity and Union Membership: A Study of Government Employees." *Journal of Applied Psychology* 62, no. 4 (August 1977): 459-462.

Knight, Thomas R. "Toward a Contingency Theory of the Grievance-Arbitration System." In David B. Lipsky (ed.), *Advances in Industrial and Labor Relations*, vol. 2. Greenwich, Conn.: JAI Press, 1985, pp. 269-318.

―――. "Feedback and Grievance Resolution." *Industrial and Labor Relations Review* 39, no. 4 (July 1986): 585-598.

Kochan, Thomas A., Robert B. McKersie, and Peter Cappelli. "Strategic Choice and Industrial Relations Theory." *Industrial Relations* 23, no. 1 (Winter 1984): 16-39.

Kuhn, James W. *Bargaining in Grievance Settlement: The Power of Industrial Work Groups.* New York: Columbia University Press, 1961.

Landis, Brook. "Labor Relations: Expediting the Arbitration Process." *Personnel Journal* 6, no. 6 (June 1982): 402-404.

LaVan, Helen, Cameron Carley, and J. Marshall Jowers. "The Arbitration of Employee Grievance in Health Care Institutions: An Empirical Study." *Arbitration Journal* 35, no. 4 (December 1980): 33-36.

Lewin, David. "Theoretical Perspectives on the Modern Grievance Procedure. In J. D. Reid, Jr., (ed.), *New Approaches to Labor Unions, Research in Labor Economics*, Supplement 2. Greenwich, Conn.: JAI Press, 1983, pp. 127-147.

_____. "Empirical Measures of Grievance Procedure Effectiveness." *Proceedings of the 1984 Spring Meeting, Industrial Relations Research Association.* Madison, Wis.: IRRA, 1984, pp. 491-499.

_____. "Conflict Resolution in the Nonunion High Technology Firm." In A. Kleingartner and C. Anderson (eds.), *Human Resources in High Technology Firms.* Lexington, Mass.: Heath, 1986, pp. 137-155.

_____. "Dispute Resolution in the Nonunion Firm: A Theoretical and Empirical Analysis." *Journal of Conflict Resolution* 31, no. 3 (September 1987a): 465-502.

_____. "Industrial Relations as a Strategic Variable." In Morris M. Kleiner et al. (eds.), *Human Resources and the Performance of the Firm.* Industrial Relations Research Association Research Series. Madison, Wis.: IRRA, 1987b, pp. 1-42.

Lewin, David, and Richard B. Peterson. "Behavioral Outcomes of Grievance Activity." Working paper, Columbia University Graduate School of Business, September 1987.

Lewin, David, and Peter Feuille. "Behavioral Research in Industrial Relations." *Industrial and Labor Relations Review* 36, no. 3 (April 1983): 341-360.

Lewin, David, Peter Feuille, Thomas A. Kochan, and John Thomas Delaney. *Public Sector Labor Relations.* Lexington, Mass.: Heath, 1988.

Loewenberg, J. Joseph. "Structure of Grievance Procedures." *Labor Law Journal* 35, no. 1 (January 1984): 44-51.

MacDonald, Lois, et al. *The Grievance Process in New York City Transit.* New York: Institute of Labor Relations and Social Security, New York University, 1956.

McKersie, Robert B., and William W. Shropshire, Jr. "Avoiding Written Grievances: A Successful Program." *Journal of Business* 35, no. 2 (Spring 1962): 135-152.

Magenau, John M. "The Impact of Alternative Impasse Procedures on Bargaining: A Laboratory Experiment." *Industrial and Labor Relations Review* 36, no. 3 (April 1983): 361-377.

Martin, James E. "Grievance Procedures in the Federal Service: The Continuing Problem." *Public Personnel Management* 7, no. 4 (July-August 1978): 221-229.

Masters, Marrick. "Federal Employee Unions and Political Action." *Industrial and Labor Relations Review* 38, no. 4 (July 1985): 612-628.

Miller, Richard U. "Hospital." In G. G. Somers (ed.), *Collective Bargaining: Contemporary American Experience.* Madison, Wis.: Industrial Relations Research Association, 1980, pp. 373-433.

Mogulof, Melvin. *Governing Metropolitan Areas.* Washington, D.C.: Urban Institute, 1971.

Moore, William R. "Justice and the Grievance Procedure in the Federal Public Service." *Relations Industrielles/Industrial Relations* 36, no. 4 (October 1981): 848-862.

Muchinsky, Paul M., and Mounawar A. Maassarani. "Work Environment Effects on Public Sector Grievances." *Personnel Psychology* 33, no. 2 (Summer 1980): 403-414.

———. "Public Sector Grievances in Iowa." *Journal of Collective Bargaining in the Public Sector* 10, no. 1 (1981): 55-62.

Nadler, David A., and Michael L. Tushman. "A Model for Diagnosing Organizational Behavior." *Organizational Dynamics* 8, no. 1 (Winter 1979): 35-51.

Neale, Margaret A., and Max H. Bazerman. "The Role of Perspective-Taking Ability in Negotiating Under Different Forms of Arbitration." *Industrial and Labor Relations Review* 36, no. 3 (April 1983): 378-388.

Nelson, Nels E. "Grievance Rates and Technology." *Academy of Management Journal* 22, no. 4 (December 1979): 810-815.

Norsworthy, J. R., and Craig A. Zabala. "Worker Attitudes, Worker Behavior, and Productivity in the U.S. Automobile Industry, 1959-1976." *Industrial and Labor Relations Review* 38, no. 4 (July 1985): 544-557.

O'Reilly, Charles A., and Barton A. Weitz. "Managing Marginal Employees: The Use of Warnings and Dismissals." *Administrative Science Quarterly* 25, no. 2 (June 1980): 467-484.

Pateman, Carole. *Participation and Democratic Theory.* Cambridge: Cambridge University Press, 1970.

Peach, David A., and E. Robert Livernash. *Grievance Initiation and Resolution: A Study in Basic Steel.* Boston: Graduate School of Business Administration, Harvard University, 1974.

Peterson, Richard B., and David Lewin. "A Model for Research and Analysis of the Grievance Process." *Proceedings of the Thirty-Fourth Annual Meeting, Industrial Relations Research Association.* Madison, Wis.: IRRA, 1982, pp. 303-312.

Pondy, Louis R. "Organizational Conflict: Concepts and Models." *Administrative Science Quarterly* 12, no. 2 (June 1967): 296-320.

Prasow, Paul, and Edward Peters. *Arbitration and Collective Bargaining: Conflict Resolution in Labor Relations.* 2d ed. New York: McGraw-Hill, 1983.

Price, John, James Dewine, John Nowark, Kenneth Shenkel, and William Ronan, "Three Studies of Grievances." *Personnel Journal* 55, no. 1 (January 1976): 33-37.

Rand, James F. "Creative Problem-Solving Applied to Grievance/Arbitration Procedures." *Personnel Administrator* 25, no. 3 (May/June 1980): 50-52.

Ronan, William. "Work Group Attitudes and Grievance Activity." *Journal of Applied Psychology* 47, no. 1 (February 1963): 38-41.

Roy, Donald. "Quota Restriction and Goldbricking in a Machine Shop." *American Journal of Sociology* 57, no. 2 (June 1952): 427-442.

Sandver, Marcus H., Harry R. Blaine, and Mark N. Woyar. "Time and Cost Savings Through Expedited Arbitration Procedures." *Arbitration Journal* 36, no. 4 (December 1981): 11-21.

Sayles, Leonard R. *Behavior of Industrial Work Groups.* New York: John Wiley and Sons, 1958.

Schatzman, Leonard, and Anselm L. Strauss. *Field Research*. Englewood Cliffs, N.J.: Prentice-Hall, 1973.

Scott, William G. *The Management of Conflict: Appeal Systems in Organizations*. Homewood, Ill.: Irwin, 1965.

Seitz, Peter. "Delay: The Asp in the Bosom of Arbitration." *Arbitration Journal* 36, no. 3 (September 1981): 29-39.

Selznick, Philip. *Law, Society, and Industrial Justice*. New York: Russell Sage, 1969.

Slichter, Sumner H. *The Challenge of Industrial Relations: Trade Unions, Management, and the Public Interest*. Ithaca, N.Y.: Cornell University Press, 1947.

Slichter, Sumner H., James J. Healy, and E. Robert Livernash. *The Impact of Collective Bargaining on Management*. Washington, D.C.: Brookings, 1960.

Sloane, Arthur A., and Fred Witney. *Labor Relations*. 5th ed. Englewood Cliffs, N.J.: Prentice-Hall, 1985.

Somers, Gerald G. *Grievance Settlement in Coal Mining*. West Virginia Bulletin, Series 56, No. 12-2, June 1956.

Spencer, Daniel. "Employee Voice and Employee Retention." *Academy of Management Journal* 29, no. 3 (September 1986): 488-502.

Stagner, Ross. *Psychology of Industrial Conflict*. New York: Wiley, 1956.

_____. "Personality Variables in Union-Management Relations." *Journal of Applied Psychology* 46, no. 5 (October 1962): 350-357.

Staudohar, Paul D. "Exhaustion of Remedies in Private Industry Grievance Procedures." *Employee Relations Law Journal* 7, no. 3 (September 1977): 454-464.

Stieber, Jack. "Grievance Arbitration in the United States: An Analysis of Its Functions and Effects." In *Royal Commission on Trade Unions and Employers Associations*. London: Her Majesty's Stationery Office, 1968, pp. 1-30.

_____. "Steel." In G. G. Somers (ed.), *Collective Bargaining: Contemporary American Experience*. Madison, Wis.: Industrial Relations Research Association, 1980, pp. 151-208.

Stessin, Lawrence. "Expedited Arbitration: Less Grief Over Grievances." *Harvard Business Review* 55, no. 1 (January-February 1977): 128-134.

Stoudemeir, Robert H. "Grievances of Employees and Personnel Administration." *University of South Carolina Governmental Review* 18, no. 2 (June 1972): 1-14.

Sulkin, Howard A., and Robert W. Pranis. "Comparison of Grievants in a Heavy Machinery Company." *Personnel Psychology* 20, no. 2 (Summer 1967): 111-119.

Sulzner, George T. "The Impact of Grievance and Arbitration Processes on Federal Personnel Policies and Practices: The View from Twenty Bargaining Units." *Journal of Collective Negotiations in the Public Sector* 9, no. 2 (1980): 143-156.

Svejnar, Jan. "On the Empirical Testing of the Nash-Zeuthen Bargaining Solution." *Industrial and Labor Relations Review* 33, no. 4 (July 1980): 536-542.

Thomson, Andrew W. J. *The Grievance Procedure in the Private Sector*. Ithaca, N.Y.: New York State School of Labor and Industrial Relations, Cornell University, 1974.

Thomson, Andrew W. J., and Victor F. Murray. *Grievance Procedures*. Westmead, Eng.: Saxon House, 1976.

Ulman, Lloyd, and Elaine Sorenson. "Exit, Voice, and Muscle: A Note." *Industrial Relations* 23, no. 3 (Fall 1984): 424-428.

Veglahn, Peter A. "Making the Grievance Procedure Work." *Personnel Journal* 56, no. 3 (March 1977): 122-136.

Walker, Robert I., and James W., Robinson. "The First-Line Supervisor's Role in the Grievance Procedure." *Arbitration Journal* 32, no. 4 (December 1977): 379-392.

Weiss, Edward C. "The Relation of Personnel Statistics to Organizational Structure." *Personnel Psychology* 10, no. 1 (Spring 1957): 27-42.

Wyman, Earl J. "Now Then, About That Grievance." *Personnel Journal* 50, no. 5 (May 1971): 400-404, 406.

Zalusky, John. "Arbitration: Updating a Vital Process." *American Federationist* 83, no. 11 (November 1976): 1-8.

Index

About the Authors

DAVID LEWIN is Professor of Business, Faculty Coordinator of the Ph.D. Program, and Director of the Industrial Relations Research Center, Columbia University. He has published six books and many scholarly and professional articles on employee relations, human resource management, collective bargaining, wage determination, and labor markets. He serves as Faculty Director of the Columbia Executive Program "Managing the Enterprise," the Columbia-IBM Personnel Institute, and the Columbia-General Motors Personnel Strategy Seminar. He also serves as a mediator, factfinder, and arbitrator, and is on the labor arbitration panel of the American Arbitration Association and the mediation-factfinding panel of the New York State Public Employment Relations Board.

RICHARD B. PETERSON is Professor of Management and Organization, University of Washington. He is the author of many books and articles on bargaining dynamics, human resource management, and comparative industrial relations. Professor Peterson is a member of the Industrial Relations Research Association and the Academy of Management and has presented several professional papers at these organizations' meetings. He is chairman of the Bargaining Group, which consists of seventy-five researchers who specialize in industrial relations and human resource management.